The Invisible Presence

The Invisible Presence

How a Man's Relationship with His Mother
Affects All His Relationships with Women

MICHAEL GURIAN

Shambhala
Boston & London
2010

Shambhala Publications, Inc.
Horticultural Hall
300 Massachusetts Avenue
Boston, Massachusetts 02115
www.shambhala.com

©1994, 2010 by Michael Gurian
This is an updated edition of a book previously published
as *Mothers, Sons, and Lovers* (Shambhala Publications, 1994).

9 8 7 6 5 4 3 2 1

Printed in the United States of America

♾ This edition is printed on acid-free paper that meets the American
National Standards Institute Z39.48 Standard.
♻ This book was printed on 30% postconsumer recycled paper.
For more information please visit www.shambhala.com.
Distributed in the United States by Random House, Inc.,
and in Canada by Random House of Canada Ltd

Library of Congress Cataloging-in-Publication Data
Gurian, Michael.
The invisible presence: how a man's relationship with his
mother affects all his relationships with women / Michael Gurian.
p.   cm.
"This is an updated edition of a book previously published as Mothers, Sons,
and Lovers (Shambhala Publications, 1994)"—T.p. verso.
ISBN 978-1-59030-807-3 (pbk.: alk. paper)
1. Mothers and sons. 2. Men—Psychology. 3. Man-woman relationships—
Psychological aspects. I. Gurian, Michael. Mothers, sons, and lovers. II. Title.
HQ759.G87 2010
155.3'32—dc22
2010009752

Michael Gurian and his colleagues at The Gurian Institute offer keynotes,
consultation, and training in education, family issues, community
development, and corporate leadership. To learn more, please visit
www.gurianinstitute.com or www.michaelgurian.com.

For my mother and father,
Julia and Jay P. Gurian,
and the Herzog family

Contents

Preface to the 2010 Edition

Since the original publication of this book (in 1994, under the title *Mothers, Sons, and Lovers*), I have received many powerful letters and e-mails from both women and men. Many have been from women who say, "Help me understand my relationship with my husband better," or "Help me do best by my growing son." The study guides at the end of this new edition are meant to provide women with help in their interactions with boys and men.

When I wrote the book, I set out to provide a course of healing and growth for men, as well as a blueprint for mothers raising sons and for women in relationship with men. As a therapist and a student of attachment psychology and human brain development, as well as a practitioner of Jungian archetypal theory, I hoped to write a book that would unveil the mother-son relationship with clarity and power. In that relationship I believed—and still believe—we each find individually, and all find collectively, the life-blood for our civilization.

The title of this new edition is no accident. It is the result of reflection on reader responses, and on my continuing clinical work. I am even more convinced than before that the initial female relationship in a boy's life remains an invisible presence throughout his whole life as a man. The power of this invisible presence, its beauty, and its constancy grow within the complex webs of love between male and female, webs that are meant to be both unyielding and flexible. By this I mean that some of the initial bonds established between a boy and his mother must stay strong throughout both their lives; simultaneously, many others must be dissolved in order for a man to become independent of his mother's psychological will, and thus take a step toward becoming the loving, wise, successful man his partner and children need him to be.

The "invisible presence" can remain active between lovers later in a man's life. In the time we call "adulthood"—when we have all ostensibly finished with childhood ways—we can still be confused by our childhood relationships. As we seek attachments with lovers, we want attachments that are immensely strong, yet do not overwhelm the pull in each person toward independent psychological strength. Many times, however, we may sense that the invisible webs woven by us and our partners were crafted long ago, long before we even came together, and we sense this from inside a cage that does not allow us our freedom to fully and gracefully love one another.

For a man, graceful love is immensely difficult, and nearly impossible, if his relationship with his mother is not fully understood. Once understood, it can become as mysteriously beautiful and practically useful to him in adulthood as it was in boyhood.

For a woman, love of a man and love by a man can become difficult, and can seem, after the initial years of pheromones and hormones and other blisses have diminished, like a trap, a cage, even a depressing nightmare. If a woman's relationship with her father and a man's relationship with his mother are not fully understood, a long-term relationship or marriage may simply not happen.

And for mothers of sons, love of a growing boy is both an immediate, hands-on experience, and also a long-term, visionary one. If a mother intimately raises her son while unaware of the psychological webs they are weaving together, she may often lack the practical help she needs in both hands-on mothering and in accomplishing her vision of her son's healthy manhood.

It is to speak to challenges faced by men, lovers, and mothers that I initially wrote this book, and now I am deeply honored that Shambhala is publishing this new edition. I want to thank Shambhala for all its wonderful books, and I want to thank my family for their constant support. My own mother and I have always had a complex relationship. I thank her for her gifts. My wife of twenty-four years, Gail, and my grown daughters, Gabrielle and Davita, have supported me as my mother and I worked through the intricate webs of our relationship.

I hope as you read this book you will feel in it not only the professional energy of a therapist but the personal energy of a man who has journeyed in constant intimacy with an invisible presence that at one time he could not understand, but that now nourishes him.

Feel free to write e-mails and letters as you are so moved. You can contact me at www.gurianinstitute.com or www. michaelgurian.com. All the best to you as you join with me and many others in working with the invisible presence. May you find much of your own purpose in life and satisfaction as a man or woman by the blessings this presence holds for you.

Acknowledgments

This book could not have been written without the support of Linda Whittenberg, William H. Houff, Julia Bjordahl and Sandy Hank, Sally Green, Jo Stowell, Jim Connor, Ron Hansen, Terry Trueman, Bob Cole, Gene Dire, Roy Carpenter, and Herm Ryans; my agent, Ned Leavitt; my editor, Dave O'Neal, who with quiet tenacity helped me find the book I had in me; my daughter, Gabrielle; and Gail, my wife, friend, and partner.

Teachers of the Sacred Psychology of the Goddess and the Hero have been crucial to my own growth and the growth of my work. In ways I cannot ever adequately trace, pieces of their work appear in my own. Chief among them are Robert Bly, Jean Shinoda Bolen, Joseph Campbell, Carlos Castaneda, Clarissa Pinkola Estes, Douglas Gillette, Jean Houston, Robert Johnson, Carl Jung, Sam Keen, John Lee, Michael Meade, Robert Moore, Carol Pearson, Starhawk, Barbara Walker, and Marion Woodman. My thanks to all these women and men.

Thanks to my Native American teachers, especially to that gracious practitioner of Shamanic traditions, Jim McNeill. My special thanks to the Southern Ute tribe and to my father for first introducing me as a young boy to Native American tradition.

This book was deeply influenced by the work of John Bradshaw, Robert Hopcke, Alice Miller, Daniel Wakefield, Warren Farrell, Victor Turner, Joseph Palmour, Linda

Schierse Leonard, Sam Osherson, Dan Kiley, Ken Druck, and Aaron Kipnis. My thanks for all your good work.

Special thanks are due David Feinstein and Stanley Krippner, whose ground-breaking *Personal Mythology* has helped men and women look inward for wisdom and growth. Their guided meditations have influenced forms in Part Two of this book.

In the end, all written and oral efforts to understand and heal mother-son relationships would be impossible without the courage of individual men and women. I have seen this courage in groups, workshops, counseling sessions, homes, schools, and special seminars. I have felt it as I travel the country doing talk shows, and I have answered this question from women more frequently than any other: "I am a mom trying to raise sons. How do I do it?" I have felt it in men's retreats and workshops around the world as men come together to explore and heal relationships with mothers.

To these men and women, who have allowed me to work with them, I give my deepest thanks.

The Invisible Presence

Introduction

He had come back to his mother. . . . Everybody
else could grow shadowy, but she could not. It was
as if the pivot and pole of his life, from which he
could not escape, was his mother.
　　　　　　　　—D. H. LAWRENCE, *Sons and Lovers*

A MAN HAD A recurring dream. He walked into the huge
front door of a large country castle after a stroll in the
surrounding woods. His own smaller house, his friends
and family, were across the forest in the village.

The man felt how empty the castle was—no kids, no
workers, no pets. Yet as he climbed the stairs, he sensed a
huge, ancient presence. He was afraid of the presence. He
adored the presence. It wasn't a lover, yet somehow he
knew he needed it to survive. It wasn't a deity, yet it was
somehow more than human. It wasn't a friend, yet it knew
him so well he needed few words with it.

The man got to the top of the stairs. He knew the
presence waited for him behind one of the huge oak doors
he was now facing. Which one? He had been in this
confusion before. He yearned for some man, his father or
some old man, to come up to him and tell him what to
do. But in this castle he had never met a man.

He went to the first door, opened it, found nothing. He
went to the next. Nothing. Then the next. He opened the

first six doors, finding nothing, becoming more and more relieved and more and more anxious.

He walked through the seventh door. There she was. His mother. Sitting at a huge wall mirror. On half her face was a smile, on half a look of rage. How could she do this to her face? Yet she did. "Close the door," she told him. "Come to the mirror."

He did as he was told. Much as he wanted to, he couldn't resist.

"Dance, my dear," she said.

He danced. He danced as he had when he was a boy, twirling, jumping, doing all the things she used to love. She clapped and he laughed. The moment of dancing was ecstatic. Following his mother's eyes, he too turned to the mirror, watching himself dance in the glass.

A wave of anxiety came over him suddenly. The dancing man he saw in the mirror was not a man at all—it was himself as a boy. Memories flooded him: memories of all the times he had come here, danced here. Memories of how much he loved the ecstatic twirling, and hated looking in the mirror.

For a moment he was paralyzed. Then he pulled off his shoe and threw it at the mirror. The mirror didn't break. He ran to the mirror and punched it. It didn't break. Nor, strangely, did he feel pain in his hands. He turned to look at his mother helplessly. She stared at him, saying nothing, inscrutable.

He fled the room, ashamed. He ran down the stairs and out of the castle. He fled through the woods, afraid, ashamed, trying to get control of himself. He arrived back at his house. His wife and family saw him running toward them. They recognized his agitation from previous times. They girded themselves, finding other things to do. He had never told them where he went or why his brief trips through the woods confused him so, but they knew the trips left him crushed for days.

The last thing the man remembered, before waking up, was the confusion, fear, and anger on the face of his wife, who watched him, as always, waiting for something from him, something he did not know how to give—something he yearned for too: something freeing.

That dreamer was me. Like most men I know, have known, work with, and discover in my research—indeed, like most men in this culture—I grew up in a family and social system that brought me manhood by default. My physiological clock struck twelve, and I became a man by growing adult male sexual organs and body hair. My social clock struck twelve, and I became a man by learning to drive a car, by leaving home, by going to college, by getting a responsible job, by marrying, by having a family. My psychological clock, however, despite my physical and social manhood, was still creeping along at about six o'clock. I was still only half-grown.

And I kept having that dream about my mother.

Like most men, I had a psychological clock stuck somewhere in adolescence. This did not make me inferior to anyone. Yet, like so many men, I felt inferior to other men I competed with and to women I loved, hiding my sense of being an impostor from everyone, creating few really close, intimate relationships. At times I even tried to compensate for the stuck clock by becoming grandiose and hypermasculine. And I had moments, even months, of loving, wise, and powerful maturity, too. I was like most men. Certain experiences—such as weddings, the birth of children, hard work and personal accomplishment, a relationship that's working well, children's successes—give us the feeling, sometimes quite prolonged, that finally the clock has become unstuck, struck twelve, and we've arrived, we've grown up, we've made it.

Then, more often than not, we come down off the high of the event, relationship, or accomplishment and feel again that we're impostors, unable to really say what a man is, how we are men, and what we really need out of life. Many of us don't face this crisis until midlife, when we worry that we've accomplished very little and have little spiritual ground to live on. Some of us start the inward journey to maturity earlier.

Some of us are lucky enough to have had our developmental needs met in the first twenty years of life, so that we can make the inward journey more for experimental personal growth than as a passage into adulthood. Some of us never make the journey at all, never admitting that our clock is stuck, that we feel isolated and like imposters, and that if we had the chance, we'd go back to our mother's mirror in a flash, since hers was the only world we ever really felt whole in.

As late twentieth-century males, men of our generation were brought up in homes by individuals who loved us but who were missing some essential knowledge about raising us and were not supported by their culture in raising us completely. When I was having my recurring dream about my mother's mirror, and as I began, in my middle twenties, my journey to mature manhood, I began to discover how warped our families have become. My discovery began with my own family, which at first I thought uniquely vague in its attention to my needs as a maturing boy. I soon discovered that my family's confusions about raising sons were much like those of most families in our culture.

My family was relatively nuclear. My father was gone most of the time, so my mother had to do the bulk of the parenting. She and I developed a psychological connection by which I supplied her emotional nurturance in the absence of my father, as much as she supplied me the nurturance a child needed. She did not know how to let go of me nor I of her. As she and I tried to separate during my adolescence, so that my psychological clock could tick toward individuation and maturity, she became scared of losing me, and I felt guilty for leaving her. Meanwhile, I learned very little of a concrete nature from my father and other men about the spiritual and emotional life of men. Most of what I learned about relating to women was confusing and still somehow stuck in relating to my mother. By the time I went to college I was still a boy, dressed in a man's body. When, in my twenties, I finally admitted this, I began a wonderful journey.

Unresolved issues in a man's relationship with his mother are profound sources of trouble in a man's life. In studies and surveys done by psychologists and researchers over the last decade, among them psychologists Sam Osherson, Dan Kiley, and Ken Druck, psychotherapist Anne Grizzle, and researchers Carole Klein and Shere Hite, we have discovered that the majority of men in this culture have unresolved problems concerning their mothers. Some of these involve a mother's abuse, neglect, abandonment, or impingement on a son's healthy individuation. Others have to do with the father's emotional and/or physical absence, which affects the mother-son relationship profoundly. Whatever their source, the problems invade the mother's nurturance of her son. The son lives out his adulthood—unless he awakens to his problems and deals with them—in a fog of low self-image, relationship anxieties, and family tension.

"In our own culture," writes Carole Klein, "we are considerably confused. Mothers are told to remain emotionally involved with their sons so that the sons have enough psychological support to fulfill society's expectations of them. Yet as a woman embraces her male child, some voices will rise in ominous warning that she may create a 'momma's boy,' the ultimate crime. As a result mothers often seem to live with their sons on the edge of pain, wanting to stay close, afraid not to pull back. Nor do sons escape their own bewildering conflict. The battle between establishing distance and clinging to dependence takes hold of a boy almost at the moment that he learns to differentiate himself from his other or sister as a male, rather than a female."

Mother-son issues that arise in boys and later affect a son's adult self-image and relationships are hard to admit, hard to imagine, and hard to define. It is easier to say we were wounded by our fathers, but about our mothers we tend to say, "She was great, no problems with her. Or if I had any, they weren't much. She took good care of me."

Yet in a culture that does not help sons separate from mothers, that puts mothers and women down, and that replaces realistic portraits of mothers and women with unrealistic stereotypes; in families that embroil sons in extreme gender war they don't understand, in which the father and elder men are so often absent from the home that the mother must do the parenting job of two (which, especially if she must work, she cannot), and that provide little extended family to support her or help the son through necessary stages of male development, we as sons grow up wounded, confused, and conflicted. We need to find ways to heal ourselves and discover who we are. We must undertake a conscious search for our own mirror. Our relationships with our spouses, partners, children, friends, and co-workers depend on our exploring the very murky and too often oversimplified world of mother-son relationships; and they depend on our healing the misconceptions, hidden aggressions, and painful wounds we have received both in our mother's world and in the larger world we grew to know, which seemed to confuse us even more about mothers, women, and Woman.

The search for a mirror of our own and the healing of our wounds involves a long process and long journey. This book invites you to make that journey. It invites women to better understand men and their own maternal relationships with their sons, and it invites men to enter an experience by which they can discover and activate healthy adult relationships, appropriate boundaries, and loving openness with intimate partners.

This book is based on some assumptions, among them that most of our mothers tried their best to raise us well, but they and we live(d) in a cultural system that led to very distinct problems in mother-son relationships; that many of us may not even have lived with our natural mothers, so "mother" to us might mean something different than natural mom; that while many mothers are willing to explore the issues raised here, many are not, especially mothers of sons who are already "grown up." Much of this exploration we must do on our own, and with some supportive friends and groups.

Both women and men dance in their mothers' mirrors. Both need to separate from their mothers' mirrors and find their own. Thus, much of what is said in this book about adult men and their relationships with their mothers, and much of what readers will experience, applies to daughters as well as sons. There is also a great deal of material that very practically informs mothers of sons how to navigate the complexities of their relationships with their growing boy-men. Yet I will speak directly to men, because the final part of this book is a quest of initiation into full manhood.

This is not a mother-bashing book. It asks readers to be honest about their mother's behavior and their own behavior in relation to their mother's; it pinpoints deep cultural inadequacies in attitudes toward mother-son relationships; and it is a book about making peace, finding a core self, and letting go of damaging legacies, including abject blaming.

Part One of this book tells the story of the stages of a boy's development in relation to his mother and within his family system. Part Two turns the story of a boy's development into manhood into an experience that explores and dramatizes the feelings of mothers, boys, men, and women. Part Two also leads any man who wishes to make it on a journey at whose end he will stand in his own mirror, different from what he was before.

The journey we'll take together in this book is based on the knowledge that to grow into self-confidence and the next healthy stage of our lives, we must confront our relationship with our mothers, and that we can do the bulk of that confrontation within ourselves. We also assume we can engage in this confrontation with our own wounds, tensions, and personal issues as our need and inspiration, certain techniques and rituals as our tools, archetypal metaphors as our aids, and ancient myths and stories as our guides.

How to Use This Book

I have used the process of this book with hundreds of people. Each has navigated the material in his or her own way. Although *Mothers, Sons, and Lovers* helps you focus on mother-son relationships, many other relationships in your life will be explored as well. The wisdom and guidance you discover within yourself will also apply to those relationships.

As this book proceeds into material about how the mother-son relationship directly affects the son's later patterns of intimacy with mate or partner, it will become clear that while most of its material applies to homosexual as well as heterosexual sons, it is nonetheless written about relationships between men and women. This is a matter of convenience. As there is not space in this book to deal specifically and adequately with the effects of mother-son patterns on homosexual relationships, I ask your patience. Also, if you are gay or lesbian, consider reading Robert Hopcke's *Jung, Jungians and Homosexuality*, an insightful book about homosexual relationships that uses archetypal psychology as its base.

If you are not familiar with the word *archetype* and/or have never looked at psychology and spirituality from a mythological point of view, take a moment now to read the part of chapter 4 entitled "The Vision Quest and the Hero's Journey." It contains valuable material on archetypes.

In my previous book, *The Prince and the King: Healing the Father-Son Wound*, I explored father-son relationships in depth, taking the reader on an archetypal journey in which he confronted his father and healed wounds he gained in his father's house. In this book the archetypal journey is about our relationships with our mothers. But because these two relationships are so intertwined—our first twenty years of life spent in the web of mother-father-son—a man cannot generally deal with one without also dealing with the other. The psychological currency we carry in our adult pockets as we try to purchase and earn happiness is a coin with Dad's face on one side and Mom's face on the other.

You can use this book in solitude, but I also suggest reading it, doing its personal rituals, and making its quest while in the company of other men, either in a men's or couples' group or with a therapist or another trusted friend. Individuals and groups, as well as counselors and therapists, will find that this book's program weaves into about a year of a man's life. Men might come together to do its program in groups that use the programs step by step, as they have come together to form Prince-King groups; therapists might form such groups. I have seen this process work well in all these contexts. The advantage of going through the process with others is that, as a hero needs his mentors to guide him and his brothers to admire him, all of us need our voices to be heard and our visions admired by others. Thus, even if you speak only to trusted friends or family members about episodes of this journey, do speak them, do articulate them.

Don't be surprised if your journey through this book takes longer than you expected. It takes time to discover *your* personal langauge, *your* personal story, and *your* own path of healing. Deep work is slow work. It is only in life-styles as fast-paced as ours that we have been able to convince ourselves otherwise.

It is my hope that in reading this book and accepting the journey, you'll get a deep sense of what the male inner world looks and feels like. If the lessons of dream, mythology, and archetype are valid, that inner world is not a world of chaos; it is a world of cosmos, of intricate structure.

PART ONE

How a Son's Relationship with His Mother Affects the Rest of His Life

---

Men do not often discuss their unresolved feelings about their mothers. While they play a key part in their relationships with other women, these emotions are often hidden away out of our awareness. Men's deepest feelings toward their mothers remain some of their best-kept secrets, even from themselves. Yet a large part of what men expect from women, and of themselves as men, dates back to their childhood experiences with their mothers.

—KEN DRUCK, *The Secrets Men Keep*

COMMENTS FROM A MEN'S GROUP

All I know is, I'm happily married twenty-one
years. Women make sense to me. Except when
Mom's in town. I just don't understand what happens to me. It's not like it's any big thing, but still,
I go all weird and soft. My wife tells me I turn into
a kid. It really causes problems in our relationship.

—HAMID

Every woman I've ever really known, deep down
really known, turned me into a momma's boy.
Some time or other, it just started happening. Then
they have the gall to tell *me* I've got "unresolved
issues" about my mother. They're the ones doing
it to me.   —BILL

I don't have a clue about women. They don't make
sense the way Mom did.   —ALLEN

I'm on my fourth marriage. I was in counseling
after my second and after my third. Both times the
counselor helped me see how I had issues around
my mother. Either I'm trying to marry her each
time or divorce her each time. I don't know which.

—KEVIN

I guess what I've kind of discovered in life—even
though I know it's dumb—is that except for Mom,
a man really isn't ever going to find someone he
can trust. We try and try, but when everything's
said and done, we've got to just take care of ourselves, and hope for the best, and put flowers on
Mom's grave.   —ANTHONY

Chapter 1: Searching for the Man in the Mirror

> Early on we experience women as the ones who fill us up, who comfort and take care of us, without having an opportunity in growing up to learn how to fill ourselves and to feel full while truly separate from women.
>
> —SAM OSHERSON, *Finding Our Fathers*

WHO DO YOU SEE when you look in the mirror? Do you see a man you are proud of, a man you know well, a man you trust?

You shave the face of an adult male. Naked before the mirror, you see the body of an adult male.

But do you see a *man?*

Do you find yourself confused about how to be intimate and often worried and guilty that you're not doing relationships right, raising your kids right, loving others right?

Do you find yourself easily distracted by the escape that substance, work, love, and television addictions provide, and by the fashions of people you don't really know or trust?

Do you feel inadequate and unable to understand why, and ever-ready to sacrifice your sense of yourself for some idea of what you should be that someone else—especially a spouse, partner, or parent—tries to impose on you?

In every mythology of mature heroism, an adolescent has grown into manhood and reached maturity when he has developed capacities for deep intimacy, wise seeing, and powerful self-trust. A *man,* the story goes, is loving, wise, and powerful. Mature heroism does not necessarily mean a man has developed these qualities to perfection. Mistakes are built into mythological journeys. Mature heroism means when the adult male looks into the mirror, he sees a man who has been nurtured in and then earned his manhood, ready and willing to assume its responsibilities and recognize its joys, prepared for its sufferings, filled with a sense of his own worthiness, and humble with awe at the spiritual world that contains him.

I'll never forget what one man said to me in the early stages of a men's group I led: "Spiritual life? That's for priests and Sunday school."

Yet in most tribal cultures—and in our own ancestral cultures—people spend a third of their day in prayer, ceremony, rite, and ritual—in "soul time."

We grow into adulthood with significant problems in at least one of the three key components of mature manhood. Striving to be loving (able to be intimate), wise (able to live discerned values and engage in life as a search for meaning), and powerful (able to live in personal empowerment), we fall short in one of these, and spend much of our lives presenting a false self to cover our sense of inadequacy; pretending to be intimate but really fearing it; pretending to know what the world needs of us but really feeling very dumb; pretending we have personal power by disempowering others.

SEARCHING FOR THE MAN IN THE MIRROR

As males in a culture that fears and forgets spiritual growth, brought up in the highly industrialized twentieth century, taught that material gain is the way to prove we are men, we have lost contact with tribal training of males and mythological blueprints of how males need to develop. Most of us grew up underfathered and overmothered. We got locked into relying on our mothers for our emotional bedrock; yet we must separate from our mothers and discover a male mode of feeling. It should come as no surprise that the vast majority of us come into adulthood confused, feeling defensive toward women's overwhelming affection, and feeling abandoned by men's lack of intimacy with us.

It should also come as no surprise that when we read a book about these issues or become involved in counseling or groups or church activities or any other personal growth work, or when through a failed relationship, job transition, period of depression, parent's death, child's birth, or any other crisis/transition point, we look in the mirror for a long time, we see as much unfulfilled boy there as confident man. We have not been initiated into manhood. We are still a Prince, not yet a King. More and more studies, more and more psychologists, and more and more of our own friends, spouses, and acquaintances are noticing that yearning boy inside of us, calling us to look in the mirror and see him too. Seeing him need not be a source of shame. It need not be a reason for the reflex of denial. Seeing that young, yearning Prince is the beginning of a wonderful journey.

THE SURVIVAL MODE

A man in his early fifties once said to me, "When I hit midlife crisis, I hit it hard. I lost everything important to me—my wife, my family. I had to really look at things, at myself. I looked back at my life and felt like I had signed some kind of hidden agreement when I was born into the man's world. It was as if someone said: if you stay emotionally and spiritually half-developed, you'll get all the material success you want. Which I got. But inside I was empty."

Most of us, by late adolescence, have signed this agreement. The agreement says, "We'll let you work your way up to the top of the world, as long as you cut off any sacred yearnings along the way." When we do get to the top, we discover a world ruled by the survival mode—we will have to make money, dress well, and be clever in order to retain our place, a place we'll never be satisfied with anyway. Like a machine that will spend the rest of its life jumping back and forth in a concealed frenzy between lover, money, and personal appearance, we guard "the top of the world" without realizing we're only protecting a socially powerful but internally disempowering survival mode.

For many of us, midlife crisis is the first time we see the man/boy in the mirror and realize we're living in survival mode. We come to that midlife moment when our instincts kick in to remind us that we are mortal—it is time to take stock of where we are in the life journey. We may be dissatisfied with this life, but we made an agreement, we feel locked in; and we find our culture provides few ways out of the agreement.

The first step in tearing up the agreement is to recognize how family systems and cultural imperatives have locked us into that agreement. We recognize that while we were searching for initiation into manhood, Dad was mostly gone, Mom hung on too long, there were few mentors around, and we were left to find wisdom teachers among boys a couple years older than us, or on television, in films, and in other forms of popular culture. We were badly initiated into manhood, and this fact haunts our lives.

WHAT IS INITIATION?

Social systems, lack of ritual education, patterns of male isolation from feeling, and lack of psychological separation from mothers have put a wall between older men and boys, a wall we explore in this chapter; but within us there is still the instinct to link with each other as men—to construct that link so strongly that it can never be severed—through a boyhood and adolescent series (not just one *bar mitzvah*) of ritual experiences of manhood. In these experiences, the boy is put through (or finds himself in) ordeals and tests of manhood, ritual tasks which, as Robert Moore puts it, initiate the boy "into the mysterious world of male responsibility and male spirituality." Through this long series of initiatory experiences, the boy seeks to be accepted as a man by his family and community and, most important, by himself.

Without these experiences, he is not capable of healthy and mutually nurturing relationships with women. If he is not initiated away from Mom into the world of men, women still seem like Mother to him, even in his forties, even as he knows an adult male cannot open (and close) himself to Mother-Woman the way he used to. Without healthy initiation, the grown man is not prepared for the harsh realities of male life and remains an adolescent.

At a talk I was giving about initiation, a man said, "So what? So maybe we're not initiated too well in our culture. What's the concrete disadvantage of that?" In the same group was a Vietnam veteran who for the first time realized why he went to Vietnam: "I was eighteen and didn't know what a man was. I joined the army, thinking the army would make me a man. I made a terrible mistake. Why couldn't I have become a man back home?"

If we are not initiated, we get locked into adult-adolescent modes of intimacy. The uninitiated adolescent approach is to experiment rather than to commit; to act out anger, sometimes violently, because a man does not yet know how to control his anger; and to avoid "embarrassing" displays and dialogues of deep feeling.

If we are not initiated, we get locked out of personal fulfillment. The uninitiated adolescent approach to personal growth is to conform to what others say is moral and spiritual, without seeking his own wisdom—or to rebel completely and turn away from all spiritual searching.

If we are not initiated, we misunderstand power. The uninitiated male nurtures either a void of self-image, in which he feels a constant sense of not deserving what he earns, and/or a boyish grandiosity. His confusion about personal power often results in his exercising "power-over" others and the environment. In the mythology of the Bible, humans were given by God the power to guard, protect, and lead the whole ecological system—God expressly told the Hebrews to nurture the environment in a "power-with" style. God spoke in the mythos of the Old Testament to initiated men and women who for millennia did protect and preserve the environment. Architecture, art, and design "served" nature. Only recently have we left boys and adolescents so uninitiated that man/boys are leading our cultures, and destruction of the environment is possible.

If a boy is not well initiated, he will nonetheless find

unhealthy, shadow ways to be initiated. A gang initiate murders a rival gang member on a New York street and says, "See there, now I'm a man." In a culture that doesn't understand initiation, drugs and alcohol become initiations for young men. In Oliver Stone's film *The Doors,* Jim Morrison, son of a disengaged father, rebellious, spiritually hungry for real manhood, sought initiation by Native American medicine men in his visions. Drugs and booze, the tools he ultimately relied upon for initiation, for vision, for breaking through to the other side, destroyed him. Many men feel their lack of initiation less dramatically—they just go through life in survival mode, without self-trust.

Separation from Mother: A Crucial Initiation

The objective of healthy family life is to teach a growing child to individuate, that is, to trust himself. To learn this, he must first bond with and trust his care givers; and he must separate from the care givers and feel his own power. Children are constantly pulling away from parents and coming back to them and pulling away again. The parent (and mentor) must put as much kindness and firmness into the pulling-away time as the coming-back time. Bonding is thus about *both* attachment and separation.

The separation from the mother is the most anthropologically studied separation initiation in an adolescent's life. Separation from the mother is not necessarily about a boy living apart from his mother—although it can include this, as when a boy goes to live with Dad. Many young men move out of the house for college, military, or other reasons, but still have not psychologically separated. Separation from the mother primarily implies that the son is no longer ultimately dependent on the mother for these elements of his psychological life:

- development of a core self, which he will bring to his adult life
- development of his view of masculinity
- development of personal rituals that will help him function in day-to-day life
- development of personal rituals for feeling he belongs in the universe
- development of personal vision of his life's purpose
- development of his emotional language
- development of his view of femininity
- development of healthy communication and conflict styles
- development of a sense of safety in the world
- development of personal boundaries

Unfortunately, most of us, as John Lee says, never really had the experience of separation from Mom/intimate fathering by Dad/mentoring by initiated elders. Still dependent on Mom/Woman for our core self and much of our other developmental needs, we suffer terrible confusion in our sense of what and who we are as men. This confusion severely affects our marriages and love relationships.

The break with the mother, supported in traditional cultures by rituals and ceremonies, is unsupported and unnoticed in our own. Fathers don't even know they are supposed to be involved. Fathers do alter somewhat their interaction with us as we enter adolescence, but not very much, and not in rituals that connect them and us to our masculine spirituality. We are still attached to our mothers, trusting them for our nurturance, not ourselves; we are not ritually bonded with our fathers, yet yearn to trust them for our nurturance. Fathers do not lead us toward *deep* male self-trust, so we turn to male mentors to teach us healthy male spirituality. We bond and separate with coaches and teachers and again learn a great deal, but now our troubles in initiation are compounded: we are still attached to our mothers, we are still yearning for our fathers, and we move through the time of our mentors too quickly to heal these lost initiations.

We grow to love and have families of our own without the kind of trust in our manhood that we desperately needed to learn during adolescence, especially in the act of separating from Mom. Robert Bly talks about how every boy must steal the key to the wild man's cage from under his mother's pillow; separating from our mothers is a primordial door we must walk through if we are to learn about huge and deep parts of ourselves that our mothers have not been able to show us.

Almost fifty years ago, Joseph Campbell clearly saw our culture's loss of mythological blueprints and loss of male initiation rituals; he saw the direct connection between our self-destructiveness and our neglect of essential male development patterns, especially healthy and respectful separation from Mother. In *The Hero with a Thousand Faces,* he wrote, "It has always been the prime function of mythology and rite to supply the symbols that carry the human spirit forward, in counteraction to those other constant human fantasies that tend to tie it back." Those fantasies, he explains, generally relate to fantasies of constant care and attention during boyhood with Mom. As he puts it: "We remain fixated to the unexorcised images of our infancy, and hence disinclined to the necessary passages of our adulthood . . . In the United States there is even a pathos of inverted emphasis: the goal is not to grow old, but to remain young; not to mature away from Mother, but to cleave to her."

The cult of youth we live in has become more pronounced since Campbell wrote this in the 1940s. Our cultural confusion about initiation and an adolescent's separation from his mother has only increased. Yet as I talk to mothers, I find that many sense how important all this material about initiation really is.

A mother's job—even as she teaches, nurtures, disciplines, and supports our search for manhood—is very much to hold back the coming of manhood. At a workshop I was doing on mothers and sons, a mother of three sons put this wonderfully: "My sons are in their teens now. If I really knew all the longings and confusions they feel, if I knew all the amoral and dangerous things they do, if I ever knew all about their sex lives and their fantasies, I'd go crazy. Let's face it. I can't know about those. I can help explain the crazy things their girl friends do. But I can't make my boys into men. I've done my part. Now it's up to Dad, and the boys themselves."

Another mother said, "I wasn't hard on my boys. I taught them well. But I just couldn't help pampering them, especially when life was hard for them. My husband and I always had fights about this. Even when the boys were teenagers, I hated to see them in any kind of pain. My husband said pain was OK, it was good for the boys. He was more right than I realized then. The boys will always love me, I know that. But it did them good to move away and stop calling home and find themselves. One day, finally, I just had to learn to stop calling them all the time, stop worrying about them, stop worrying that they were getting hurt all the time. I just had to let them get hurt and take care of it themselves."

There is a difference between maternal and paternal nurturance. This woman was sensing that difference. Recently in this culture, we've tended to say women are nurturing and men are not. In fact, women and men are both nurturing; we just have very different styles of nurturance. Men can gain by learning more of the maternal style of nurturance, just as women are gaining political ground by learning the paternal. Neither style is more right or wrong, and both have their flaws. The son, as he is being initiated and separating from Mom, tends to need more of the paternal style.

The maternal style is based on the mother's sense of the child being "hers." She carried the child in her body, and the child seems like a part of her. Even mothers who adopt have told me they feel this possessiveness and lack of separateness between themselves and the baby. The paternal style is based in the father's physical separateness from the child.

Given a situation where both parents love their children unequivocally, and neither side of the family suffers from too much addiction or dysfunction, the mother's style of nurturance tends toward emotional rescue of the boy, immediate forgiveness of his flaws, and less harsh discipline than the father's. She is tacitly saying to him, "You're a part of me and maybe the best part of me, and as long as I can clutch you to me, you'll be fine. Your very existence is my reason for respecting you." The father's style of nurturance tends to say to the boy, "You are not a part of me. You have my love, but you need to *earn* my respect in your life journey as a boy and as a man. You will ultimately earn this respect by doing what you must to live your vision with personal responsibility, and by being a loving, wise, and powerful man."

These two styles of nurturance can go awry, get out of balance, and cause huge problems for children. The mother can become *smothering,* the father *authoritarian*— the mother in her way crushing the son's core self by controlling it too much, the father in his way crushing it by forcing the son always to be "doing" and doing as Father knows best, rather than seeing what the son sees in himself and helping the son nurture that vision. Or the father can be passive and distant, forcing the mother into the position of trying to fulfill both roles, trying to operate in both styles of nurturance, a burden no mother deserves. Or any number of other dysfunctions can invade the family system so that the son does not get a balanced dose of the two styles of nurturance.

When the son starts separating from his mother around puberty, he is yearning for more of the paternal style. He may fear it—it may be the harder style—but still he yearns for it. Developmentally, Mom needs to let him go so he can experience that style of nurturance. Before puberty and the onset of manhood, he was able to experience both styles without too much confusion. But as his physical, psychological, and social clocks all begin to move more quickly toward his accomplishment of mature manhood, he needs to hear the message, "It's time you earned respect, rather than had it given to you." If a single mother is raising a son alone, adolescence is when she needs to switch her style of nurturance, and/or help the son find an emotionally healthy elder man who will make him earn respect and feel separate but not alone.

The archetype and metaphor of the Warrior helps us see this clearly. Although the word *warrior* conjures up for some people a very narrow definition—destroyer, killer, rapist, pillager—that is not the Warrior we mean here; rather, that is the Shadow Warrior, the Warrior run amok. The kind of Warrior I am talking about is the kind Carlos Castaneda described in *Tales of Power*. "The basic difference between an ordinary man and warrior," explains the Yaqui shaman Don Juan, "is that a warrior takes everything as a challenge while the ordinary man takes everything either as a blessing or a curse." The warrior is grounded in himself, meets life head on. The uninitiated adolescent is outward focused, vacillating between high and low depending on what's thrown at him, unable to self-lead.

When tribal cultures initiated their young men as warriors, they were initiating far more than the ability to kill (that ability was a small piece, and a last resort). Primarily they were initiating qualities of discipline, assertiveness, teamwork, altruism, loyalty to a cause, self-protection, and protection of others. To inculcate these things into the youngsters, separation from the mother was not only required but became part of the teaching experience. *If a son could successfully separate from his mother—the one person in the world who had most protected him from having to learn the warrior qualities—he had taken the first leap into those qualities.*

This is the razor's edge that separates a mother and a son. It is very painful. In every culture we know, part of the core development of a child is his knowledge that there is a safe place and that safe place is Mom; there is a place where he can feel whole and warm and settled—that place is with Mom. Having that place of safety and wholeness, he survives the suffering that fate and crisis throw at him. A child must have this feeling to flourish in childhood.

But to grow up, he must be able to survive fate and

crisis by developing his own safe place and place of wholeness. It must be a place *he* controls, from within. It will not ultimately work to transfer the puppet strings of his safety and wholeness to a wife or partner, because she can leave him, just as Mom can die. To grow up, a child must be able to make himself feel safe and whole. He must be led by other emotionally healthy and spiritually vital men into the mysteries of manhood.

Ritual Initiation

There are three psychological actions in the male initiation process:

1. attachment to and separation from Mom
2. attachment to and separation from Dad
3. attachment to and separation from mentors, who function as transitional and auxiliary parents, as children grow to maturity

There are three simultaneous interpersonal activities of initiation:

1. a boy's search for his own vision, personal powers, and talents
2. unforgettable lessons in personal, family, and tribal responsibility
3. experimentation with lovers

And there are three spiritual/emotive goals in the initiation process:

1. to learn and accept lifelong rituals that will bring intimacy with a spiritual center (what many cultures call a "soul" or "sacred self")
2. to negotiate new and mutually empowering boundaries with the feminine

3. to develop a commitment to others and the earth (altruism)

In our culture we initiate fragments of these, and we end up with fragmented men. We initiate much more by shaming and competition than is healthy. We do not understand developmental patterns enough to nurture the attachments and separations that individuation requires. We do not give children clear signals and teaching about what is appropriate experimentation with lovers and what isn't. We fill children's lives with so many gadgets and stimulants that each new generation becomes less clear on where personal responsibility begins and ends, and how to achieve it. We do not support our children's spiritual search, nor do we teach them that life is a journey—we teach them that it is a set of goals to be discarded once reached. We do not help children discover ways to kiss the earth and nurture their own divine connection with all things.

In some very deep and hidden part of ourselves, our culture has developed in this direction with the very best intentions: because we want the best for our kids, we want them to have more than we did, we don't want them to suffer the restrictions we did, *we don't want them to have to become adults*. At its core, materialism takes any culture in the direction of adult adolescence. By its very nature, reliance on material goods for social and personal accomplishment is a reliance on a pace of productivity that only the young can keep up with, and only the adolescent or young adult, who has the time and lack of responsibility to be hedonistic, can fully enjoy. This culture's virtual destruction of rites of passage was either the chicken or the egg of industrialism and materialism—we'll never really know. But of one thing we can be sure: the lack of ritual initiation in this culture is one primary factor in our remaining psychologically adolescent throughout our lives.

A *ritual initiation structure* has four main components:

1. a safe place
2. an elder, trusted by the initiate
3. a tacit sense that the ritual rises from and is supported by the community to which the initiate belongs
4. a tacit sense that the ritual connects the boy to the sacred world

The safe place can be a functional, therefore emotionally safe, family home; or it can be another place made safe through blessings, however the initiate and elder/leader define them. In families, "blessings"—safety and sanctity rituals—are less formal than in church or sacred wisdom circles (evening dinner-table conferences, tucking a child in, bedtime story), yet can be immeasurably binding.

If mother or father is the initiator, the family system itself is supported by the community. If a ritual elder is the initiator, he cannot be some sort of quack, unsupported by the community; he must be a medicine man or qualified mentor. Thus the elder is trusted by both the student/child and the community.

The ritual initiation teaches the boy his sacred interconnectedness with community and nature. It reminds the boy that he is not alone, that there is a sacred connection between his evolving self and the evolving human community that he will serve and that will serve him, and the greater circle of nature, at once loving and giving and destroying and indifferent, in which he and his loved ones lead their difficult lives.

The structural characteristics of ritual initiation mirror in a microcosmic way what the boy, once a man, will experience macrocosmically, in his uncontrollable and unprotected adult world; yet at the same time, the structural components of ritual initiation show the adolescent that when, later in manhood, he suffers pain, fear, shame, and grief, there is a community, a support system, a safe and sacred place within himself, in his family, in his church or sacred circle, in the woods or somewhere else he considers safe, to which he can go for support and growth.

During ritual initiation, the boy is told medicine stories (stories that teach and heal); is put through ordeals and tasks; receives symbolic or real wounds during these tasks; sometimes receives ritual humiliation from the parent or elder; returns fom the tasks and is received with questions about the experiences and ceremony. There is no winner or loser in this ritual initiation. Each boy grows at his own pace, although parents and elders will certainly push a boy to work hard and extend his boyish boundaries beyond fear into self-empowerment.

The importance of communication and stories cannot be underestimated in ritual initiation. A parent who humiliates and shames a son without teaching reasons and lessons through communication and story is not adequately teaching. Even "the strong, silent type" father must tell stories, even if he can't reveal his emotions to the son directly.

A Native American vision quest is a revealing example of ritual initiation. It is the model for the ritual experience I will guide you through in Part Two of this book.

I first came in contact with the vision quest ritual when I was thirteen and spent a year following my father and his Ute friends around the Southern Ute reservation of New Mexico. My father worked on the reservation, and I noticed a very positive and empowering quality of contact between boys and some older men that I didn't experience in my own culture. It was a quality of contact only possible among individuals who understand ritual. We left the Southern Ute reservation, but my brief initial experience with that culture did not leave me, and I have spent much of my life understanding the mythology and practicing the ritual of that experience.

The ritual initiation of vision questing is a spiritual integration of the young initiate's separation from his mother, his ability to survive for three or ten days in the wilderness alone, his bloody scratches and cold sleepless nights, the discovery in himself of physical prowess and ways to battle fear, the bond he feels with other men, the stories he hears and visions he sees, and a spiritual integration he proposes to his elders on his return from the journey—a spiritual integration for which he has only a remedial felt-sense after his return and for which he needs interpretive help from his elders.

Usually this spiritual integration becomes a part of the adolescent boy as he goes through many vision quests and other experiences, a youth who wanders away from his tribe but always comes back, at some point, to remember home. The goal and center of his learning is the vision quest structure itself: that a boy throughout his growing up will make journeys, external and internal, and have visions of who he is through his dreams, his seeing, the workings of his body, his education. These visions need to be interpreted with wisdom and admired for their courage. They are seen as tokens of the boy's manhood, suitable to find their place in the circles of men and women he seeks to join, suitable to give him strength as he leaves the protection of his family and becomes a man in his own right.

Most of all, the boy is taught through this vision quest to trust his inner world and look to it for guidance. He is taught his sacred self in metaphor and experience. If, for instance, he has a vision of Hawk on his quest, he has found Hawk to be the sacred carrier of his inner voice. Perhaps the boy will take on a new adult name with Hawk in it. When he must make a difficult decision a year from now, he will go back and try to summon Hawk again. He is really summoning, in whatever his personal ritual of meditation, prayer, or contemplation, his own inner voice—first and most powerfully revealed to him as Hawk in the structure of ritual initiation.

In learning his vision and powers on a male-led quest, the youth is taught to develop a sacred self outside the realm of his mother's world. This is not a call to destroy the visions she has given him and helped him see, nor is this a call to disrespect his mother—just the opposite. It is a call to understand boundaries. Everything in the universe has its place and time. Human life, like the ecosystem of which it is a part, is lived in cosmos rather than chaos. In his mother's world he can never really figure out who he is, so he must spend some time away from it.

The intense disrespect with which boys nowadays try to separate from their mothers is tragic. Given so little help managing the separation and making the quests of initiation, boys dump on moms. "When he turned thirteen or so," one mother told me, "he called me names, he made fun of me in public. He did everything to humiliate me. He's twenty-nine, and he's still doing it." To some degree, unless they are taught otherwise by elders or unless their mother is pretty dominating, boys will separate themselves through disrespect. They know few other ways in our culture. In a culture that has all but destroyed ritual initiation and has incorporated female inferiority, we can expect this disrespect of Mother to continue. And, because disrespect of Mother is an incomplete separation at best, we can also expect men to practice it on intimate partners onto whom they project the maternal.

THE ADOLESCENT HERO

In adolescence, our yearning to belong in the society around us and to be initiated into the world was so strong we tried everything we could, often overdoing it, to push against Mom, to belong among the other boys (often doing things with them Mom wouldn't approve of), to be loved by girls (certainly doing things with them Mom wouldn't approve of!), to "become a man." In our social setting, we measured status by how good we looked, often measuring our "looking good" by adopting a style that rebelled against Mom's vision of us. We preened in masks of mature manhood, most of these borrowed from peers and popular culture. We sought to be "noticed" above all else. Even if we were very shy adolescents, we hated our own shyness because it didn't fit the qualities of other adolescents. We sought self-image in what was popular around us. We sought self-image in what wasn't Mom. We yearned for men to come into our lives and take us by the arm and lead us into the world of men. We hungered for our father's attentions, but at the same time, he was either absent, or his vision of what we should be seemed to be an extension of Mom's, so we tended to rebel against both Mom and Dad simultaneously. Dad was not well enough trained to realize that in our rebellion is our cry for him to separate himself from Mom and come into our lives at puberty with fierce attention and subtle teaching.

Even as we rebelled against Mom in our adolescence, we were afraid of leaving Mom's world. When we become afraid of someone or something, we could still go back to Mom, and did. When we wanted our everyday needs met, from food and laundry to clothes and new shoes, Mom was always there. When we felt sad and alone, we hoped Mom noticed and consoled us.

In the tension of mother-resistance and mother-desire lives every adolescent and every adolescent hero. As Robert Moore and Douglas Gillette have put it, the adolescent hero "is overly tied to the Mother. But the Hero has a driving need to overcome her. He is locked in mortal combat with the feminine, striving to conquer it, and assert his masculinity." The adolescent hero tends toward extreme behaviors of bullying and cowardice. He turns to his parents, trusted elders, older boys and lover-girls to help him develop beyond this "mortal combat" and these extremes. He finds little healthy help.

Killing a lot of men or at least beating them up, sleeping with a lot of women, making a lot of money, remaining ever-young (nineteen, twenty, late adolescent), remaining "the best," avoiding embarrassing intimacy—these were the qualities of the adolescent heroes, the Princes disguised as Kings, we got from popular culture and from the boys around us. These were the qualities we taught each other, the grandiose "no dream is impossible to reach," "I'm all powerful" feelings. The creators of popular culture, for their own psychological and marketing reasons, catered and still cater to these feelings. Like most adolescent boys, we believed during the second decade of our lives that the adolescent mode of love, tending toward prolonged infatuation and sexual conquest, then dissatisfaction and emotional distance, was the most appropriate. In most of our lives there were not initiated, emotionally alive men with enough spiritual sense to slow down and wonder what their inner voices were, and help us wonder about ours.

To say "in most of our lives" is not an exaggeration. A decade of studies show that 80 to 90 percent of men of our generation did not have relationships of intimate trust with their fathers, and that 95 percent of boys learn by age nine to cut off all feelings except anger. So, like most boys around us, we strove to break away from our moms by doing dangerous things, by disobeying her, by treating her with disrespect, by feeling our own power and fighting against hers. Yet we had few initiated male role models to learn manhood from. In that void, filled with popular culture heroes specifically created to entertain rather than teach children, we did what everyone around us was doing: we became adolescent heroes. We learned to move always with the terrible speed of a boy who can't wait to grow up and be known as a man, even if he does not feel like a man.

Popular culture—this entertainment landscape of Princes disguised as Kings that initiates our children (children watch seven hours of television a day)—is, of course, a thing of our own production. If we, as men and women, were conscious of what boys need to mature into healthy Kings, we wouldn't create and support a popular culture— our society's substitute for the tribal story—that teaches men never to leave adolescence. Mothers would help their sons break from them, perhaps in some cultural equivalent to the Pygmy ceremony in which mothers beat their adolescent sons with sticks to force them toward their fathers. Fathers would be intimate with the sons. Mentors would do their part. The social structure would support mature, intimate relationships—it would facilitate soul time. Boys would not have to feel that adolescent heroism and survival modes were the best they could do. Men would not have to wait until midlife crisis, "second adolescence," when many of us rush back toward adolescent desires, to see how much self-destruction could have been avoided in our adult male lives.

The mature counterpart of the adolescent hero, the Mature Hero, gains his maturity when he makes the journey out of the survival mode, stepping out of the need for ego fixes and ego approval. Films like *Casablanca* and *To Have and Have Not* depict Humphrey Bogart's transformation from adolescent to mature hero. By the end of both these films, he has decided to do what he believes in and do it with courage, rather than to remain socially comfortable, in a survival mode. The Kevin Costner character in *Dances with Wolves* could be characterized as a mature hero. He develops within himself a spiritual mode and lives it authentically, even though that authenticity means danger and sacrifice.

The mature hero searches for wholeness in the inner life, which needs external approval less than it needs sacred ritual spaces and tasks in which to develop and other mature people to help nurture it. The mature hero gains his life when he sees his existence as a vision quest, not a conquest. The mature hero gains his heroism and the Prince gains his Kingship by making a journey through the most frightening wilderness of all—his own.

THE ADULT/ADOLESCENT: THE BOY/MAN IN THE MIRROR

When a boy is not initiated into manhood, what does he feel like? How does he act? Go back a few years. Picture yourself in junior high school and high school. Take out your yearbooks and remind yourself of what you looked like. Your adolescence will drift back to you. It was a very strange time. Even if you were one of the very popular kids, you may still remember the loneliness you felt inside. Nearly everyone remembers that loneliness, that fear of life that marks our culture's way of doing adolescence. When an adolescent male is not initiated, does not separate adequately from his mother, does not learn manhood from his father and other men, and thus remains in confusion about how to be a man and how to love mature women, he carries that fear of life into his adulthood.

Consider the following list of characteristics. Be honest with yourself about which of these fit your present life and relationships.

1. You want to prove you are a man whenever possible, especially in the company of women or men you consider superior to you.
2. You go out of your way to court danger, just to prove you're not afraid of a damned thing.
3. You sacrifice intimacy with family and others in order to accomplish professional goals you believe, consciously or unconsciously, will give you security in the world.
4. You are addicted to work, alcohol, drugs, relationships, and/or sex.
5. You approach new women/partners in your life with extremes of longing and terror. You tell her and others your most intimate secrets, then wish you never had, and soon turn away from her.
6. You are unable to commit to intimate relationships for more than a few months, or a year or two.
7. You constantly explain yourself, especially your

emotional actions and reactions, worrying over how even the smallest comment will be "heard" by others. You find yourself cleaning up emotional messes you've made, constantly feeling you have created a crisis with a companion, child, parent.

8. You have difficulty feeling comfortable with closure in your relationships. You have difficulty letting go of parents, intimate partners, friends, children.

9. You react to others' criticisms and their moods with childish responses, that is, with immediate fear that you are unloved by the critic. Sometimes this leads to early termination of relationships.

10. You assume you are primarily at fault for glitches and problems in relationships.

11. You assume you are rarely or never at fault for glitches and problems in relationships.

12. You avoid solitude and soul time, avoiding vacations, filling quiet time with television or busy work, and avoiding time alone in the woods or other activities of solitude and closeness to nature.

13. Even if you tend to be a silent man, you fill your time and thoughts with activities.

14. You fulfill the tasks of your everyday life out of guilt and a sense of duty, rather than out of a passion for life.

15. You have a terrible fear of death. Often this fear manifests itself as your avoiding even talking about the subject, and grows more from a fear of life than a fear of death.

16. You feel your vision is inadequate compared with the visions and ways of others. You are easily convinced that your rituals and ways of loving, being,

and doing are inherently flawed and inferior to other people's.

17. You unconsciously and constantly ask women/partners to show you you're OK.
18. If you are a son of a divorce, you still feel guilty for your parents' problems, unable to extricate yourself from a triangle with them.
19. You expect women/partners to do most of the changing to accommodate problems in your relationship(s).
20. Your feelings for intimate partners vacillate between affection and resentment, with very small things pushing your anger buttons more than you would like them to.

If three or more of the above statements feel deeply familiar, you are probably operating out of more fear of life than you want and need; and you probably were not adequately initiated into manhood, into your own vision. You are probably still locked in some adolescent patterns, many of them still surrounding your relationship with your mother.

Fear of life is a part of living. Because we are so small and life and the universe are so large, we cannot help but be afraid. Mythology and ritual have been our spiritual tools to manage our normal and essential fear. They turn fear of life into a passion to bond with life, adapt to life, and find the piece of the huge whole which is our own. Ideally, throughout our boyhoods, we discover and are taught myth and ritual. We do not realize yet that they are essential for managing our fear. Mom is still always present and manages most of our fear for us. In adolescence we feel the urge to separate from her, and we simultaneously become old enough to understand the necessity to manage fear and discover joy through personal vision—through one's own participation in and modification of cultural mythos and trival/family rituals.

If we are not initiated—if we are not supported in making a shift away from Mom's management of our fears to our own management of them through Father's vision, Mother's adult vision, mentors' visions, and our own vision and powers—we move into adulthood still locked in our fear of life, unable to feel adequate, secure, intimate. We may find subtle or obvious ways to go back to Mom to manage our fear—never moving out of her house, or marrying a woman who substitutes for her; or we avoid our fear by never admitting it and punishing (distancing ourselves from) anyone who comes close to us, and therefore to our fear.

Thus, one of the most dramatic influences of adult adolescence in your life will probably be in intimate relationships, especially relationships with women and intimate life partners. It is very important that we do the work of connecting our fears of women with our mothers. It is in a boy's early relationship with his mother that he first opens the doors within himself to the female. In his boyhood with her, he learns very well what the feminine is like, but does not quite know where masculine begins and feminine ends. Ideally, in his separation from his mother, he learns the boundaries between the masculine and the feminine without crushing the feminine. And as he pursues relationships with women in adulthood, he finds the feminine in the form of a new Goddess, an adult woman, his peer, with whom he can be safe.

In the real world we live in, a son grows up in confusion about where his mother's energy ends, his own energy begins, and his lover/mate's energy fits in. His father and elder men offer him little help. His mother doesn't want to let go of him, for fear of the danger and lack of support he will confront outside the home. The son thus remains in an archetypal adolescence, fighting the internal battle to break from his mother. He is never initiated as a Sacred Warrior. He learns a "mother tongue" for his emotional life but not a "father tongue." He stays trapped in the uninitiated warrior, finding himself in self-destructive patterns of codependence, emotional shutdown, isolation, and violence within a decade of adolescence.

It is as if we are naked over a gorge, one foot still on the side of the gorge where Mother lives, the other on the side of the gorge where lover/mate lives, the two sides of the earth gradually moving farther away from each other so that our psychic body is being split in two. As our legs are stretched apart more and more, our genitals hang less and less protected. Our manhood, year by year, becomes more and more vulnerable. As we move through early adulthood, we may escape dealing with this condition for a time—enjoying girl friends, distracted by climbing the social and job ladder, perhaps getting married and having children. But at some point, we will realize how stretched and near breaking our psychic body feels, and how cruelly vulnerable our manhood feels.

With our psychic body in this schism, our daily life and relationships get more and more confused. We tend to act more and more as an adolescent would—confusing sex with love; trying to prove we're men at every turn; turning away from conflict in committed relationships in the hope that it will just go away; relying on narcissistic self-aggrandizement for self-image; being distracted by the shine and verve of material goods; placing our lovers and mates on pedestals, then tearing them down when they do something imperfect; trying to conform to what the mass of people, fashion, and culture tell us a man is.

The son's journey out of his schism and deeply unhealthy masculine vulnerability begins as all spiritual journeys begin: with a leap of faith and a belief in magic. He must let himself go, fall into the dark gorge, land safely in a river down below, and let it take him on a journey through an inner wilderness where he will discover who he really is. He cannot make that leap until he sees his mother very clearly and feels the mother-son conflict within himself.

THE MOTHER-SON BIND

The vast majority of men I work with, and the majority of men in national studies, admit to needing to work on boundaries with their mothers, feelings of guilt about their mothers, and confusions about a wife's/partner's role in relation to their mother's role. Even men whose mothers are dead often report major unresolved issues with their mothers. Often these issues revolve around a lifelong emotional dependence on Mom that sons carry into adult relationships with partners and spouses. But this is not all. The mother-son bind occurs when we, as adult adolescents, yearn to destroy our emotional dependence as much as retain it. When we are in this bind toward women, we use women as mothers with whom perennially to play the role of separating adolescent—on the one hand asking our wives and partners for deep nurturance, and on the other pushing our partners away with all our might.

Consider this list of experiences and behavior. If three or more of the statements on the list fit you, you are probably more caught in the mother-son bind than you realize.

1. When your mother comes to visit, you become like her child again, in obvious or subtle ways. Your family complains to you about it, or you just know it and wish it didn't happen.

2. When you prepare for your mother's visit, you get a knot in your stomach just thinking about it. As the day of her arrival comes closer, you get more and more nervous.

3. When you face a crucial decision, you go to your mother for help or wish she could help you with it, despite the fact that you also wish you could make the decision on your own.

4. You wonder now and then, as if from a kind of free-floating anxiety, whether your mother thinks you've made it.

5. You will not let anyone say anything negative about your mother. You feel you must protect her at all costs.

6. When you are around your mother, you feel it is your job to interpret the world for her.

7. You never quite feel you've done enough for your mother.

8. When you must choose sides between your wife/partner and your mother, you tend to take your mother's side.

9. When you consider confronting your mother about something, your first feeling is guilt—she did so much for you, how can you cause her stress now?

10. You avoid confronting your mother about issues important to your life "to keep the family together," "because she has had enough stress with

Dad to last her a lifetime," or "because it won't do me any good anyway."

11. When you see your mother and interact with her, you have difficulty seeing her present accomplishments as a woman—you still see her primarily as *your* mother.

12. You wouldn't admit it to anyone, but you still fear your mother terribly. She can say just one or two things and push your buttons.

13. Your mother still embarrasses you in public. She does this very consciously, still treating you, in subtle ways and through subtle gestures and words, as she did when you were a boy; or she does it unconsciously, doing the things she did years ago that drove you crazy with shame.

14. You expect your wife/partner to do the primary emotional work in your relationship.

15. You expect your wife/partner always to be around to take care of your needs and make things right for your life to flourish.

16. You might not admit it, but you operate on the assumption that it's OK for your wife to provide for your needs more than you provide for hers.

17. You are a good little boy. You are hyper-responsible, unable to let go and have fun. You feel extremely guilty when you don't get everything just right and take care of people's needs just right.

18. You fear intimacy with a strong partner. You prefer passivity in her.

19. You fear intimacy without a domineering partner. You want her to tell you what to do in the relationship.

20. As you answer questions about your mother, go

through this list of experiences, or think about exploring mother-son relationships, you feel immediately defensive of your mother, yearning to put the book away and say, "Leave her alone. She's sacred. Everything's fine."

Among the hundreds of men I've shown this list to, most have agreed that they participated to some degree in #20. It takes us a long time to cut through our defensiveness concerning our mothers. It is not just defensiveness, it is also self-preservation—we feel that if we criticize our relationship with her, we might lose the one thing we could always psychologically count on in this world. Yet we must risk it.

In the next chapter, we will explore what the first ten years of our lives feel like as we live in our mother's house. How did the personal myths by which we live our adult lives develop in our families? These personal myths become clearer as we peer through the looking-glass and see our mother's world, remembering what it was like to dance in her bright and beautiful mirror.

Chapter 2: Dancing in Our Mothers' Mirrors

> The development of a self is fraught with danger.
> How does the child discover himself within his
> mother's care without losing himself to her?
> —JAY GREENBERG AND STEPHEN MITCHELL,
> *Object Relations in Psychoanalytic Theory*

I WAS DOING A radio talk show recently on the topic of mothers and sons. One caller, a business professional, wife, and mother of two sons, called in, at first with specific questions about how to treat her two sons, who were ten and six. As our brief conversation unfolded, however, it became clear something else was on her mind.

"It actually has to do with my husband and his mom," she said. "See, I love my husband. A lot. And he loves me. But see, there's always been something going on between him and his mother that gets in the way of my love for him and his love for me. I can't really describe it. I just know I don't want my son to be attached to me at the hip when he's forty."

"How is your husband still attached to your mother-in-law?" I asked.

"I don't know," the woman said frankly. "I don't know why I say attached. Most people would think he's not attached to his mom at all. He talks to her only once every couple months. We live three thousand miles from her; we see my in-laws only once a year. Like I said, it's hard to define. But for instance, when he does talk to her, or when she does come to visit, he changes so drastically. He becomes a kid again. And when she's not around, he seems confused about how to talk about her, how to treat her. Sometimes he's very generous and loving when he talks about her; other times he's mean, cuts her down, bitching about her like he's punishing her. He's usually so even-tempered, but about his mother, some small memory will set him off."

"How old is your husband?" I asked.

"Forty."

"When it comes to the emotional life of your home and family, who does most of the emotional work?" I asked.

"I do."

"Even with him?"

"Oh, yes. He's not the best at getting into his feelings, though he's getting a lot better. But still, I sometimes see him as a third son, an older son."

"So in your mind, in terms of how he relates to you, what emotional age would you put him at?"

"He's kind of like a teenager with me; his emotions go up and down with me."

"Is it the same up-down dynamic with other people, friends, colleagues, with your sons? Is it up and down with them the same way it is with you?"

She paused a second. "No. He's so . . . so 'together' with most people. He's a great father—and he's a good husband, don't get me wrong. He's successful in his work. He's even-tempered, respected. There's just something unique about the up-and-down feelings he has toward me. He adores me sometimes, and then other times it's like he's punishing me for something, distancing himself for some reason, and neither of us understands it. We went into counselng together, and we've talked about it with our counselor. We haven't really gotten to the bottom of it. But today you were talking about mothers and sons, and I just wondered if there's a connection."

There is a deep and profound connection. How often is the man's superimposition of his mother's face onto his wife's—and his wife's quick surrender to that motherly role—a root cause of divorce? How often is a man's distancing pattern connected to unresolved issues involving his mother?

These are essential questions not only for family intimacy but for global life. The way we raise our sons affects all aspects of culture. Only recently are we beginning to identify men who are wandering in mother-son conflict, attached to their mothers yet needing to separate; or separated from their mothers yet still yearning to be attached. The caller on the talk show had realized, preconsciously and before she even called in, that her husband was still dancing in his mother's mirror. She was confused by it and didn't know what to do.

First Attachment: The Invisible Cord

From long before conception, we were dancers in our mother's mirror. She dreamed that we danced within her and without. Drifting off to sleep, she wondered what it would be like to love us, afraid of the responsibility, exhilarated. When we lay within her, she felt we were a part of herself. As men, we can barely imagine this feeling a pregnant woman comes to know so well. We danced against the sides of her womb, and she giggled and wept with emotions she had never before experienced. She sat or stood naked in front of her mirror, staring at the changes in her body, the growth of her child within her. She called our father in, who kissed her belly there before the mirror, and perhaps they both stood there naked, at one with spirit and life, creators.

Our mother looked in that mirror and imagined us and wanted the world for us. She wanted to be perfect for us. She wanted us to be perfect. And after we were born, she stood at the mirror, holding us in her arms, showing us to ourselves. We didn't know what we were seeing yet. She and we were still one. As we grew into early boyhood, for us and for her there could be no more beautiful thing in the world than her huge and wonderful mirror, before which we danced, sometimes with her, our arms and hands linked, our bodies twirling together; and sometimes without her, as she sat back in a chair admiring us, watching our talents emerge.

As we grew up in her arms and in her castle, our mother was, in archetypal terms, like a great nurturing Goddess— the Mother-Creator, the Sacred Queen, the wise Crone, and the beautiful Maiden all in one. She created us, she was partial ruler of the household, she held the wisdom of the ages, and she was as beautiful and striking a woman as we would ever hope to meet. We were *attached* to our mothers (or other primary care-givers) in a unique way. Our ancestral cultures and their mythologies have symbolized this primal attachment in figures like the Greek goddess Sybil, with her multiple gigantic breasts that feed and nurture the world, or the medieval Christian *vièrge ouvrante* in which, when the sculpted cabinet of the Virgin Mary is opened, Jesus is seen within, a small figure wrapped in her much larger chest.

DANGEROUS ATTACHMENTS

What we need in the very early stages of life is profound attachment to Mom, for we live very much by her love and attention. Without her deep attachment to us, especially in the first six months of life, our ability to relate to others is profoundly damaged. Our ability to trust depends on healthy attachment to our mothers during our infancy. If there is abuse, neglect, abandonment during early attachment, we are deeply wounded. Although this should be common sense to everyone, abuse and neglect of children by mothers is increasing year by year.

The most strenuous challenge to healthy mother-infant attachment is our economic system. As mothers are pulled further and further away from their infants by the necessities of work, sometimes after only six weeks of maternity leave, children may suffer later relationship troubles. When the mother is removed from the child in the first months of life, the child risks personality disorders, especially borderline, schizoid, and narcissistic disorders. The studies proving this tragic tendency are overwhelming, yet our culture ignores them in search of material values (and fiscal survival) that erode family intimacy. To blame mothers, as so many find it easy to do, or to blame fathers, is convenient but superficial.

The primary cause of the problem is that this culture has forgotten the essentiality of children. We live at such a distance from our basic survival and spiritual needs that we see children as by-products of marital unions, rather than as essential features of our tribal, family, and personal continuity. With the extended family destroyed in our culture, fathers absent from homes or emotionally withdrawn within them, and mothers bringing their own wounded childhoods to their children, mothers are raising kids in a kind of loneliness, isolation, and exhaustion that invites guilt, overreaction, neglect, and abuse.

World mythology, a record of human psychological development, has told us for millennia what we as a very young and very destructive culture believe we can forget: that some form of extended family must support the birth of every child and the mother's healthy attachment to the child; and that unless a mother and infant attach in a very profound way, whether the child is strapped to Mother's back while she works the fields or sits beside her in his bassinet while she hums him to sleep—or, abandoned like Moses by one mother, is immediately taken up by another primary care giver who loves him—he will become destructive, either to himself or others.

The Dream of the Lost Child

Recently, a single mother visited her children's pediatrician because her two-year-old son seemed "behind the other boys" in his development and generally listless. After substantial testing, the pediatrician found nothing the matter with the son's intelligence or motor skills, but he did discover signs of abuse and neglect. He referred the mother to state agencies, and from there she entered counseling.

In counseling, the mother revealed a recurring nightmare: she and her son were walking in the city; she got distracted by something, just for a second, and her son disappeared. She searched the busy and crowded streets but couldn't find him. She would wake up sweating, sometimes weeping. As her counseling continued, the mother disclosed her childhood—she had felt abandoned by her father, who was gone from the home for weeks on end, and by her mother, who had a retarded son and two daughters to care for.

Who was being lost in her dream? It was her child—but she also felt lost and afraid, even more now that she had the lonely responsibility of a child. The pressure of her own past was impinging on her relationship with her son. She was abusing and neglecting him and then forcing herself on him, out of guilt, in inappropriate ways. He was taking on the symptoms of her troubles.

In his relationship with the world in general, and especially with his mother, the child, as Swiss child psychologist Alice Miller puts it, "has a primary need to be regarded and respected as the center—the central actor—in his own activity." Child psychologist Margaret Mahler explains it in this way: "The infant's inner sensations form the core of the self. They appear to remain the central, the crystallization point of the 'feeling of the self' around which a 'sense of identity' will become established." This sense of identity is developed in relationship to others, especially mothers, who nurture it—who are attuned to the child enough to mirror the child's inner world. The infant cannot mirror his own inner world yet; he is simply not capable. His inner being is the responsiblity of another, usually his mother.

He is very narcissistic in his demands to have his physical and psychological needs met. The mother and other care givers must do their best to respect his narcissism. If he is not allowed it in his infant years, he will throughout his life look for what his mother could not give him at the correct time—the presence of a person who is completely aware of him and takes him seriously, who admires him beyond all others and attends him whenever he desires her.

When a mother abuses, neglects, or impinges on a child, he senses very clearly that he is not the center—his mother's wounds and needs are the center. In this situation, he risks becoming an abusive, dangerous man. In his future relationships with women and partners, he risks dysfunction. If there have been problems in his first years of relationship to the Goddess-Mother, he will fear being neglected by the Goddess or abused or devoured by her later. So many of us men bring this low-grade fear of women to our relationships with them.

ABUSE

Although it is often popularly assumed that men are the primary abusers of children, studies show this not to be the case. The *Handbook on Family Violence,* the *Journal of Social Work,* and numerous national studies indicate that mothers are the most likely perpetrators of child abuse, and male children the most likely victims. There are many reasons for this trend, but primarily, mothers are with kids more than fathers and have more chances to abuse; and sons, given their hormonal makeup and the fact that society encourages their expressions of anger more than daughters' anger, tend to act out more than daughters, requiring more discipline—discipline that often turns into a mother's verbal and physical abuse.

This society is doing a great deal to come to terms with child abuse, but it must do more. As Alice Miller, the Swiss psychologist, has put it: "There is no one person in the whole world who abuses children without having been abused as a child." In mythology, abuse of children is often symbolized by parents eating their offspring. In the archetypal psychology of mythological stories, when a mother, like the Celtic Mother-Goddess Ceridwen, abuses her child, she is devouring his soul, his core self. When Ceridwen rails at her son Gwion, beats him and hurts him, he turns into various animals to escape her, but she turns into predatory animals that can eat his animals. Finally, he turns into a seed and she into a hen, and she devours him.

The abusive mother, whether in mythology or in the household, devours her son's soul—his core self. One of his great journeys in life is to retrieve his soul from the depths of the Goddess's belly. Few journeys are more frightening. As our social structure becomes more and more stressful and provides mothers with less and less support for their mothering, mothers are more and more on their own, and children are devoured more and more. The more beaten and abused a child is, the more his core self will suffer, hide, and make him act in inappropriate, often dangerous ways. Many intimacy problems can be traced to abuse and other mother-son problems in the infant (and later) years. If you were abused, you must get help in working through that abuse. Your life and your relationships will profoundly change.

NEGLECT AND ABANDONMENT

Although abuse is the most easily documented and most dramatic suffering of children at the hands of their mothers, neglect is equally pervasive. In its most extreme form, neglect becomes abandonment.

Studies show that child neglect is increasing as teenagers have children at younger ages, more drug-addicted mothers have children, fathers are being drawn farther from homes, mothers are being pushed into the work force earlier after their children's births, and parents spend a little more than half the time with their kids that they spent twenty-five years ago.

Day-care centers are flourishing, doing their part to fill the gap left by overworked parents. But especially in the child's first two years of life, day-care centers cannot completely substitute for a mother. A day-care worker recently told me about parents of a two-year-old boy, CJ. They had called to ask her to keep CJ until 11:00 that night. They wanted to go to a party. The day-care worker had been asked by the parents to do this kind of thing many times before. It was illegal for her to keep the child that long. Yet it was clear to her, based on her knowledge of the parents, that if she made waves they might take CJ to a day-care center that wouldn't take care of him as well as Jane did.

Day-care workers and therapists are functioning in our culture as substitutes for the grandparents, uncles, and aunts of the extended family. As extended families break down, we take our kids to day-care instead of Grandma. We ask counselors to help with family and personal problems instead of asking Uncle Carl or Aunt Julia. We are creating a new extended family system, and it is a very workable one. But it still requires parents to realize that once they have children, nothing is more important in their lives than creating a safe, nurturing, intimate environment for those children.

Nothing.

Abandonment by a mother, a mother's coldness to her children, a mother's neglect of a child's needs because her own have been unfulfilled and take up most of her energy—all these profoundly affect the fragile and growing son. I have worked with men whose mothers died when they were young. The men were not allowed to grieve over the mother's death, or did not know how. I've worked with men whose mothers were cold to them, unable to show emotion, or constantly distracted. The core feeling in all these sons is abandonment. These men unconsciously fear the fate that befell Linus, a character in Greek mythology who was abandoned by his mother and, before he reached full manhood, eaten by dogs. The neglected child, feeling abandoned by the Goddess, lives in fear of others and the world, cannot trust, and dies an early death, psychologically speaking—he is eaten by dogs. He lives and breathes and works and even marries, but without the capacity to trust, he is not alive for others, or even, truly, for himself.

IMPINGEMENT

Abuse, neglect, and abandonment are obvious and very dramatic causes of the lost child, but there is another that we are just coming to understand—*impingement*. Says D. W. Winnicott, the child psychologist who pioneered many of our present views of infant psychology, "The infant must start his life by existing, not reacting." He must exist in his mother's castle, protected, fed, and mirrored there. His mother must react to his deep emotional needs. It is not his job to react to hers.

This distinction in infant psychology we see in adult psychology as "being vs. doing." The infant must be allowed to simply be—to discover the world as he needs to, and especially to learn his own inner world as he needs to. It is very difficult for primary care-givers, most of whom are mothers, to allow this to happen, unless they are educated that they must, or are brought up without impingement as children, or intuit the need to let their son "just be." It is very difficult, as any adult knows, to keep one's own emotional needs to one's self in the company of a child. Children seem to cry out to us to project our hearts and souls onto them. And many of us, having grown up in profoundly dysfunctional families, unconsciously use our children to heal our own wounds.

When we as parents do this to our children, however—especially in their infant years, when we are most confused and exhausted and vulnerable—we risk damaging them. They need us to teach them how to find themselves; they are damaged when we teach them how to help us find ourselves. There is no doubt every child helps every mother know herself better. But this self-knowledge on the mother's part must not be the primary goal of the mother-son relationship. The child's psychological survival must not depend upon meeting his mother's needs. "The major consequence of prolonged impingement," say the psychologists Jay Greenberg and Stephen Mitchell, "is fragmentation of the infant's experience. Out of necessity, he becomes prematurely and compulsively attuned to the claims and requests of others. He cannot allow himself the experience of formless quiescence, since he must be prepared to respond to what is asked of and provided for him. He loses touch with his own spontaneous needs and gestures, as these bear no relation to the way his mother experiences him and what she offers him."

This fragmentation is a split between the core self and a false self. "The (child's) true self," Greenberg and Mitchell continue, "the source of spontaneous needs, images and gestures, goes into hiding, becomes detached and atrophied. The false self provides an illusion of personal existence whose content is fashioned out of maternal expectations and claims. The child becomes the mother's image of him."

How can he find his core self while responding to his mother's needs? Rather than finding his own Hero, he takes on the role of reacting to the Goddess, gaining his heroism by being *her* hero. The child tries to pull away. The mother feels psychologically abandoned by the child. She pulls at the child even harder, invades his system with her own.

What is called "impingement" during the child's infancy is often called "overmothering" or "a mother's domination" as it continues into the son's boyhood, adolescence, and even adulthood. Fathers and others will express their frustration at a mother's impingement, overmothering, and domination by telling her, "You're making our son into a Momma's boy," "You never let him be himself," "You're always in his face."

Once I got into a heated argument with a woman at a women's health conference at which I spoke on mother-son issues. The argument was about impingement during boyhood. The woman, a mother of three, was angry at me for saying a mother impinges on her children when she devotes herself to their care: "You're advocating that a mother be detached from her kids. That's a typical male attitude."

This woman and I were involved in a language dilemma critical to dealing with mother-child relationships. I was criticizing *how* a mother (or any primary care-giver) devotes herself to her children; the mother at the conference heard me criticizing *that* she devoted herself.

A mother's burden is very difficult. She must be devoted to her child, yet it must be responsible devotion. As the primary care-giver, she must realize that if she neglects her child, he will suffer immeasurable. She must also realize that if she impinges on her child too much, not letting him find his own way, he will not develop a true self and will risk personality disorders—moving through life unable to achieve intimacy, unable to set appropriate boundaries for himself, and unable to find fulfillment. The mother's risk of impinging on the child increases in direct proportion to the child's urges to separate from her. As her son gets older, needing to separate and individuate as much as cling to her, her impingement takes on a kind of urgency, confusing the boy as she holds him back or clings to him.

IMPINGEMENT DURING SEPARATION

There is a children's book, *The Runaway Bunny,* based on fairy tales of mother-son relationships, written in the United States in the 1940s by Margaret Wise Brown. It begins,

> Once there was a little bunny who wanted to run away.
> So he said to his mother, "I am running away."
> "If you run away," said his mother, "I will run after you.
> For you are my little bunny."

The bunny describes to his mother the various things he will turn into in order to run away; the mother describes what she'll turn into to keep him from running away. All her transformations indicate how completely her powers surpass his, and how utterly she will impinge on him: when he becomes a trout to swim away from her, she becomes a fisherman; when he becomes a rock on a mountain, she becomes a mountain climber; when he becomes a crocus in a hidden garden, she becomes a gardener. At one point, the little bunny says he'll become a sailboat. His mother says, "I'll become the wind and blow you where I want you to go." As the story reaches its climax, the little bunny realizes there is nowhere he can go and nothing he can transform himself into that is not part of his mother's circle of power. Resignedly, he agrees with his mother that he must just stay where he is and "be your little bunny."

To develop a true core self, the son must be able to transform himself into things his mother cannot control. The impinging mother insists the boy remain "her little bunny." She is afraid of his transformations, especially during his separation, for they will ultimately take the boy away from her. She negates them by doing everything for the boy and overprotecting him, by not letting him out of her sight, by dominating his vision of the world.

In the wake of a destroyed extended family, a lack of mentors educated in the ways of male initiation, distant, overworked fathers, and the necessity of mothers working away from children—causing many to impinge on their children out of a sense of guilt for having abandoned them—this culture is abandoning mothers to the impingement dilemma. Mothers feel terribly alone, confused about what constitutes appropriate and responsible devotion, and locked by their social and family situations in extremes of one or the other. Although impingement is destructive to both daughters and sons, its destructiveness to sons has a peculiar edge to it—for the son, if impinged on too severely, will not be able to discover what a man is separate from Woman. And especially if, for whatever reason, the mother-father-son triangle gets distorted and dangerous in the family, he will grow up deeply wounded, unclear on his boundaries, overreliant on his mother and women to define him, and unable to develop a true male self.

MOTHER-SON-FATHER:
THE FIRST LOVE TRIANGLE

For about a century, more has been written about the love triangle that exists between mother, father, and son than perhaps about any other triangle. Freud pointed out that a mother and son are so bonded at birth, the father is a kind of intrusion. Often the son projects onto the intruding father his fantasies that the father will hurt or ruin the first bond the son knew, in the womb and after the catastrophe of birth. Often the son feels like his mother's lover. These things are normal.

Mothers and fathers have the terrible burden of negotiating between themselves appropriate responses to the son's normal, frightening, and exciting fantasies. If they do not negotiate responses that nurture all three occupants of the triangle, the family is left deeply wounded.

Every man, in his journey of the soul, must look back at his boyhood and feel just how his mother and father handled this triangle. He will probably discover that his family's version of the first love triangle affected him deeply, that his parents didn't understand it well enough to protect him from its extreme form, and that he was wounded by it.

Psychologically, in families in which fathers are absent or emotionally withdrawn, sons feel they have participated with their mothers in killing off their fathers. They feel a preadolescent surge of power at having accomplished this early ascendancy, but that surge is not enough to engender their growth into manhood.

With every generation, as fathers pull farther away from families and mothers fill the gap more assiduously, neither parent realizing the effects of this impingement on sons, sons get locked deeper and deeper into adult adolescence, operating in adult relationships out of shame at being unable to fully work out their own emotional issues, fear of living adult lives for which they are unprepared, and guilt for never doing enough for Mom.

In mythology the story of the dysfunctional mother-son-father triangle is told this way: Once there was a young family—mother, father, and son. As the son grew, he and his mother got closer and closer while his father was elsewhere most of the time. When his father was home, he was busy and not too friendly. One day his father just seemed to disappear. He came around again, once in a while, then disappeared again each time, for longer and longer periods.

The son went through the rest of his life, even after he'd married and had a family, taking care of his mother, the first Goddess—which was what his father was supposed to do—relying on her for sustenance, and searching for his father, the Sacred King, the secret master of his young blood. He wanted to ask this Sacred King why he had left his son alone in confusion.

Never finding his father, his mother never letting go of him nor he of her, the adult son was not respected by the world, for the world never saw that he had become a man of the world—a loving, wise, and powerful King in his own right. He became a troubled ruler of the land he owned, sometimes overworking himself to prove himself, other times depressed and distant, brooding in a cave. His inconsistency, moodiness, and lack of deep love for others made even his wife and children wary of him. They did not know what he wanted from them.

This man had a son. He watched his son grow. The son seemed to remain close to his mother, almost as if he didn't trust his father. The father knew things were going terribly wrong again but couldn't understand what to do about it. He prayed to the gods, but they never came to help him. One day he went off to live in the cave, visiting home now and then, moving his life away from the mother and son. Like his own father, he disappeared. He left his son to dance in his mother's mirror. The son, like him, would grow up with no choice but to stay in his mother's mirror, or to disappear.

In *The Prince and the King,* I explored in depth the father's role in his family. The father is absent, distant, abusive, or passive in 80 to 90 percent of families. He is drawn away from the family by this culture's training of males—his life is a life of work "out there" and little intimacy back home. His father was this way, and so was his grandfather. The culture is economically and socially set up, even founded, on the presence of the father outside the home and his absence within it. He is guided to addictions, unhappiness, and an early grave.

The disengaged father leaves his son deeply wounded. He plays a large part in keeping the son a Prince—an adult adolescent. He does not pass his Sacred King—his spiritual ground, masculine birthright, empowering discipline, and peace of mind—into his son. The son wanders through life hungry for intimacy with a father who did not know how to give the son a foundation for healthy and rich manhood.

In *The Prince and the King,* the exploration of the father-son wound held, as one of its basic assumptions, that in the first love triangle mothers participate in the father-son relationship. Our present exploration of how mothers wound sons is predicated on our common agreement that fathers participate in a mother-son relationship—specifically, they participate by their absence, distance, abusiveness, or excessive passivity in most of our homes. Thus, part of the mother's wounding of her son is done in direct (and usually unconscious) proportion to the absence, distance, abuse, and passivity she suffers in her relationship with his father and, if unmarried/divorced, her lovers and new husbands. Because of past wounds of her own, peculiar challenges she faces with her son, pressures on her from society, and stress from the presence or absence of her mate, she sends messages that distort her sons's development. Once the son is past infancy, most of these messages impinge on the son's development of a core, individuated male self.

In his book *The Peter Pan Syndrome,* psychologist Dan Kiley describes the covert messages one son receives in his parents' home. Mom is there much more than Dad. There is tension between Mom and Dad over conflicting needs. She needs more from him, he feels unable to give more. The tensions the parents feel are not directly confronted. Rather, the mother tells the son not to be like Dad, who has few feelings and barely loves his family. The father tells the son women don't really understand boys or men, so he should just leave her alone. The mother tells the son always to be there for her. The father tells the son to do as he says and be like he is.

The son is brought into the mother-father conflict by being the substitute object of his mother's anger at and need for nurturance from her distant husband; and by having cut off his feelings and curbed his behavior so Mother will stop her bitching and Father can find some peace. Kiley summarizes the messages the boy's heart and mind are wrestling with as he goes upstairs to bed: "I hurt my mom because I'm like my dad, who can't stand to have me hurt Mom. Dad doesn't love us like his work because he doesn't have feelings. Mom can't understand me, and I make her pick on Dad. I'm supposed to protect her, but that means I have to use my feelings to do what Dad doesn't do. To protect my dad, I have to shape up and not be like him."

Kiley explains the damage to the son: "The covert messages do most of their damage as the boy tries to make sense out of the senseless. Imagine the pain and turmoil that assault this boy's mind. The knot in his gut condemns him as a culprit; the scream in his head points the finger of blame solely at him. Must he not illogically reason that he is the originator of the pain in the people he loves most? By the time he's ready to fall asleep, whatever self-esteem he managed to accrue that day is most assuredly destroyed."

MOTHERS' MESSAGES ABOUT DAD AND MEN

In the mother-son-father triangle, mothers hold far more power than they may realize. What are some of the messages mothers pass on to sons about fathers and men? Let's explore specific ones many of us heard as boys, and messages boys hear now too. As we explore these messages, push beyond any protectiveness you may feel toward your mother. Push beyond it into clear memory and clear thinking. Even if the message your mom gave you about your dad was altogether true, explore how the message nonetheless wounds males. Women and men must both be honest about these messages, for the sake of our children.

Fathers are not inside the most important emotional loops. Or: "We don't really need dad anyway." Recently a woman said, "My husband complains to me that the kids and I don't seem to need him. All he feels like is a meal ticket, no matter what I do to reassure him. The problem is, most of the time I don't feel like we need him either."

Another woman said, "So much of the time I just wish Jack wouldn't come home at night. His presence upsets the family routine. Oh, it's not any one thing he does. It's just that the kids and I have a good thing going without him. And, truthfully, he's tired, he's cranky. He's more work than he gives back. I'm ashamed to admit it, but sometimes I just want to say to the kids, 'We really don't need Dad anyway.' "

These sorts of comments are not as uncommon and exaggerated as we might think. In our family lives, a father's necessity often is in question. In our world, a father feels unclear about his role as a man and father, forced to be gone at work, then exhausted and feeling guilty when he's home. He takes on less of a role at home because he must take on an overwhelming role away from home. Home comes to need him less and treats him as such.

The poet Lord Byron, more than a century ago, wrote *Don Juan,* an epic poem about a man whose life is profoundly affected by his relationship with his mother, his mother's dislike of his father, and his father's exile from the home. Donna Inez is Juan's mother and Don Jose his father. Donna Inez is a very strong woman married to a man who is respected outside the family, in the social sphere, but passive at home. He clearly does not satisfy her. He is, in his wife's view, the kind of man "a lady could brain with a fan." The poem reads like an account of many families:

> Don Jose and the Donna Inez led
>   For some time an unhappy sort of life
> Wishing each other, not divorced, but dead;
>   They lived respectably as man and wife,
> Their conduct was exceedingly well-bred,
>   And gave no outward signs of inward
>   strife.
> Until at length the smother'd fire broke
>   out,
> And put the business past all kind of doubt.
>
> For Inez call'd some druggists and
>   physicians,
>   And tried to prove her loving lord was
>   *mad,*
> But as he had some lucid intermissions,
>   She next decided he was only *bad.*

Soon, Don Jose dies. Donna Inez celebrates. Now she has the son to herself. And now she raises him without the obstruction in the house of a man she dislikes. Don Jose's name is now rarely, if ever, brought up in the family. He has been virtually erased.

Later, Don Juan will grow up to be addicted to fame, work, and love. He will fill the hole left by battered, exiled, and destroyed masculinity with desperate substitutes. Learning as he grew that life is better without Dad, and that Dad is not needed, he, like so many of us, learned that masculinity is intrinsically flawed. He spends most of his adult life trying to redeem Dad, fix the flaws, escape the pain.

Especially in the circumstance of divorce, mothers often say to their children, whether directly or through other means, that Dad is not needed. Sometimes Dad is so deeply dysfunctional he is dangerous to the family, making other healthy male role models a necessity for the son's complete development. But more often than not, Dad is the only available father, and a more than adequate role model for his sons. If forced, many mothers who previously disbelieved that their sons need a man around, will admit it, especially as their sons near puberty and "seem to go nuts." As one woman said to me, "For a while after my divorce I felt great ragging to Jeremy about what a jerk his father was. But during Jeremy's teen years, I had to change my tune. Jeremy needed something from his father I just couldn't give him."

While much of the $25 billion in back child support is owed by men who are irresponsible, much of it is also owed by men who have felt pushed out of their families by women who are angry at them. They exact their revenge, however misguidedly, by withholding money.

Paul Shaner, a Seattle social worker and custodial father, talks about the cultural and maternal bias against divorced fathers: "When I became a counselor in 1972, it was clear that the unwritten rule for divorced dads was that they should pay their child support and visit the kids for three months, but then should drop out of the way. The mother might be planning to remarry and the stepfather wouldn't want him around. There was thought to be something wrong with a man who resisted this trend." Have things gotten better for divorced fathers? Some say yes, some say no.

In Shakespeare's *Hamlet* this is beautifully enacted. Hamlet's mother joins Hamlet's uncle to kill Hamlet's father. Hamlet's wrath, confusion, and death evolve from that killing. In Act III, Scene iv, Hamlet can see his father, who is now a ghost, but his mother cannot. His mother has killed off the father in her mind. The father is still alive in the son's mind, but a ghost. Hamlet rails at his mother, amazed and furious that she can't *see* his father anymore.

Hamlet makes literal what is going on psychologically in the son of a mother who "kills" the son's father. She is crushing the son's own male spirit in ways she does not wish to do and does not realize. She is telling him his father was inadequate, worth nothing more than to kill and replace. Yet Hamlet is his father's son. He has inherited his father's body and soul. He has no choice but to cleave to his father, to become somewhat like his father.

Whether the family is intact and the mother is angry at her husband's work addiction or emotional distance, or it is in transition and the mother is angry at what she considers her former husband's inadequacies, or she is angry at men in general, a mother who teaches her son that the father is unnecessary robs the son not only of a father, but also of his own emerging masculine ground.

For most of the first two decades of his life, the son's healthy emergence into manhood depends on modeling after his father (or other primary male care-giver) and receiving healthy, positive messages from father, mother, and culture about masculinity. Many of those messages, especially as they are received in the family system, come from his mother. When she turns on the father, the son, deeply attached to her, will turn on men.

Even despite the fact that she has been hurt by her husband or partner, she might say to her son, "He did not satisfy *me*, but that doesn't mean he can't be a good father to you." This allows the son to develop a relationship with the father that can, at least in part, satisfy him. She will probably find that the more she protects her son from her anger, the better able he is to hold male boundaries in his later life. She may also find that her son, especially as he nears puberty, would gain things by living with his father that she is already finding it difficult to provide. And from this, she might find that the father will in fact take on a more intimate and responsible role in raising his children the less she convinces them that he is not needed.

Men Are Inherently Flawed.

"Men are pigs!"

"Men suck."

"The best man's a dead man."

"All men want is sex."

"The world would be better off without men."

"Men are good for nothing except drinking beer and barking orders."

"Men have ruined the world. If women ran the world, it would be . . ." (fill in the superlative).

"Male culture is destructive, female culture is constructive."

"Just get enough sperm to last a few generations and then kill off all the men, that would solve the world's problems."

The list of male-bashing comments made by women (and some men) is endless. Aaron Kipnis, in his book *Knights Without Armor,* quotes Donald Buzzone, who does research on television commercials: "Ads with male-bashing themes work. They seem to do more to turn females on than they do to turn males off." Whether the man can't choose his own toothpaste without his wife's help or has his eye on one thing only, sex, or kills and rapes and murders in nearly every television program and movie, we are in a time of male bashing, and it is getting worse.

Sons pick up negative images of men from the culture; then mothers attack men, reinforcing the new cultural stereotype "the villainous male." Once again, the sons suffer. They hear the culture's messages about men, especially those from their mothers. If the culture is bashing men but the mother and father hold onto positive images of masculinity, the son will probably weather the present cultural storm. If, however, the father is pushed (and/or opts) out of the emotional life of the home, and the mother participates in male bashing at his and other men's expense, the son learns what he is taught: men are inadequate. It takes very little time for him to learn that men are unnecessary, and still less to realize he is male and be ashamed of it.

This culture seems to hold onto the illusion that because women have been oppressed by a social system that both men and women fostered but in which men held economic power, therefore all men are fair game for insult. Mothers who participate are damaging their sons (to say nothing of their daughters, who will never trust men)—they are doing exactly what they despise about oppression: generalizing genders, exaggerating a particular gender's perceived faults into genetic predispositions, and condemning the gender.

A boy is wrong to become a man. Or: "Don't turn out to be a man." Recently, my wife and I joined another couple and their sixteen-year-old son to watch the thriller *Mortal Thoughts.* In it, Bruce Willis plays a drunk, violent man. Two women collude in killing him and, in the end, confess their crime to authorities. Somewhere toward the end of the film—in which all male figures verge on villainy—the mother beside me whispered to her son, "Whatever you do, Justin, don't turn out to be a man." The comment was made in front of the boy's father, in front of all of us. The mother shot it from the hip, unaware of its danger; unaware, too, that her freedom to make it grows largely from a culture that has convinced itself men and masculinity are villainous. The boy's father, accustomed to comments like that from his wife, said nothing. The boy grinned a kind of "Sure, Mom" grin. The moment passed.

When a mother convinces her son that his father is inadequate and adds to that by showing the son how inadequate and villainous all men are, she negates the male soul. In negating the father and all men, she allows the son nothing organically male to grow into.

A son whose father gets killed off in the family system will suffer Hamlet's fate, or find a dysfunction that will allow him psychological survival.

THE DEVOURING MOTHER AS THE SON GROWS TO PUBERTY

Most of the destructive messages a mother gives a son in relation to a disengaged father are messages that tear men and manhood down. These messages tear the male soul, and the son, as he grows up and realizes the male soul is his soul, hates men, doesn't trust men, and even becomes self-destructive, so powerfully can a father's absence and a mother's anger influence him. When his mother dislikes, hates, puts down, turns away from, does not respect men, and when the son remains, as he does in so many families in this culture, psychologically attached to and in collusion with her, how is he to grow beyond adolescence? What manhood is he to grow into? Manhood has been devoured by the Goddess, found lacking, spit out. The son spends a lot of time looking at the pile of spit seeds, even touching them, ultimately confused by them.

From the son's point of view, his mother's acted-out anger at his father devoured the *principle* of masculinity and the *father's* soul. The destructive messages she gives her son—as he hits puberty—such as, "Be my little man," "I know what's good for you better than you do," "Make my life worthwhile," and "Don't ever leave me"—are messages that devour the son's *own* soul.

World mythology, in exploring the devouring Goddess, warns its audience to respect the Goddess who gave us life, but also to recognize the awesome power of that Goddess to devour us. Just as it warns the gods to keep their boundaries or the consequences will be lethal, it warns the Goddess-Mother to keep hers. The Goddess's ability to devour can be manifest in her ability to devour her sexual partner in "the little death" of intercourse with her, as in Chinese mythology; the Earth Mother who opens up the land in an earthquake and devours her children, as in Native American mythology; the mother who eats her son, as in the Celtic myth of Gwion Bach; or as the three Fates, who control human death and destiny, in Greek mythology.

Just as there is in every man some of Chronos, the father who ate his sons, there is also in every mother some devouring Goddess. The great tension for a mother raising children, especially sons, is to balance her respect for the son as an individual with her awesome power to consume and devour the son's fragile masculinity in her femininity. What messages about himself does the devouring Goddess give that impinge so deeply on his development that the son grows up feeling his core-self is devoured?

Mother Knows Best. Always. Or: "I know you better than you know yourself."

A mother must teach her son morality—but can she teach it so heavily and rigidly she crushes his sense of experimentation and free expression? A mother must do things for her son and indulge him—but can she do so much for him that he will never be able to separate from her, or live without some woman (or intimate other) always doing for him?

A mother must give her son her vision of the world, her sense of who is enemy, who is friend, what is valuable, what is not—but can she push her vision on him so completely that he never develops his own? A mother must protect her son—but can she protect him too much?

A mother will sacrifice for her son and ask in exchange that her son provide for her, protect her, be there for her, bring gifts back to her, and never leave her—but can she sacrifice so much that she asks too much in return, so that her son is never able to find out what gifts are his, not hers, what world is his, not hers?

Mothers must help sons develop healthy foundations, but they often go too far. Once at a workshop, a mother and grown son both talked about the son's pre-adolescence. The son said, "She was always hovering over me. I felt like her shadow was always over me. I felt smothered." The mother said, "I know. I was. I did smother you. I was just trying to be a good mom. I was afraid, so desperately afraid, something would happen to you, or you'd get hurt or you'd become a bad man, and I'd be at fault." The mother grew into midlife feeling always on the edge of guilt and failure. The son grew up feeling smothered, dominated, overmothered.

Overmothering, especially as a son's puberty enters the

relationship, dangerously enmeshes a mother's identity in the son's and the son's in the mother's. In all mother-son relationships there is enmeshment, but it becomes dangerous when, as Jungian analyst Guy Corneau warns, the mother "imprisons his identity into remaining a son and making the same sacrifice as she did herself." As the years go by, the son puts up some fight against the overmothering, but he ends up just letting it happen, feeling the common feeling of boys in adolescence—guilt about wanting to pull away from her, guilt about not being a good enough boy for her, guilt about no longer wanting to let her have her way with his feelings, guilt about not having fulfilled her wishes, guilt about how Dad has treated her, guilt about having caused the divorce, guilt about not being able to make her happy.

Robert Duncan wrote a poem, "My Mother Would Be a Falconress," that helps answer the question, "What does overmothering feel like to an adolescent son?" Here's the first part of it:

> My mother would be a falconress,
> And I, her gay falcon treading her wrist,
> would fly to bring back
> from the blue of the sky to her, bleeding, a
>   prize,
> where I dream in my little hood with many
>   bells
> jangling when I'd turn my head.
>
> My mother would be a falconress,
> and she sends me as far as her will goes.
> She lets me ride to the end of her curb
> where I fall back in anguish.

I dread that she will cast me away,
for I fall, I mis-take, I fail in her mission.

The falconress is the Goddess-Mother, awesomely powerful, overwhelming. When a mother's intimacy confuses
us—when she consumes our boundaries in her overmothering—we feel, as the falcon does, that we should only go
out to the curb of her will. But at the same time, it is our
urge to go beyond. In fact, to accomplish many of the
missions she tacitly gives us, we must go beyond her will.
We are confused. We fall back, unable to go beyond her,
and unable to fulfill her missions as we want to.

She would bring down the little birds.
And I would bring down the little birds.
When will she let me bring down the little
    birds,
pierced from their flight with their necks
    broken,
their heads like flowers limp from the stem?

I tread my mother's wrist and would draw
    blood.
Behind the little hood my eyes are hooded.
I have gone back into my hooded silence,
talking to myself and dropping off to sleep.

For she has muffled my dreams in the hood
    she has made me,
sewn round with bells, jangling when I
    move.
She rides with her little falcon upon her
    wrist.
She uses a barb that brings me to cower.

She sends me abroad to try my wings
and I come back to her. I would bring
    down
the little birds to her
I may not tear into, I must bring back
    perfectly.

I tear at her wrist with my beak to draw
    blood
and her eyes holds me, anguished,
    terrifying.
She draws a limit to my flight.
Never beyond my sight, she says.

She trains me to fetch and to limit myself in
    fetching.
She rewards me with meat for my dinner.
But I must never eat what she sends me to
    bring her.

Like the falcon, we find ourselves longing for freedom. We want some of the power the Goddess has. We want to bring down the little birds too. When will she let us?

She won't. We are bound to her, hooded by her, silenced. We often find that her power muffles our dreams. So controlled by her, we take on her missions and dreams and forget our own. We cannot escape her. We are her handiwork to such an extent that she truly seems to know us better than we know ourselves. She has eyes in the back of her head. We seem loud in our movements, jangling. She always knows where we are and how to call us back. She has barbs that make us cower. She knows just what to say to hurt us, shame us, remind us of her power. We create very high expectations for ourselves. We must bring back little birds and bring them back perfectly. Many of us learn perfectionism from our mothers, and when we do not perform adequately for our wives or partners or others, we feel ashamed. Many of us don't even realize why we feel a constant shame, especially with women, that we are not satisfactory.

Adding to the shame is the confusion of pulling away from Mom's mothering, a pulling away that always draws blood. The guilt we feel at drawing her blood is immense. We hurt her when we don't allow her to live for us, to do for us, to smother our vision with the hood. Her response is to hold us tighter and tell us never to go beyond her sight. She teaches us to fetch but tells us to bring home what we fetch. Don't eat it on the way. What she sends us to get and to do—the mission she gives us—is ultimately hers. We must not steal it from her.

> Yet it would have been beautiful, if she
>   would have carried me,
> always, in a little hood with the bells
>   ringing,
> at her wrist, and her riding
> to the great falcon hunt, and me
> flying up to the curb of my heart from her
>   heart
> to bring down the skylark from the blue to
>   her feet,
> straining, and then released for the flight.
>
> My mother would be a falconress,
> and I her gerfalcon, raised at her will,
> from her wrist sent flying, as if I were her
>   own
> pride, as if her pride

knew no limits, as if her mind
sought in me flight beyond the horizon.

Even as we were being overmothered—even as we are
tearing away at her wrist and drawing her blood—aren't
we like the falcon, wishing that we didn't have the urge
not to be mothered; wishing we didn't have the urge to
make our mothers bleed; wishing, most of all, that we
could be satisfied with being her pride, the part of her life
that makes her whole?

Ah, but high, high in the air I flew.
And far, far beyond the curb of her will,
were the blue hills where the falcons nest.
And then I saw west to the dying sun—
it seemed my human soul went down in
        flames.

I tore at her wrist, at the hold she had for
        me,
until the blood ran hot and I heard her cry
        out,
far, far beyond the curb of her will
to horizons of stars beyond the ringing hills
        of the world where the falcons nest
I saw, and I tore at her wrist with my
        savage beak.
I flew, as if sight flew from the anguish in
        her eye beyond her sight,
sent from my striking loose, from the cruel
        strike at her wrist,
striking out from the blood to be free of
        her.

And at some point we do tear away from Mother. We move out of the house. We tell her off. We begin to disrespect her. We make fun of her. First we tear away in our inner vision of ourselves flying high, escaping her. Then we tear at her wrist again, hurting this time with more power than we had as little boys—adolescents now and able to make her cry out as we tear. We are wonderful flying boys who fly to the horizon, flying away, yes! but somehow still tearing, locked into tearing, at Mother. How can this be? How is it that even flying away from her we still feel gripped by her, the guilt? How is it that no matter how far we fly we don't feel free of her?

> My mother would be a falconress,
> and even now, years after this,
> when the wounds I left her had surely
>   healed,
> and the woman is dead,
> her fierce eyes closed, and if her heart
> were broken, it is stilled
> I would be a falcon and go free.
> I tread her wrist and wear the hood,
> talking to myself, and would draw blood.

Sons of a culture that specifically teaches mothers to smother us with affection, to gain status by loving us perfectly, to feel guilty and at fault when we do even the slightest thing wrong, we grow up and our mothers die, figuratively or literally, and still we know her heart is broken, by us, by Dad or by life, and we feel guilty, and we are still treading her wrist, blinded to who we really are, knowing the pattern we learned in our overmothering—to live with a false self; to tread the Goddess's wrist (and if Mom is dead or we've moved out of her house, we find a new Goddess-Lover's wrist to tread), and in our confusion about feeling so bound, to draw blood, the Goddess's blood, whenever the feeling of mother-domination returns to us.

To truly be men, we do not need to separate from the feminine—we need to separate from Mother. If we are overmothered during boyhood, our chances of separating from our mothers without lifelong irresolution and confusion go down exponentially. We will find a way to fight the smothering mother by doing exactly what will oppress and reduce her femininity. Promiscuous, exploitative sexuality, hypermasculinity that becomes abusive—these are just the most obvious ways. Less obvious is the push-me, pull-me relationships we will get into with spouses and partners.

It is important for every man to look in the mirror and decide with integrity whether he is still trying to free himself from his mother's smothering—still basing his self-image on his mother's image of him; still blinded to the world he needs for his mature existence; still yearning to prove to his mother he has power; still not living as a man who knows the depths of his own passion and healthy power.

A Good Son Fills the Role of the Man His Father Isn't—the Man His Mother Needs in Her Life to Feel Whole. Or: "Be my little man."

One man, Jay, spoke to the men's circle on a men's retreat. He remembered being told by his mother when he was about five or six and all the way into adolescence that he, the eldest son, needed to be the man of the house. "Be my little man," his mother told him, "and I'll always make things right for you." Her husband was gone most of the time. Without knowing it, she made her eldest son into his substitute.

In my work I have discovered that Jay's experience is the experience of many men. An unwritten contract is effected during a boy's childhood—usually in the void left by a disengaged father—in which the mother and son become psychological peers and lovers; yet the son is still the son and must take her orders. The son becomes a substitute husband, yet remains a boy. Later in his life he will relate to women the same way: half-man, half-boy.

Anaïs Nin, in *Delta of Venus,* explores what Guy Corneau has called "the mother/son couple." She writes about a man, Pierre, who was raised by his mother and a nurse. His father died at sea. Pierre's mother "loved only to find a replacement for the man she had lost. She was a born mistress. She treated her son like a young lover." Pierre, for his part, "loved the voluptuousness of his mother. . . . At ten he was already initiated into all the preparations which a life filled with lovers demanded. He assisted at his mother's toilette, watched her powder herself under the arms and slip the powder puff into her dress, between her breasts. . . . As she dressed she talked about the man she was going to meet, extolling to Pierre the aristocratic nature of this one, the charm of another, the naturalness of a third, the genius of a fourth—as if Pierre should some day become all of them for her."

Nin puts in blatant psychosexual terms a circumstance that goes on below the surface of so many mother-son relationships. It is based in the mother's desire and power to mold the son into the male nurturer—emotionally, spiritually, psychologically (and sometimes physically)— that she cannot or does not find in the husband or lover she knows as a peer. She molds her son into the man she wants a man to be for her. He is, especially before his separation from her around puberty, relatively incapable of resisting her power to mold him.

Many of us, without realizing it, were thus molded by our mothers. We were taught to take care of her emotional needs. We were taught to be her little man. When Dad was inadequate, we stepped in with our innocent emotional desire to heal Mom. We became her Hero. Often Dad became the villain.

In gaining the role of Lover in his mother's mirror, the son will gain a certain kind of power he does not understand. His confusion about his mother will be augmented by confusion about his father, and his father's confusion about him. When a father feels he is losing out in the mother-father-son triangle to a son who is taking his place with his wife, he will usually respond by punishing the mother and son. He may become harsher to the son, more authoritarian, forcing his wife to protect the son more and more. He may force the son into a certain profession or mission in life, often one he knows the mother won't approve of. If his temperament moves him toward more self-effacement than authoritarianism, the son, seeing his father's self-destruction, may feel ashamed of his father's "weakness," and will often make it his mission to redeem his father, or "not to become like Dad." Whatever the outcome of the father-son relationship in the triangle, up to and including the father's leaving the home and leaving the mother and son to their relationship, the son will have lost his core self to a Lover relationship with his mother, will have lost his father, and will be locked into a confused and lifelong adolescence.

A Good Son Is a Son Who Fulfills His Mother's Unfulfilled Goals Or: "You're what makes my life worthwhile."

We live in a culture that is *oppressive* to women and *repressive* of men: women are, for the most part, allowed to feel their feelings but not allowed to gain economic and political power, whereas men are allowed external power but little feeling-life. In the mother-son relationship, a son learns, even if only by sensing it, that part of his burden in life will be to make his mother's life, which is socially unfulfilled, worthwhile.

When in mythology the Goddess is oppressed—by being killed, imprisoned, buried alive, or exiled—the whole community suffers. Often, a Hero's task is to rescue the Goddess, who holds the deed to the community's happiness. Fairy tales, wisdom tales, and medicine tales about men who develop into Warriors and Kings by doing great deeds, including rescuing a princess, are tales about the necessity of men unchaining the Goddess within themselves and in the world, in order to be whole. A primary message men receive in fairy tales is that you cannot have a functioning kingdom without a free feminine.

Our culture's oppressiveness to women and to the feminine affects the mother-son relationship in a similar way. Sons grow up knowing that part of their imperative in life is to rescue their mothers. For sons whose mothers are in constant danger, the development of a core self is put on hold, sometimes for a lifetime, as they strive to rescue Mom and to live for her—something they cannot psychologically accomplish, but will give their souls to, so deeply are they attached to her.

In the Biblical story of Rebecca and Jacob, you might remember that when Isaac first meets Rececca and falls in love with her, she is a very beautiful and very powerful figure. As their marriage goes on and they have two sons, Esau and Jacob, her importance and self-confidence recedes. Esau becomes the favorite of Isaac, Jacob becomes the favorite of Rebecca. Esau, being older, will gain the family's birthright when Isaac dies. Rebecca and Jacob collude to trick Isaac and rob Esau. Rebecca orchestrates the trick, Jacob executes her plan, Esau is robbed, Isaac dies, and from that trick the kingdom of Israel is divided and at war.

Within Isaac's and Rebecca's family, Rebecca's best remedy for the oppression and unfairness that has taken over her life is to collude with her favored son against his father. Her son helps her regain her power. The result is a wedge driven between father and son and brother and brother. The Goddess-Mother, oppressed, is the one rescued and fulfilled, but her rescue and fulfillment lead the son to great suffering and leads his community into deep division. Where mythology teaches us that oppressing the Goddess is dangerous to a community, it also teaches us that a son's collusion with her to steal her power back is equally dangerous.

As in the Rebecca-Jacob story, the son's psyche is deeply divided by having made the mother's fulfillment its mission; it is not healed or growing. The division sends the Kingdom of Israel, which the son inherited by his deceptions, into war. Part of Jacob's mission, including the famous wrestling-with-the-angel story, is to grow into his own core self, removed from collusion with his mother, and make peace with his brother.

Researcher Carole Klein found a nagging feeling of guilt in men she interviewed—guilt for not having fulfilled Mother's needs. One man, a salesman, told Klein: "No matter what I did, what accomplishments I laid at her feet, I always felt it wasn't enough. For a long while, I thought it was because I wasn't going after a profession with real prestige, but now I understand there was no way to really satisfy her, because her own ambitions had been so frustrated."

It is natural for any parent to push children toward accomplishments. Many men who have accomplished a great deal—like Pablo Casals, Andre Gide, Bo Jackson—had mothers who pushed them. It is dangerous, however, when the mother pushes the son to accomplishments, actions, and relationships whose primary reward is the mother's. When this occurs, the Hero lives to reward the Goddess-Mother, not to find his own life. He will spend the rest of his life proving himself worthy. He will tend toward addiction. He will bring to intimacy a deep, abiding wound.

WOUNDED AND DANCING SONS

Sons whose mothers have given them the messages we've just explored reach adolescence both wounded and dancing. Our mothers have devoured, or eaten away, parts of our masculine psyche. Our fathers have done little to help us regain those parts, or to help us resist the devouring. We are limping, unconscious of our own pain because it came from the Goddess, the one who loved us more than anyone. How could she have hurt us? She was our mother! Most of us never realize that our core self is undeveloped, superseded by some form of a false self; nor that this devouring was something the cultural and family system arranged for both of us, mother and son, to experience.

Even as we are devoured, we are still dancing for our mothers. We still grow up in her house and in her garden. We still obey her, help her with the shopping, make her proud, work for her, live with her. Our dance becomes a limping one, but we are still in our mother's mirror, and still, even as we begin to limp, and even as others in the world begin to shame us for our limping, she generally does not. We look wonderful to her in her mirror.

As we approached puberty, our bodies became maturely male, our desire for feminine love moved away from Mom and toward girls, and our deepest (and most confusing) desire was to become a man separate from Mom. However unconsciously, we began to notice our limping, and that we were still dancing (being forced to dance) in our mother's bedroom, before her mirror. We felt ashamed. We wanted something else. We wanted to be initiated into manhood.

Don't Go. Or: "I'll always care for you."

In a men's group, a man in his forties recalled: "I remember getting injured playing football. I remember I wanted to see the doctor alone. The gash was on my thigh, right by my groin. I begged and begged my mother to let the doctor examine me without her there. She thought I was silly. We went in there and I had to take my clothes off. I had a few pubic hairs by then. In front of the doctor she clapped her hands. 'Oh, look, my little boy's becoming a man!' I was so embarrassed I couldn't speak. I think even the doctor was embarassed. She never got it. She never understood I just didn't want her there."

It is difficult for anyone who has not experienced the separation of a child to understand deep down how terrifying and painful that separation is. It feels like the death of the child. The separation anxiety a mother feels as her children grow up and away from her was acknowledged by our ancestral and tribal cultures as something to be respected and worked through in supportive ceremony and ritual. She was not abandoned—in fact, she was the object of respect, affection, and comaraderie—as she let her son go to the men.

But she had to let him go. In many puberty and initiation ceremonies for boys, she was an active participant in sending him to the men. If her son didn't want to go—if he cried for his mom to save him from the arduous tasks and more difficult world of the men—her heart might feel as if it were breaking; but she had to force him away from her. Among the Hopi, the Ndembu, the New Guinea tribes—wherever we look, this separation was ritualized. A mother could not hold onto the son by saying, "I'll always care for you," or, in the inimitable way a mother has, "Don't go," with the implication, "You're hurting me deeply by leaving."

Does the fact that tribal culture ritualized the separation mean mothers in tribes didn't hang onto sons? Of course not. I recall during my two years in India that separation from Mother was ritualized, yet some mothers still ran their sons' homes, giving sons and daughters-in-law little power. In every culture, whether separation is ritualized or not, it is not always successful. Whether mothers want to let go or not, they do not always do so. It is very much the job of the tribe, culture, husband, and other elder men to help the mother make the separation from the son.

In our culture, however, the problem is far worse than in most others, continuing beyond the son's adolescence, as he comes to dance in his lover's mirror, asking his lover to sustain his inner life and resenting her for it as if she were a dominating mother—never finding an emotional mirror of his own.

Chapter 3: Dancing in Our Lovers' Mirrors

> Our mothers send us forth as incomplete human beings, do-it-yourself-kit human beings, ready for a woman to assemble to her specifications. The wife has the unfair and inherently unworkable task of raising the boy into a man, while the man without a model [and with incomplete separation from Mom] thinks he can only become a man by running away from mama. This dilemma turns marriage into a cruel joke, and one that is passed from generation to generation.
>
> —FRANK PITTMAN

A FRIEND OF MINE, in his mid-forties, once told me a story:

"When I was seventeen years old, a strange thing happened at our breakfast table. My brother, gone to college, had already moved out of the house. My sister was staying with friends in another city. My mother, my father, and I ate alone at the breakfast table. Usually, my father read the paper and my mom and I talked, or all three of us read the paper.

"That morning, though, I recall lifting my spoon to my mouth, and I recall my mother looked up from her own plate and asked, 'Son, have you had sex yet?'

"My father just stared at her. My mother kept looking at me, wanting an answer. I ate my spoonful of oatmeal, my brain whirring.

"My mother spoke again, trying to help me out. 'Now I don't just mean you've experimented with girls—I mean, have you actually had your penis inside a girl and ejaculated?' By now I was beet red, not only because my mother had asked me, but because she had asked me in front of my father. I knew like all boys know: not to have been laid meant I wasn't a man. I wasn't going to let either of my parents know I wasn't a man.

" 'Sure,' I said, 'Jenny and I did it.' My family had lived the year before in another city. My rapidly scheming brain figured my mother would never see Jenny again. She'd never be able to check up on whether I'd 'ejaculated' into her or not.

" 'Jenny, huh?' my mother nodded approvingly. 'That's good. I'm glad to hear it. Because sometimes I worry you're not maturing the way a boy should.'

" 'I'm fine, Mom,' I said. She must have heard the pleading in my voice. Please Mom, drop it!

" 'I hope so,' she said. 'I'm the one who made your Dad a man, and I'm glad some nice girl could do it for you.'

"And we went on eating our oatmeal. I'll never forget that conversation as long as I live. No one even believes it happened. I tell other guys about it and they just laugh. 'No way! Your *Mom* said all that?'

"But it really did happen."

The man's family was like most of the families we grew up in (though most moms weren't so overtly inquisitive!). His father was a nice guy but overworked and emotionally aloof. His mother did not often have power to make decisions outside the home, but she basically ruled the emotional life of the home. Dad was called on at times to discipline and to plan trips and to earn the money the family needed and to do well in the economic and social sphere so the family could be proud.

Underneath all this was the deeper agenda. The mother sensed her son wasn't finding his own way in life; she sensed her husband wasn't helping him much; and she sensed that she and her son were still too close. Even though she considered herself a very "moral and upright" woman (her son's words) and even though she had, a year before, insisted her husband talk to her son about sex and encourage abstinence, she believed something that became more compelling as she watched her son live an unhappy adolescence, something most of the culture around her assumed: that, when all is said and done, after all the adolescent boy's acting out and seeking danger and rebellion, a boy *really* knows he's a man by loving/conquering/seducing a woman.

My friend's mother had given her husband his manhood, and she hoped some girl/woman would give her son his. The relief she felt when her son told her he had had sex was something he's never forgotten. "It was," he said to me, "as if she was off the hook now. She could feel OK that I was finding my own way."

We are born into our mother's arms, we spend a decade dancing in her mirror, we seek separation from her, we barely separate, we find during adolescence that we're still dancing in her mirror. We want desperately to be free of her mirror. We determine that the best way to achieve this is to love another girl/woman besides Mom. Our hormones and desires are already sending us in that direction anyway. And our pop culture, the older boys around us, our fathers, even our mothers (despite their hanging on to us, and generally their reticence in saying it) have taught us that to be free of Mom, to be free of the Goddess-

Mother, to find ourselves and a mirror of our own, we must impress, seduce, conquer, protect, and (if the woman insists) cleave to a girl/woman, the Goddess-Lover. Once we have done that, everyone tells us, we will be men.

Yet when we do this, we leave our mother's mirror for our lover's mirror, and, in our deep heart's core, we become dancers in women's mirrors for the rest of our lives, still yearning to find mirrors of our own. We are no better off, in a psychological sense, than when we were boys with Mom. Women become for us not women, but substitutes for Mom. On the surface it may appear, because we are so successful at projecting false selves to the world, that we are "independent men." Women are the ones, we would contend, who are dependent on the other sex for their self-image. In fact, beneath the surface, we men are not independent—we often do not have a spiritual/ emotional life without women. Men without spouses have shorter lifespans than men who have spouses. Men are twice as likely as women to commit suicide after a divorce.

Why Do We Love?

Every man must ask himself why he loves his mate or lover. When the initial hormonal, sexual, and romantic surges have subsided, it becomes possible to answer this question honestly. As the relationship grows, extends in time and communication, and even produces a family, the question becomes crucial. The longer a relationship lasts, the longer a shadow it grows—more and more gets hidden in that long, dark bag the relationship drags behind it.

What is hidden in your relationship?

The crucial question we must all ask of our romance is: Do I love predominantly for the *content* of the relationship, or do I love predominantly to get my *self-esteem* fed? The *content* of a committed relationship includes comfortable companionship, intellectual stimulation, nurturance and support, sexual ecstasy and comfortable intimacy, procreation/nurturance of children. We all seek affection to feed our self-esteem, but the question is, do I love this woman or partner because without her I have no sense (no mirror) of my core self, or do I have a core self and love her because she is the mystery my core self needs—both to nurture me and I to nurture—as I continue to grow?

If I am predominantly involved in love-relationship(s) to feed my self-esteem—to keep me feeling adequate about myself, to keep me from being lonely, to keep me from feeling like a boy, to keep me from feeling pain—I have probably been emotionally wounded in the first twenty years of my life by mother, father, or both. If I seek love predominantly to feed my self-esteem, I am probably still embroiled in an inappropriate psychological link with my mother. I had most of my self-esteem nurturance during my boyhood through her. I am now transferring that pattern onto a woman/partner. As I moved through adolescence, a very blurry male mirror at best was shown to me by my father and elder men—certainly not a loving, wise, and powerful male mirror which, through my own journey, I could make my own. Rather, I was taught to find new women to mirror me. Until I find a mirror of my own, as men are invited to do in Part Two of this book, I will continue this pattern.

In this culture, men and women both have to struggle with the urge to ask their partners to control their own self-esteem. As adults we live in a triad of primary life-projects that mirror us: mate, children, and work. The very competitive work systems for which men are mainly trained rarely allow us to feel competent—in fact, Warren Farrell has discovered that the majority of American men feel on the edge of failure at any given moment. Most men have no intimate male friend, lack intimate trust with their own children, and feel emotionally inadequate with mates. Males in our culture live in a state of constant emotional defense—hypervigilance. As George Taylor has put it, "It isn't true that men don't have feelings. The truth is, men have no safe place in which to feel." Our self-esteem constantly at risk, we turn in boyhood to our mothers to save us and then in adulthood to mates on whom we've projected all the best qualities of Woman, most of which— sexual contact being the primary exception—involve mothering and nurturing of others' self-esteem.

This reliance on women to feed our self-esteem will probably (and has probably) worked for us for months, even a few years on end. But at some point—unless we marry a woman willing to give up her emotional life to meet our needs—our relationship will begin to break down. We will feel trapped between constant apology to her for our weaknesses and failings, our heads down, as if apologizing to Mom, and constant rage at her, as if she held us too close, like Mom used to do when we were trying to grow up and away from her.

At some point in relationships based in self-esteem needs, our families will collapse. We will feel—after a divorce or breakup we barely understand the roots of— more unsafe than we felt before. We'll try many ways of avoiding our hurt—addictions, rage at women, and sui- cide—often not realizing that the key to finding fulfilling love is hidden, as it was as we began adolescence, in making an initiatory journey away from our mothers, toward our fathers and other men, and deep into a manhood that respects women for who they are, not for the role we project on them, and teaches us the kind of self-respect no one else can give us, not even Mom.

It is crucial for each of us to go into relationships cognizant of why we are seeking the relationship, and how that "why" relates to our mothers, the first, most powerful goddesses in the first years of our lives. If we are seeking the relationship for self-esteem-building rather than content, we will probably find ourselves in debilitating behavior patterns—like oppression of women, codependency, and sex and love addiction—patterns we can identify, and transform, with hard work and a long initiatory journey.

THE MOON CHILDREN

As an aid to exploring your dominant mode of loving, let me tell you a story, The Moon Children. See what part of it reflects your life and loving.

There is a young prince, son of a king and queen who rule a nation on a plateau that sits about three thousand feet above the sea. Between the towns of the plateau and the sea below are sheer cliff walls.

Like everyone in the kingdom, the young prince grew up with stories about the Goddess of Love who, the culture believed, lived in the moon. The prince and the culture he lived in believed that the mysteries of the night, of loving, of childbirth, and even of the tides were secrets of the moon.

Like all young men of the kingdom, he had grown up waiting for the day he would play his part in the moon-light. Like everyone in his kingdom, he had stood on the cliff's edge looking down at the water, seeing the track of the moon on the water, wondering what great powers could be his if only he could touch it there, on the water. The legends of his people called the track of the moon on the water Aluna. The legends of his people, legends that had been passed down for centuries, told of a young prince who would one day climb down the terrible cliff to the ocean's edge and there discover a way to touch the track of the moon on the water—to touch Aluna, the Goddess of Love. When Aluna is touched by the young prince, so the legends said, the curse of life would be removed from the kingdom: no more drought, no more disease, no more death, no more suffering.

As the story begins, the prince stands on the cliff's edge, strong, feeling well trained to make the hazardous journey, ready to be the one who fulfills the prophecy, finds ultimate love, touches the track of that moon goddess as she lies out white and beautiful on the ocean.

But, as he ought to be, he is afraid. Many young men, some his peers, most of previous generations, have climbed down the cliff to the ocean. None have ever returned. The king and queen are frightened too. The prince has asked his father for permission to make the journey. His father has refused his permission, more than once. The prince has gone to his mother, and she, too, has refused, even more frightened for his safety than her husband. If you even try to make the journey, his father has threatened, we will disown you.

The prince comes away from the cliff's edge and goes back to the castle. He has made a decision. He finds his mother and tells her he will go despite what his parents say. She tries to convince him not to. But she can see he is determined. She can do nothing to stop him. She wants to go to her husband and get him to force her son to stay, but the prince tells her if she does that he will never speak to her again. Without her husband's knowledge, she packs her son a pack, filled with necessities. Begging him not to go, she sees her son off that night. The kingdom hears of the prince's rebellion, and some of the braver souls, who do not fear the king's wrath, make a small bonfire and a celebration at the cliff's edge. The prince puts the pack on his back, and as dawn breaks, he says his goodbyes and begins the climb down the sheer cliff.

As he climbs, his father is still nowhere to be seen. His mother's tears echo in his ears. In his mother's backpack, the prince has hidden a small ornament his father gave him years ago when he was a boy—something to remember his father by. It is heavy, made of gold.

Already the climb is difficult. The voices at the top of the cliff recede, and the wind and the cries of seagulls pierce his ears. For the first time in his life, his mother's and father's world behind him, he feels a strange and powerful aloneness. The climb gets more and more difficult.

As his first day of climbing ends, his muscles feel like jelly. And that night, unlike most nights, there is no moon. He cannot continue climbing, for he can see nothing. He can only remain fastened by trembling fingers and toes to the side of the cliff. This is the case the next night as well. By the end of the following day, he has climbed perhaps two thirds of the way down. He has thrown off all the weight he could—all the tools he carried, all heavy clothing, even the items in his mother's pack. He hangs onto the gold ornament his father gave him, his mother's pack (though it is empty), and just the barest clothing. That night he again hangs to the side of the cliff by tiny juts of rock, delirious from lack of sleep, his muscles ready to give up at any moment.

But the next day comes, and he manages to climb down further. He falls onto the sand at the bottom of the cliff, collapsing in exhaustion and relief. He sees the bones of other young men who have fallen. He crawls to the water's edge and falls asleep.

As the first part of the story ends, the young man has left his parents' world. His leaving has destroyed the unity of his family home, but he felt he had no choice. Even despite his father's distance, he keeps his father's gold ornament. He keeps his mother's pack, although it is empty of everything except the ornament. He has made the arduous journey away from his parents' restrictions and lives—or so it seems. In making the journey he feels alone but, too, he is poised for adventure. He has survived the climb downward. He is at the water's edge, ready to figure out a way to touch Aluna, commune with the Goddess of Love, find happiness, and save his kingdom from all suffering.

When he wakes up, it is dusk. He is sore, still trembling, but touched by joy. Like all young men, he has no doubt he will be able to achieve his goals, touch Aluna, and find his future, and very soon.

But as he sits at the water's edge, watching the moon rise, as he watches darkness shroud the ocean and Aluna appear shimmering on the water's surface, he sees no way to get out to the track of the moon on the water. He gets up, walks around. He explores the beach, looking for enough driftwood for a raft. There is not enough. The more he explores, the more he knows he cannot swim out to the track of the moon on the water. He sees no evidence of other young men on the beach, no matter how far to the east or west he walks. They must have swum out and never come back. The sharks will have gotten them, or the sheer arduousness of the swim.

Hearing something to his left, he turns to see a traveler coming towards him. This is definitely not someone from his own kingdom. He hails the traveler, tells him his mission, asks if the traveler has seen others like him. Have they been successful at communing with Aluna?

"Of course," the traveler responds. "It's not hard to touch the track of the moon on the water. Not hard at all. But it will hurt a little." And the traveler gives instructions. "Through your arduous efforts, you have climbed down into a land of fantasy. You now have certain powers; what you imagine will be so. In order to get Aluna's attention, you must close your eyes and bring to your vision all the women you have known—your mother, your sisters, women you have seen, girls and women whose fine company you have enjoyed. As you bring them to your mind, they will appear here on this beach. You must then take a knife, which you will imagine, and cut off all their hair. Once you've done that, throw their hair on the water. It will form into a net. The net will slowly move out to Aluna and entrap her light and bring it back here to shore. Can you do that?"

The prince nods. This makes some sense. How can he attract or entrap Aluna if so many other women still occupy his mind? He must cut off their hair. He must show Aluna he knows she is the supreme and only Goddess.

The prince closes his eyes. He imagines his mother, his sisters, a girl friend, others. When he opens his eyes, they each appear. The traveler is gone. The prince tries to speak to his friends and family, tell them what he has to do.

They stand mute, without resistance. He knows their hearts are hurt as he cuts their hair, but he has no choice. As he cuts the hair off each girl and woman, she disappears.

When he has finished, elated, he throws the hair out onto the water. For a moment—perhaps in real time, in our time, that moment is six months, or a year, or five in a man's life—he feels successful, he knows this will work, for the hair is forming into a net on the surface of the small waves, moving out toward Aluna!

But then, as quickly as the net formed, it begins to dissolve. Have I done the ritual incorrectly? he wonders. He has done what the traveler said to do. What's wrong? Why is the net dissolving so rapidly?

The hair laps onto shore like seaweed. The prince sits back down, imagining the women again, his mother, his sister, his girl friend. None appear. He closes his eyes, trying again, and again, without success, to bring them back. Meanwhile their hair lies all around him, lifeless on the shore.

THE MAN WHO CUTS OFF WOMEN'S HAIR

When in a mythological story a person cuts off another's hair, the action implies domination, the removal of the victim's power and beauty. Probably the best-known example of this is the biblical Samson and Delilah story. Central European myth and fairy tale, from which The Moon Children springs, has the same archetypal and symbolic association. The prince is coached by the traveler in patterns of domination and achieves this domination by cutting off women's hair. Many of us, especially in our adolescence and early adulthood, are coached in this pattern without realizing it. Perhaps our mother was dominated by our father. Perhaps we had little spiritually vital and emotionally mature male initiation, so we listened to and watched the other older boys who carried on their relationships by insisting their girl friends do as they wanted them to do. Many of these older boys verbally or even physically abused the girl friends when the girl friends did not do as they were told. Even if the boys treated the girl friends well in public, when the boys were alone with us, many of the older ones talked about how they were the man in the relationship, the girl was just a girl, and the "man" did what he wanted with her. In watching and sitting with these boys, we learned to cut off women's hair.

Perhaps we were abused by our mothers or someone else during our boyhoods and grew into adulthood wounded, needing to defend against intimacy by cutting off the hair of people who came close to us, people who might get so close they could penetrate our defenses and touch our wounds. Often, Ken Druck has pointed out, our domineering attitude toward women grows from our need to punish lovers for our mother's abuses, sins, and crimes.

> Men may find themselves becoming unusually pushy, defensive, angry, overly sensitive, and frustrated with little or no provocation. Something their wives or women friends do or say suddenly lights a short fuse inside them. The anger, frustration, and confusion that may result is but the ghost of those feelings they had years before in encounters with their mothers. These youthful emotions will continue to haunt them and the women in their lives until they learn to recognize them for what they are and face their feelings toward their mothers.

The man who cuts off women's hair may hit his partner, yell at her. He will try to convince her she's wrong, ugly, or stupid. He will tend to blame her for all or most problems in the relationship. He will withhold from her the feelings and things he knows she needs most, keeping her in her place, keeping her emotional expectations of him low, and allowing him to remain in control of how much emotion flows between them. He may purposely stay away from home and from her, giving his time to everything but her. He may respond with extreme jealousy when others pay generous attention to her.

The man who cuts off women's hair is dancing in his lover's mirror and punishing her for the power she has to make him dance there.

The prince is sitting at the water's edge, the hair all around him. He is hurt, ashamed, unable to call back the women. He does not know what to do. Then he hears a voice saying, "Ho there!" He opens his eyes. It's another traveler, coming from the other direction. This traveler sits down next to him.

"You look pretty sad," the traveler says, smiling kindly. "I bet I know what's just happened to you." The traveler accurately describes everything the prince has just gone through.

"Well, what happened?" the prince asks, irritated. "Why didn't the net work?"

"It was not meant to," the traveler says. "My brother, who gave you those instructions, was merely sent to test you. The Goddess of Love needs to know if you have the strength to love her alone, above all other women. You have proven you have that strength. Now you are ready to meet Aluna. I have been sent to show you how."

Eagerly, the prince listens as the traveler describes what he must do. "In this land of fantasy, you have exquisite powers. To embrace Aluna, you must reach your hand deep into your chest, pull your heart out of the cage it rests in, and hold it in your palm in front of you. Aluna will see, by your actions, that you are capable not only of holding her supreme above other women, but also you are capable of giving your whole heart to her. When you hold your heart out to her, she will come for it, and take it, and you will have succeeded in your goal. Now close your eyes."

The prince closes his eyes, understanding what he must do. He has proven his loyalty to Aluna by cutting off the women's hair. He has put the real women he knows in their place so that the supreme Goddess can occupy him fully. Although it hurt the women, still they were not really hurt, for he had imagined it all. And now he must prove his utter servility to love, to Aluna, the Goddess of Love all men desire to serve—the creature all men wish to give their hearts to.

He plunges his hand into his chest. Amazingly, his hand pushes through his flesh, like a fist through soft ground. He wraps his hand around his heart and pulls it out. He holds it out to the moon in his hand, feeling it pulse there.

For a moment—a moment that might be a year or five or ten in a man's life—he feels the rightness of his actions. He opens his eyes, and it seems the moon is moving closer to him. For a moment, he knows this will work!

But then the moment passes. The moon stays where it was, as does the track of the moon on the water. His heart dries in his palm, and his chest feels empty.

He puts his heart back in his chest. Now he's angry. It is an anger that distracts him from the sorrow of having hurt the women of his life; it is an anger that distracts him from the feeling of emptiness he felt when he tore his heart out and offered it to the moon. The anger turns, after a time, to grief.

HOLDING OUR HEARTS IN OUR PALMS

How many of us have done this? How many of us have given ourselves up in the fleeting hope that we would be loved? Codependency is the popular term for this kind of love. Codependency implies the surrender of our core self to serve the needs of another. This is very different than, for instance, a warrior's surrender of his time and energy to the needs of the king, queen, or divine teacher. In that surrender, he keeps his core self—he enlists it to a higher cause. In codependency—when we hold our hearts in our hands—we surrender our boundaries, our self-image, our own needs. We hope and pray that the surrender will be rewarded. The warrior knows his surrender will be rewarded. Even if he dies, his spiritual vision of the world tells him his core self (his soul) will remain intact.

The man who holds his heart in his palm will put his heart out there where it can shrivel and die, and even if he is rewarded with a wonderful maternal nurturance by his mate, he will also feel lost in emotional dilemmas and schisms that eat at him and at his relationship. If his mate does not grow tired of mothering him, he himself will probably grow tired of being mothered.

Digging our hands into our chests and pulling our hearts out for our lovers is not the same thing as "emotional openness." Each of us accomplishes intimacy by a walk on the razor's edge between loss of boundaries on the one hand and withholding of affection on the other. Love is hard and painful because it hurts to walk this razor. We must be emotionally open yet simultaneously capable of not losing our individuated selves. When in mythology a man pulls his heart out and places it before a woman, this action is not seen as the proper antidote for emotional distance. Rather, it is seen as inviting the cutting or crushing of the heart. For a man or woman to pull their heart out of their chest or engage in another act of similar vulnerability is to invite clear danger.

A man who holds his heart in his palm has allowed a pattern to be set up in his relationship(s) in which his partner withholds her most nurturant feelings until he "earns" the right to them. He probably has deep and unresolved issues with his mother. He has grown into adulthood constantly worried about letting women down the same way he let Mom down, wanting always to do the right thing for women the way he wanted to do the same for Mom.

A man who holds his heart in his palm probably had very little initiation into manhood; he will not have learned much about the male mode of feeling. He spends his life recreating the boyhood in which he learned how to feel from Mom, now learning how to feel from women and their mirrors. Because he has not learned how to feel from men, he will never know if he's being intimate the way a *man* is intimate. He will feel confused about what his boundaries are as a *man*.

Sometimes as men we find ourselves cutting off women's hair and holding our hearts in our palms almost simultaneously. We cut women down, keep them in their place, punish them in one moment, but in the next, especially with our primary partner, we beg her to love us, make life sweet for us, take care of all our needs. Still locked in issues with our mother, still dancing in her mirror, still trying to separate from her, meanwhile trying to do what our lover wants of us, dancing in her mirror, and projecting our mother's mirror onto hers, we hold our heart in our hands, and that doesn't feel right. We cut off her hair, and that doesn't feel right. We vacillate.

A man who pulls his heart out of his chest and holds it out to his lover is saying to her, "I am willing to dance only in your mirror. I will dance in no other mirror, especially not my own." He must take a great deal of responsibility for the responses his partner will have to this voluntary self-negation. If and when she begins to dominate him, he must look closely at how he does not hold his own boundaries, how he is dependent on her for his self-image, and how he has bought into the fantasy that love comes to a man who sacrifices himself (his core self) for the Goddess who, if only he will someday get it right, is waiting to reward him with bliss.

The prince, you'll remember, had cut off the women's hair, felt the moment of bliss, been disappointed. He has tried pulling his heart out of his chest; he has felt the moment of bliss, but again it doesn't last and doesn't bring him any closer to the Goddess of Love. He feels angry, afraid, numb.

Into these feelings comes a third traveler. The prince hears him coming but does not even look at him. The traveler sits down next to him.

"Get outta here," the prince hisses at him.

"I understand how you feel," the traveler offers. "Hear me out. I have sat where you sit. I know you are angry and hurt. But your ordeal is almost over. On the quest for real love," the traveler says, "you are put through tests. The first will always be evil and hurtful to others, the second will be hurtful to you. None of my brothers has been wrong. You came to this place a naive young man. You did not know the extent of your powers. My brothers have shown you the extent of your powers. My brothers have shown you how to hurt others and how to hurt yourself. Now I will show you how to achieve what you came to achieve, for now you are ready."

The prince silently vows not to be naive again. He does not jump at the chance to hear clever advice from this third traveler. "Leave me alone," he says, "I'll find my own way."

"I'll leave you," the traveler says, rising to go. "But when you can't find your own way do this simple thing, bend down to the water's edge and drink. This is a land of fantasy. You can drink the water until you have drunk the whole ocean into yourself. The track of the moon on the water will then be within you. Think about it." And the traveler is gone.

The prince sits and stares at the moon, at its white reflection on the water. He thinks: Could this traveler actually be right? Isn't it worth at least trying his advice? What can it hurt? What if I could really drink all the water and get Aluna to come into *me,* to be a part of *me?*

Looking around, seeing no one about, the prince gets on his hands and knees and puts his lips to the water. He sets to drinking the ocean. It goes down his throat, and more of it goes down and more of it goes down. He drinks and drinks and drinks. His eyes see the water level decreasing, yet his body keeps taking the ocean in. He begins to see fish and water life, coral and underwater hills, and still the water goes in. He sees the track of the moon on the water disappearing, and he knows it is disappearing into him. He allows himself to feel a wonderful ecstasy as the last drop of water touches his lips.

The prince feels powerful for a long moment. He feels filled up and complete in a way he never has before. He knows Aluna is in *him* now. What a feeling that is! Oh, the moment lasts!

Then something begins to happen—a feeling of terrible bloating. The moment of ecstasy is passing too quickly, passing into a feeling of explosion. The prince tries to hold the water, but it comes flooding out. It pours back into the ocean bed.

The prince lets it out but then bends down again, begins to drink. He was so close to real ecstasy this time, so close to Aluna. He must make this work.

He drinks again. He drinks it all up. He feels full, complete, whole . . .

Then the bloating, the flooding out. And so he tries again, and again. Drinking, letting water out, drinking . . .

Finally, he sits back down. He was so close, so close.

The prince begins to weep. He has never felt so empty, so much like a failure, so stupid. He cannot understand whether he is following the instructions incorrectly, or whether the travelers are liars, or whether the legend is impossible to fulfill. He feels very small, as if he is a pawn. He does not feel he has any real power to determine his destiny.

DRINKING THE OCEAN AGAIN AND AGAIN

The prince has tried to cut off the women's hair and, with the net of their hair, entrap the Goddess of Love. When that didn't work, he offered his own heart, holding it out not only for the Goddess of Love to take, but for anyone else to grab as well. That didn't work either. Now he has taken the path of consuming—the path we might call sex or love addiction—the path of drinking the ocean and bringing the Goddess of Love into himself. She cannot exist inside him. Nor can he hold her in for too long, because with her comes the whole huge ocean.

And, of course, we know what he doesn't realize at first: that she never comes into him at all. Just because he has drunk the ocean that mirrors love does not mean he has drunk love itself. Without the ocean there to mirror her, love still remains up in the moon, sacrosanct, waiting for the reflective surface to return.

The prince feels the ectasy of consumption for a moment; he feels the power and control of having removed darkness from love, for as he drinks the ocean, nothing on the ocean floor can hide. It is all wriggling there for him to see.

But he has removed all mystery too. And he is soon bloated by his consumption, forced to spit the ocean back out, catch his breath, try again, and again, and again, until he feels the futility of his addiction, his consumption, his search for eternal triumph.

The man who drinks the ocean again and again moves from relationship to relationship, leaving each relationship when the infatuation and ecstasy are gone. He finds 'em, feels 'em, fucks 'em, and forgets 'em. He sometimes wakes up in the morning knowing in his deep heart's core that this is not mature love, there is a better way, he's still stuck in adolescence . . . but he finds these moments of clarity dissolve at the sight of a new woman to consume.

The man who drinks the ocean again and again relies on sex as his primary form of intimacy, and on conquest-intimacy as his primary mode of building self-image. He may be very "sensitive," able to talk well, to convince women he really cares about them. But his relationships still won't last more than a few months or a year. He may even have been married for a number of years, but throughout the long-term commitment his eyes never stop straying. He carries on extramarital affairs, some of them nonsexual but affectionate to the point of robbing his primary love relationship.

The man who drinks the ocean again and again has been wounded deeply in his boyhood. It is probable that in his relationship with his mother he was abused, neglected, abandoned, impinged on, raised in her alcoholism or other addiction. His attachment to her was probably stunted, incestuous (sexually and/or psychologically), confused by abandonment. Because it was not an attachment based on trust, his separation from her was all the more confusing. He grew up yearning for her to love him and sees her reflected in the many mates he finds. As an adult, he is yearning, through many lovers, to prove to his mother that he is worthy of feminine affection.

As the story of The Moon Children continues, the prince looks down in the water and sees reflections of his parents. He wishes his father was the kind of man who could have given him permission to make this journey and some gifts that would help him know what to accomplish and how to accomplish it. He wishes his mother were with him now to take care of him, for she has always loved him and always will. She is the only person he has ever really trusted. Especially after what the travelers have done to him, he thinks maybe she's the only person he will ever trust.

He weeps for his father and mother. He weeps for his

loneliness. The prince stares out at the track of the moon on the water. To be a man, he senses now, is to be alone.

He looks up the beach, his eye startled by movement. Coming toward him is a dwarf, a tiny man, hobbling up the beach. This must be another kind of traveler, he thinks numbly. I should just kill him, but I am too tired.

The dwarf greets him and sits down. In a rasping, old man's voice the dwarf asks, "What are you doing here?"

"Don't you know?" the prince answers. "All the others have known."

The dwarf shakes his head, moving his hands in the sand like a child making a sand castle. He forms a turret, he sculpts a wall, saying nothing.

"You really don't know?" The prince can't believe it.

The dwarf shakes his head. "I was just walking up this beach and saw you sitting here so sadly. I thought I would try to help. What are you doing here?"

This dwarf must have no fantastical powers, the prince thinks, if he doesn't even know why I'm here. The dwarf isn't really worth talking to.

But the prince begins to talk. He doesn't think at first that he'll really say much, but in his sadness and loneliness he tells the dwarf everything: how he set out to remove the curse of life from the kingdom; how he met three travelers; how he did what they said but nothing worked; how he feels he's lost his soul; how the track of the moon on the water still remains far from him. "If this is love," he tells the dwarf, "I want none of it."

The dwarf nods. "I see. Now your mission is to touch the track of the moon on the water, yes?"

The prince nods.

"And why don't you swim out to the track of the moon?" the dwarf asks.

"Because all the other men must have done that, and they must have died. I see few bones, few skulls on this beach. They must have all swum out. When the water was all inside me, I saw the monsters that lie at the bottom of the sea. I value my life; I cannot swim out there."

The dwarf stands up to go. "I am not the wisest of men," he says, "but it seems to me you will never accomplish your goal here on this beach. You have two choices, but only you can make them: climb back up to the kingdom, or swim out toward Aluna. Not all the young men have died, I can tell you that. You'll find most of them on islands out there."

"They must have died," the prince exclaims, seeing no islands on the horizon. "The curse of life has never been removed from my father's kingdom."

"Nor will it ever be. Love is not the remedy of all pain and fear. Your father's prophecy was wrong. If you seek love, you must swim. To swim, you will have to throw off that backpack, for it will weigh you down. You will have to throw out that gold ornament, too, for it will weigh you down. All the powers you need are now within you."

This is a strange and different song. Throw off his mother's backpack? Throw his father's gold away? Swim out into the water where all is unknown and dangerous?

The dwarf says, "I will be on my way. Best of luck to you."

The prince watches his back until it disappears up the beach.

The prince knows he cannot climb back up to his parents' world. What is left but to swim out? Maybe there are islands out there he just can't see from here.

The tide is coming in. The water begins climbing up his legs. The prince lets the cold chill of the water touch his ankles, his calves, then his knees. It sends a chill through his body, a chill up from his thighs. The water climbs up beyond his thighs now, touching his genitals. The chill moves through his whole body.

He slides into the water. He begins his swim. After a few strokes he pauses, treads water, looks out toward the horizon. How strange! There are islands. And they are within swimming distance! Why couldn't he see them from shore?

He sees villages, ports, other swimmers. He swims hard toward one of the islands. Getting closer to it, he sees people coming to the beach to welcome him. Very close now, he recognizes an uncle, and another, and other young men from his village. The swimming, although it exhausts him, excites him. He finds he has magic in him, magic in the form of constantly renewed strength to swim.

Safe, he drags himself up onto the beach. He is embraced by his relatives. He hears about the men's experiences with the travelers, and how they had to swim out in the end. He hears about many young men who never made it to the island—some still wandering far down the beach, some trying to climb back up the cliff and falling, some swimming out in fear, losing their strength, and drowning.

He asks where the women came from and hears that the prophecy in their land was that a princess would descend the cliffs of their world and touch the track of the sun on the water. The women who tried to fulfill this prophecy met travelers who led them astray. But finally some of them, like the prince and his uncles, made it to the islands.

That night, as a welcoming ceremony, a great dance is held. All the people on the island dance in the moonlight and welcome the prince into his new world.

So the prince finds a new world once he gives up his fear. He finds his new world once he gives up his mother's backpack, his father's ornament, and his own naiveté. He finds it once he gives up the immature and dysfunctional ways of loving that any young man falls into when he does not get the support and initiation he needs from his father and does not separate from his mother. He finds it once he gives up the dysfunctions of the family he was brought up in. He finds it once he gives up the useless prophecy about love—that love of the Goddess-Lover, like a mother's love of her infant, can seem to remove all pain and suffering from the male kingdom.

When he was living in his fear of life and a deep yearning for approval—his mother's backpack clinging to him, his father's ornament at his side—he was susceptible to the three fantasies of intimacy by which all of us men have at one time or another tried to be intimate, escaped intimacy, or convinced ourselves real intimacy was impossible. While all of us have probably done all three in our lives, and combinations of them, we will each tend toward one of the dysfunctions primarily. And that dysfunction will most probably be linked to unresolved issues with our mothers. To move beyond the dysfunction, we will have to step out of her mirror and never go back. We will have to change our perception that love and intimacy are the sacred text of the feminine, a text we men can only learn through certain actions of worship and control of women-mothers, actions we rarely understand.

FINDING A MIRROR OF OUR OWN

In Part Two of this book, women are invited to see male initiation dramatized and men are invited to make a journey that will weave itself into about a year of a man's life. In it men and women will discover a mythic frame and mythic vision that men have used throughout the ages to work through their relationships with their mothers, feel the influence of their fathers in that relationship, discover their dysfunctions in the face of the feminine, and come through with new heroism and a mature mirror of their own. If, as you read Part One, you saw pieces of yourself, then the guided journey that follows has the potential to alter the future of your life.

It is hard work. It is hero's work.

Native Americans say, "What we do affects the next seven generations." As we take the journey of initiation—as we work through memories and feelings we have about our mother's abuse, neglect, overmothering, abandonment, alcoholism, or other shadow—and as we work through the separation process from her emotional hold on us and our society's addiction to that hold, we make the journey not only for ourselves, but for our relationships and children as well. At the end of the journey, we are free to feel the kind of self-trust we cannot feel now, locked in the adult life of a Prince. At the end of the journey, we are free to dance in the moonlight without guilt or shame.

PART TWO

Healing the Mother-Son Relationship

A Guided Journey of Initiation

All my life I had been looking for something, and
everywhere I turned someone tried to tell me what
it was. I accepted their answers, though they were
often in contradiction and even self-contradictory. I
was naive. I was looking for myself and asking
everyone except myself questions which I, and
only I, could answer.

—RALPH ELLISON, *The Invisible Man*

Chapter 4: Beginning Your Heroic Quest

Human beings are storytelling animals, myth-
makers and spinners of tales that give us the only
answers we will ever get to the perennial questions:
Where did I come from? What is the purpose of
my life? Who are the heroes? What should I do?
Am I alone? What is taboo? How am I hurt? How
may I be healed?

—SAM KEEN

IN THE REMAINING CHAPTERS of this book, I will guide you
on an odyssey through your own internal landscape, your
memory, your present relationships, and your future potential. The quest you embark on will be a search for
information, understanding, inspiration, and recovery.
You will be asked to perform a series of tasks, some very
difficult, which will constitute an intense journey of initiation into the next stage of your manhood.

The goal of this personal odyssey is ultimately the
journey itself: to rediscover and to live what is core and
"authentic" within yourself. This authentic self, this soul,
the Hindus believe, is like a brilliant jewel. In the personal
odyssey of this book, that jewel has four facets for men: to
resolve issues with Mother, to complete healthy separation
from her, to balance masculine/feminine elements, and to
resolve issues in intimate partnerships with women. All

these begin with and relate to your relationship with your mother. In taking significant experiential steps toward the goals of a healthy mother-son relationship, you'll have an initiatory experience like none other.

This personal odyssey involves ceremony and ritual, ordeal and accomplishment. It involves connecting to your pain, grief, joy, and strength. And it involves the return to sacred stories. We'll continue to find challenges, "medicine," and our own archetypal patterns in working with and through stories from around the world. These stories will help us through the initiation process in some very specific and some very subtle ways. Any woman or man reading this journey will better and more deeply understand how a boy becomes a man and a man becomes a lover. If you choose to take the journey, you will have the experiential challenge of actually moving through the archetypal stages of the Goddess-Hero quest.

The Vision Quest and the Hero's Journey

A vision quest is a Native American ceremony in which a boy seeking separation from his mother and initiation into full manhood—or a man seeking initiation into deeper manhood—makes a spiritual journey into a potentially dangerous wilderness. He faces ordeals that challenge his defenses and fears. After a few days he slows his life down, learning the rhythm of the wilderness. Undistracted by others, he seeks visions—experiences and projections of his hidden inner life. His fearful, incipient goal—just to survive and tell the tale—gradually becomes a more important goal: to know himself. When he returns from the physical ordeal and the spiritual journey, he returns to the safety of mentors who help him interpret his visions. Even months or years later, he recalls the vision quest and feeds at the trough of that deep personal experience.

The "hero's journey" resembles a vision quest. In myths and fairy tales all over the world, whether North American, African, Mideastern, European, Asian, Australian aboriginal, whether ancient or contemporary, we find resemblances in the ways boys move through the hero's journey into healthy manhood. That hero's journey has definite goals: to initiate the boy into sacred manhood—to teach him what is sacred within him and how to let that flow while teaching him what is shadow within him and how to control that shadow. As he is learning to be a "hero," he is initiating the constellation of archetypes that constitute the Hero. Specifically, he learns how to use his anger and assertiveness in productive ways—the Sacred Warrior; how to use his abilities to explore without wandering away from commitments—the Sacred Explorer; how to create and use tools and ideas for the betterment of the world and connection to mystery—the Sacred Magician; how to love openly, freely, trustingly—the Sacred Lover; and how to feel spiritually centered, and, through that confidence, to bless, parent, and lead others—the Sacred King.

THE GODDESS AND THE HERO

In archetypal language, the mother-son relationship is a story about a Goddess and a Hero, a hero who is at first *her* hero, then becomes his father's hero, then becomes his own, meeting and integrating a new Goddess.

It is no accident that the mythic literatures of countless cultures tell this same mother-son story, whether it be the

---

Greek story of Perseus, the Sioux tale of the Stone Boy, the Hindu creation story of Indra, and thousands of others. Standing and acting as Hero, his skills, nurturance, intelligence, and compassion result from a balance between his masculinity and femininity. Standing as a man, he is no longer ruled by feminine energy (Queen, Crone, Maiden), nor must he rule it. He has become a mature Hero—capable of sharing power with the feminine.

That a Hero is an integration of masculine and feminine has been taught in folk mythology all over the world, but it has been barely noticed in the persuasive and institutionalized interpretations of our culture's grand-scaled but archetypally limited guiding mythology. The integrated version of the Hero has also been lost in the glitter of our popular culture's stereotypical heroes. Both our institutionalized mythologies and our popular stereotypes are flawed because they are so limited, so lacking in diversity.

In the "other" mythic system—the folk and fairy tales—the Hero's integration of the Goddess and Feminine energy is an essential part of his strength, longevity, and wisdom. In the folk and fairy tale traditions we rely on most heavily in this book, we find a Hero whose journey is far richer than the stereotypes and monotypes many of us grew up with. Such will certainly be the case as we explore the quest of Perseus.

The Epic Tale of Perseus

We will explore the dual-development of masculine and feminine elements in the Hero through the epic story of Perseus, his mother Danae, his mentors Athena and Hermes, his adversary Medusa, and his lover Andromeda. Their story will become our archetypal map. If you had more than one mother in your childhood—perhaps a biological and an adoptive mother or stepmother—you will want to make substitutions and adaptations so that the story fits your life.

Perseus was the son of Danae. Danae's father, Acrisius, kept her locked in a dungeon because an oracle had told him he would have a grandson who would kill him. Zeus, the god of all gods, came down to the dungeon in a golden rain shower and impregnated Danae. Perseus was born. When Acrisius discovered the boy, he put his daughter and her infant son in a wooden chest, casting it into the sea.

As the story begins, the mother is the victim of her father's fears. Her fertility and creativity are negated by a shadow masculine presence. A sacred male presence helps her retain a portion of her creativity, resulting in her son, Perseus. She is punished for this again, and banished, left alone to do the best she can with her son.

Many of our own mothers were like Danae, to lesser or greater degrees. Many of our mothers were held back and had their self-images and creativity negated by shadow masculinity in our culture. Many of us are like Perseus, fertilized by sacred masculinity, but feeling cut off from it; knowing, much better, the shadow masculine and the absent masculine presences.

Danae and Perseus did not perish, although they suffered. A fisherman, Dictys, found their chest caught in his nets. He released the mother and son. Too poor to give them a home, he took them to his brother, King Polydectes, who accepted them and raised Perseus.

Life with this new father, Polydectes, very soon became difficult. Polydectes taught Perseus a great deal, but Polydectes desperately wanted Danae to marry him. She wouldn't. Much of Perseus' boyhood and adolescence were spent protecting his mother from Polydectes. Perseus and his mother remained very, very close throughout his adolescence.

In the next stage of her life, Danae is again relatively powerless. She and her son spend his boyhood and adolescence in the home of a man who provides for them but whom they cannot ultimately trust. They can trust no one as much as they trust each other. In Polydectes' home, Perseus learns many skills and develops into a strong, smart young man. Much of his skill and strength is used to be for his mother what no man, including her present male protector and provider, has ever been.

Similarly, many of us developed relationships with our mothers that were in some way substitutes for what they weren't getting from our fathers. Even many of us who had abusive, nonprotecting, neglectful mothers often still hold our mothers up as the ones we could rely on. We learn many skills from our fathers, but primarily it is our mothers to whom we cleave.

There are two versions of how Perseus set out on his quest for the Medusa, just as there are two versions of how frightening Medusa was. In one version, Polydectes sent Perseus off to kill Medusa (one of the sisters of Gorgon) in order to get rid of him so that he, Polydectes, could marry Danae, unimpeded by her son's presence. In this version, one look at a Gorgon turned a human to stone. In the second version, Perseus himself suggested he go kill Medusa and bring back her head. In this version Perseus wanted once and for all to prove he was Polydectes' equal. And in this version, one look at a Gorgon caused a human's immediate death.

Whichever version pleases you, in both the idea is the same: Perseus sets off on an adventure that will take him to a confrontation with a Shadow Goddess. He has to separate from his Goddess-Mother and discover himself.

Because he has been forced into a life of constant intimacy with his mother, with his mother dependent on him and he on her, and with no healthy elder men to help him negotiate his separation, Fate forces the separation—it forces his journey of initiation.

In the same way, many of us do not separate, do not resolve issues with our mothers, want to hurt them and adore them with equal energy, remain in the limbo of feeling guilty for leaving them and wanting to protect them eternally. Something, perhaps a crisis in an adult love relationship or the experiential process of a book like this one, forces us to make the journey. A primary piece of the work we will have to do is confrontation with the shadow side of the Goddess, including work with the shadow side of our mother and our relationship with her, as well as work with the shadow side of women and the feminine we experience in our lives and loves.

Perseus' journey to the Gorgon sisters and his confrontation with the Medusa was supported by two mentors, Athena and Hermes, who gave him a sacred shield and sacred sword. The journey they aided took him to the Gray Women, whose eye he had to steal to find out Medusa's location; also to the Maidens, who gave him gifts—magic sandals, a magic bag, and a cap of invisibility—to help him defeat Medusa. When he finally confronted Medusa, he was supported, ready and far wiser than when he set off.

At this point, Perseus' journey becomes very much the journey of a Sacred Warrior. He is focused on the confrontation to come. He is mentored by a female (Athena, the goddess of wisdom and war) and a male deity, Hermes. He makes a number of sacred connections before he faces his Medusa. He learns the wisdom and vision of the Crone. He spends time with the Maidens, learning from them what they have to teach him about femininity and femaleness. He carries gifts with him—in archetypal terms, he learns many of his own sacred gifts, and many of the significant and sacred gifts of the feminine, before he faces the Medusa.

Perseus' journey is like ours but also painfully dissimilar. Our adolescence and young adulthood are generally not as well mentored as his. We often find ourselves facing the shadow side of the feminine without preparation. Often we don't face it at all, becoming passive. Or we wrongly believe it is everywhere around us, ready to devour us at every turn, and thus we seek to dominate even the sacred side of the feminine with hypermasculinity and aggression toward women. Half our culture preaches the warrior's journey for men without really knowing what a sacred warrior is—leading to a shadow warrior in men, and attendant violence and domination. The other half of our culture preaches the negation of the warrior's journey, again without really knowing what a sacred warrior is— leading to the negation of healthy male empowerment. Without learning what our gifts are, and what the gifts of the feminine are, through an initiation process, we enter adulthood and get locked in constant power struggles with the feminine.

After cutting off the Medusa's head, Perseus' adventures continued. He fell in love with and rescued Andromeda, who, like Perseus, was a victim of a family curse and a deity's intercession (in her case, her mother's vanity brought a goddess's wrath on her family, and Andromeda was forced into a serpent's dungeon). His adventure ended with his return to his mother and a new relationship with her. Polydectes looked at the Medusa's head and was turned to stone/killed. Dictys took over the kingdom. Perseus tried to make peace with Acrisius but ended up killing him, through a twist of fate. Perseus did not feel he could take over the kingdom of a grandfather he had killed. He and Androm- eda parented a new dynasty elsewhere.

Perseus is a different man after his long journey and culminating confrontation with Medusa. He has healthy powers now he didn't have before. He knows significant pieces of who he is, what his vision and values are, how to balance the masculine and the feminine. He is separated from his mother. He has initiated a number of the mature archetypes within himself. Truly a man, he is ready now to responsibly, compassionately "fall in love." He falls in love with a woman who is an equal—as symbolized by the similarity in their family backgrounds and the deity's sacred incursion into their family histories. In rescuing Andromeda from the serpent, Perseus is also doing the symbolic act of heroes throughout world mythology—he is rescuing his own femininity. And, finally, after resolv- ing issues with his father(s), he becomes King. He be- comes the masculine giver of blessings and leadership to the realm, and Andromeda gives the feminine blessing and leadership.

In the Perseus' journey is both the real and the ideal of the mother-son/Goddess-Hero quest. Our own lives, marked by pieces of this journey, have been bereft of others. Many of us have found our Andromeda before we really confronted our mother, separated from her, re- solved our issues with her. Many of us have found our Andromeda before we faced the Medusa. Many of us have not accomplished Kingship, whether within our own psyches or in our families or workplaces, because we have not been able to resolve issues with and confront our fathers. The journey Perseus makes is and can be our journey. We can do what Perseus has done, rooting our growth and healing in suffering, as Perseus did, and in the joy of new manhood.

As you accomplish equivalent tasks to those faced by Perseus, you will move through the archetypal stages of the Goddess-Hero journey. You will find hidden in your own life, unremembered and unintegrated, some of these labors already achieved—and you will find other pieces of the journey beginning now. Take as long as you need to make this journey. I suggest you weave it into your life over a one-year period.

SEVEN AFFIRMATIONS OF A MAN'S HEROIC QUEST

As you move through this process, you may want to refer back at times to these affirmations. For this process to be effective, it needs to be woven through your life, returned to at some personal ritual time you set for yourself, away from family and commitments.

James Hillman has connected personal growth with "slowness." Slow discovery honors your inner voice in a way that quick change does not. Until we slow down, we cannot get to the depths of our spiritual selves. Your personal odyssey work needs this slowness, this ritual rhythm. And because it needs that, precepts will be forgotten. When you need to, repeat these seven affirmations to yourself as a way of bringing yourself back to the objectives of your inner search.

1. A man is a loving, wise, and powerful male adult. I strive to live in the fullness a man deserves. I strive to live with spiritual connectedness to my deepest self,

my friends and family, and my surrounding world. I strive to live in more than a survival mode. I strive to know my sacred self.

2. The human unconscious is a mythological story. It unfolds in my outer life with chaotic, day-to-day complexity, while unfolding in my inner story with the epic simplicity of mythology. Certain universal myths and "medicine stories" reflect my inner story.

3. My outward behavior and inward yearnings are guided by countless personal and family myths I rarely articulate. Many of these ensure my survival and the survival of my loved ones. Many of these enhance my spirituality. Many of these inhibit survival and inhibit spirituality.

4. My personal myths are not written in stone, just as wounds are not permanently damaging. I can change my personal myths. I can heal my wounds.

5. Not all damaging personal myths and wounds respond to personal odyssey work. Some need twelve-step groups, men's groups, transformative therapy, even hospitalization. I need to seek help when I need it. I will make the right choice about how to pursue my self-growth.

6. There is no such thing as a perfect man. We are all wounded. We gain strength by honoring our wounds. I am wounded. I gain strength by honoring the wounds I received in my mother's house.

7. Because our culture has turned away from the magic of the inner story toward the radiant distractions of external stimulation, I must look inward toward the dark center of my being, where my sacred self lives.

Practical Techniques and Tools of Your Quest

Personal Rituals

All significant human growth needs ritual. A ritual is a personal or communal act, using symbolic objects and sacred places, that marks an important event or process. All societies and all human beings create and discover rituals. You already have many rituals in your own life, but you may not have enough *sacred* rituals.

Ritual Space

Ritual space is where we slow down to a ritual rhythm and are thus able to hear the truth, however we define that word. We create and discover ritual spaces more than we realize. A ten-minute session every morning on the toilet with the bathroom door closed may be the only peace and quiet you get all day. Even that mundane act can become a kind of ritual place for you.

In seeking personal growth, the ritual space needs to be sanctified not only in the feeling of peace and safety it gives you, but also in the content of the actions you do in it. The weekly lunch you have with your wife to discuss important family matters can be a ritual space and, if uninterrupted by phone calls and outside stresses, can settle for that hour into a ritual rhythm. It can feel very safe. The ritual time and rhythm of therapy can feel very safe and is very sacred.

In working with this book, you will want to discover a quiet place where you can do the meditative, memory, and writing work of the quest, a little bit at a time, uninterrupted by family or work concerns. If you do the work of this book in the context of a men's group or therapy, then that group or office becomes ritual space for this spiritual journey. If you do the work on your own, make sure to find a place of peace. If you can go out into the woods, someplace away from anyone else, your ritual space and ritual rhythm will be all the more connected with the original landscape, the natural world, from which your body and mind originate.

Finding a safe time is part of finding a safe place. Many rituals, like journal writing, go deepest into the self when they are done at a similar time every day. You need to find the time of day when your mind and heart are most open, most imaginative, and least distractable.

Sacred Acts and Objects

For your writing process to have significant power, and for you to be able to move as easily as possible from your busy working life to the slower rhythm of the inner story, you need to discover symbolic objects and acts around which to focus your transition from busyness to slowness. When the truth stick is passed from one man to another, as it is at the beginning of some Native American men's councils, it is done not only to hear where each man is on this particular evening, but also as a way of slowing things down, of making the transition from the nonsacred space of the busy life to the sacred space of the ritual world.

Maybe you'll always write with a certain kind of pen. Maybe you will write on a certain kind of paper. Maybe you will read a poem before you start writing. Maybe you will listen to some music, light a candle, say a few words, drum, chant. Whatever you do, find symbolic acts and objects by which to make the transition to the ritual space and rhythm. Later, as you journey, you will find and create further sacred objects.

GUIDED MEDITATION

Some of the rituals in this book involve guided imagery that requires some preparation. Whenever you get ready to do one of the guided meditations or other tasks, it's important that you've gone through some kind of personal ritual by which your ordinary mental chatter is silenced. Your body, too, must be ready to turn away for a while from its usual hypersensitivity to external stimulation, so that it can sense, for the time of the meditation ritual, its inner rhythms. Your very breathing needs to be slowed down, disciplined, and opened up in ways it has not been before. As psychologist Nathaniel Branden has put it, "Opening the breathing is generally the first step to opening the feelings. It creates a condition of stillness, a condition in which we stop running, so that our emotions have a chance to catch up with us." Take deep breaths and pace your breathing evenly as you move through the meditations.

If you already have your own style of meditation, use it. If you have never meditated before, always remember to work toward three things: relaxing the body, evening out the breath, and clearing the mind.

To make the guided meditations flow more easily, you might want to read them onto a tape, then play them back as you do the process. You might also ask someone else to read them to you. If a men's group member or other man can read them to you, his low voice can resonate with sacred masculinity. Read the meditations slowly and deliberately. Avoid hurrying. Avoid losing the ritual rhythm. Stay as relaxed as you can.

YOUR JOURNAL

Some of the tasks in your quest involve journaling. A thick journal is the best way to hold all these writings together—in one volume that can become a sacred object.

Writing is a powerful experiential tool of healing and growth. Its power to raise consciousness and heal emotional wounds cannot be underestimated. If you can do a task and then write down the experience, it's as if you are doing it twice, gaining empowerment by claiming it in words.

For your journal to become a powerful tool of self-discovery and self-transformation, you must use it as a knife: pare with it, trim with it, treat it with sacredness as it reveals to you the powers you have. You are on a vision quest, and the words you use in your journal are your knife, one of your most sacred and important tools. *Journal* and *journey* come from the same root word. The knife is the warrior's ritual tool, and the journal is the traveler's ritual tool.

There are effective and ineffective ways to use your journal, just as there are effective and ineffective ways to use your knife. A journal that stresses analysis of events rather than the feelings the events caused; a journal that records other people's notions and explanations rather than your own; a journal that worries over grammar and formal English—such a journal will be least helpful in making a journey into deep imagination and deep feeling. Write freely and focus on "I feel" and "I experienced" statements.

Preparing the notebook. Find a blank notebook, relatively thick, in which you will record answers to questions, letters, memories, interviews, stories about your feelings, responses to meditations.

Draw straight lines vertically on every page, beginning at about five inches from the left or right, depending on whether you are left or right handed. Leaving this open space will allow you to come back after writing something and continue writing in the empty space a feeling or memory that was left unfinished at the last sitting.

Free write. Always free write at first sittings. Don't be concerned with surface mechanics or missing a thought. If, a day later, you want to bring out another aspect of feeling or memory, then do so in the open space. Free writing is essential for keeping an open channel to the heart. Formal and self-critical writing is good for a college paper or business memo but not for early sittings of personal odyssey work.

Record your dreams. As you get deeper into a journaling process that involves mythology, you will find your dream life growing and changing. Write down your dreams just after you wake up. Work with them in your group, with a therapist, with your partner, on your own.

A Preliminary Task

Finding your own rhythm of writing and discipline of feeling in written language will take some time. Set aside a week or two of preparation. During this time, pick a subject and write about it for twenty minutes to a half hour four days a week. These subjects should be profound and central to your life. What follows is one suggested pattern:

Day 1. *Who am I?* (Respond to the following questions.)
1. How do I look physically to myself?
2. How do I describe my personality?
3. What are my strengths as a man?
4. What are my limitations as a man?

Day 2. *What am I like in relationships?*
1. How do I look physically to my partner, spouse, or best friend?

2. How would this person describe my personality?
3. What are my strengths in my relationships?
4. What are my limitations in my relationships?

Day 3. How do I fit in my community and society?
1. Where am I headed as a man in this society?
2. Where do I want to be headed, especially where my work is concerned?
3. What are my strengths in social situations?
4. What are my weaknesses in social situations?

Day 4. What is my relationship to the natural world around me?
1. How do I explain the mysteries of the world?
2. Do I sense a presence or presences in nature greater than myself?
3. When has this sensing happened to me?
4. If it has not, is that OK with me?

In all your journal writing, experience feelings and memories that are not dominated by analytic ideas, although they may at times be explained by them. In other words, try to avoid a mind/body split, a head/heart split, as much as possible. Stick with memories and feelings as much as possible. Get a feel for the journaling process for a while before actually starting chapter 5.

GETTING THERAPY AND FINDING
MEN'S GROUPS

As you go through the process of this book, you may find yourself experiencing difficulty and pain. Old feelings concerning your mother, father, and other members of your family will arise. The wounded child inside you will relive some of the damaging experiences. The sacred self is not discovered without substantial and painful growth.

If throughout any of this you believe interaction with a therapist would be helpful, don't hesitate to make the phone call. You honor yourself by doing so. A therapist serves as mentor and ritual elder. Therapy can be a very powerful initiation ritual.

Similarly, men's groups are initiatory, especially groups headed by qualified leaders. If deep issues arise for you, a men's group might be an even more useful place to find ritual space than a therapist's office. If you can begin a Goddess-Hero group, in which to join with other men and move through the process of this book, you will find a wonderful camaraderie in your journey. If other men in your present group have unresolved issues with their mothers and in their intimate relationships, you might suggest your present group go through the Goddess-Hero process together.

YOUR FIRST TASK: MAPPING YOUR FAMILY HISTORY

You stand at the threshold of your quest. In Part One of this book and in this chapter so far, you've been sitting at the entrance to dark wilderness, hearing medicine stories and receiving inner and outer guidance about what your quest needs to accomplish, what its tools are, how you can best experience it.

When a man enters his quest, Native Americans sometimes say he has a trail of light and darkness behind him. This trail is his personal and family history, which every man brings to his quest.

At this time, as you are preparing your journal and your ritual time and space, identify important lights and shadows on your own behind-trail. Give a brief history of your life up until the present day.

- Write where you were born and where you lived as a boy growing up.
- Write who your parents were and what their family histories were.
- Write who your siblings were and are and what directions they have gone.
- Write who your first girl friend was, your best male friend, what you did in high school.
- Write of your partners and spouse or spouses.
- Write what your first job was, and your next.
- Write how you got into your present career, what you sacrificed to get there.
- Write about your own children, if you have children.

In this part of the ritual, I'll give an instruction I will not give again: curtail your free writing whenever you feel emotional entanglements entering it. If you feel yourself starting to say, "I think it was when I was four years old that I felt my mother cared more about booze than about me . . . ," curtail this. Stop the sentence. Return to an emotionally detached life history. Give the facts, names, dates, places, not much more. Many of your entries will not be full sentences, just listings and notes.

As you move beyond the threshold, you will need an emotionally detached reference to life events to serve as a frame for the emotionally entangled picture of your inner life you'll be painting and repainting throughout the rest of the journey. Later, you'll want to refer back to where you were at a given time, to your parents' and their parents' histories, and you will need that reference to be clean of entanglements.

Grief needs boundaries. Despair knows no boundaries. This is a journey of grief, not despair. For your grief to be nurtured, you need a strong framework in which to experience it. The people, places, and things in your life history constitute a strong frame. It has held you till now and will hold you till death. The "facts" about your life represent your destiny up to this point—your destiny is the framework for everything else in your life. Write about it without entanglements, and view its milestones and history with pride.

You can do more than writing here. Get a ream of large drawing paper and draw maps of times, dates, and places on it, including your parents' and grandparents' histories, a genealogy, and much more. To complete these maps, you will have to call your relatives, even your parents, and ask many questions about your family's origins. You'll need to ask where your ancestors emigrated from. You will want to ask what the emotional relationships were between spouses in your lineage—"What were Great-Grandma and Great-Grandpa like?" "What kind of a man was Grandpa So-and-so?"—but without getting emotionally entangled. Attach photos of the people you're representing as points and names on the paper. Write small statements that capture these people and places.

Then put the maps up where you can see them and add to them. You may find yourself covering a whole wall with this kind of "family album." Assert yourself in the space of your own home. Find a wall that can be yours and use it. Your whole family will benefit from seeing your history on its walls.

You don't have to finish this whole history before continuing to chapter 5. What you need to do now is to get the minimum written down and posted on the wall. If you have kids, let them help you. Have one of your kids call Grandpa and ask what Great-Grandpa did and where he came from. This whole life history project can become a wonderful game.

When you have enough of maps to serve as a frame, move on to the next chapter.

Chapter 5: Standing on the Earth and Saying Who You Are

The "call to adventure" signifies that destiny has
summoned the hero and transferred his spiritual
center of gravity from within the pale of his society
to a zone unknown.

—JOSEPH CAMPBELL

Stand on the Earth and say who You are, then enter
the Lodge. In the Lodge see your Vision and tell
your Story. They are the Mirrors in the Lodge.
After you have looked in these Mirrors, you will
walk your Path differently.

—INSTRUCTIONS OF RED CLOUD TO THE BOYS
BEFORE A SWEAT CEREMONY

THE CALL TO ADVENTURE is a call to a deeper and fuller life.
It is a call to a threshold. Beyond that threshold is a
journey that will take the journeyer beyond who he is
now, into a world he has not yet known. Beyond the
threshold is the path of loving, wise, and powerful forces,
people, experiences. If the journeyer will but answer the
call with curiosity, passion, purpose, and perseverance—
with a clear sense of mission—his rewards will alter the
course of his life.

Especially in journeys that involve male relationships
with mother and the feminine, Native American vision
questers and heroes in the Hero's Journey traditions have

known for millennia that a man must stand on the earth and say who he is before making the journey. If he does not, he will all the more easily slip into letting others, especially women, tell him who he is. Standing on the earth and saying who we are means entering the journey from a sense of groundedness. It means coming down out of the clouds and taking stock of what we're really about. It means looking into the mirror and seeing who is standing there. And it means spending some time looking in that mirror, spending some time looking past illusions about ourselves. A cursory glance into the mirror followed by a fast run down the adventure trail will probably lead more to escape and new illusions than love, wisdom, and personal power.

It is no accident that in Native American tradition, this practice of self-exposure and self-definition that precedes a journey into the feminine is called "standing on the earth." While there are a number of earth gods and green men, the earth is mainly known as the province of the Mother, Mother Earth. A quester grounded on Mother Earth is connected with the feminine as he answers the call to search for *his* particular relationship with the feminine.

The Sioux teacher Hyemeyohsts Storm tells a story in his book, *Seven Arrows,* about a tribe of people who "were Living Scattered Out all Over the World." Each of these people individually snuck down to a river where a powerful person spoke, but these people would not admit collectively to each other that they had done this. When a little boy and girl snuck down there to hear the powerful person and returned to the people to talk about it, the people told them to shut up, to stop being silly. Frightened and shamed, the children felt like strangers among the people. And in little time they were in fact ostracized. Through the intervention of Old Man and Old Woman Coyote, and after a great deal more suffering and danger, the people, who were truly the frightened and shamed ones, learned that sneaking down to the river was OK—in fact, it was where the truth was.

Storm interprets this medicine story as a story about the way parts of ourselves, symbolized by the little boy and little girl, are always sneaking down to the river inside us, trying to find out the truth about ourselves, while other parts of ourselves shame the boy and girl. Many of us feel so shamed for going to the river that we just stop going. We answer other kinds of adventure calls, mainly calls that promise us external treasures and success, but not calls that will allow us to go to the river and discover ourselves.

In this chapter, you will be led in a process by which you stand on the earth and say who you are, especially who you are in the context of mother, femininity, and love relationships. The earth is very strong and will hold you. The mirror you look into will not crack or fade. By the end of this chapter, you will have a clearer sense of who you are at this moment, as you enter this journey. By gaining this clear sense, you will know as you journey what you *need* from the journey. It will not be one of those journeys that have no real mission or get distracted by false missions.

Task 1: Finding the Man in the Mirror

In the previous chapter, you engaged in a preliminary task in which you identified your strengths and weaknesses. Review that material and then list in your journal ten things you like about yourself and ten things you don't like about yourself. These things can involve your personality, your wounds, your life-style, your profession, your relationships, how you were parented and how you parent—don't restrict yourself to any particular part of life. Hold up the mirror of your own reflection to all aspects of your life.

When you have completed this list, go to chapter 1, pages 38 and 44, and review the two lists provided there. Write in your notebook now the statements and questions that you answered in the affirmative, or that reflected your feelings and actions having to do with your mother and your relationships with women.

As you write each one of these down in your notebook, follow it with a paragraph that explains and describes how that statement or question pertains to you and your life. You'll be surprised at the insights and connections you will make just by taking a paragraph to expound on the flaw you perceive in your life. If you need more than a paragraph, feel free to take it.

One man, Bernie, wrote this about #7 from the list of characteristics.

> 7. *Do you constantly explain yourself, especially your emotional actions and reactions, worrying over how even the smallest comment will be "heard" by others? Do you find yourself cleaning up emotional messes you've made, constantly feeling you have created a crisis with a companion, child, parent?*
>
> Yes. All the time. I used to think it was because I was self-critical, and that's a good thing, or so I thought. I'm always working on myself, I thought. But a couple years ago I began to think otherwise. It's not that anything really huge happened, at least I don't think so, but I just remember thinking, "Dammit, why am I always so afraid of hurting people, or saying the wrong thing?" Now as I've been looking

at my relationship with Mom pretty closely, I've found some answers. Mom was that way. Especially with Pop she was that way, always worried he'd get mad at her. She was always cleaning up emotional messes, worrying that she'd been misunderstood.

About #10 from the list on the mother-son bind, José wrote this:

10. *You avoid confronting your mother about issues important to your life "to keep the family together," "because she has had enough stress with Dad to last her a lifetime," or "because it won't do me any good anyway."*

I was brought up to worship Mama. Even after Papa died, and we had to come together as a family to deal with some stuff, I couldn't tell her what I really needed to tell her. I'm the oldest son. It's my job to make things right. But it's also my job to protect the family, make the money stuff work out and clear up Papa's affairs. I just kind of got paralyzed when I had to tell her she couldn't spend money the way she used to. Papa wasn't an easy man. Why shouldn't she enjoy her life now he's gone? But there was no money left. And Mama can be real mean, real mean. But I just can't stand up to her.

Task 2: Tracing Your Lover's Personal History

In mythology, and in the psychology of male archetypes, we often talk about the Lover—the part of ourselves that is capable of unconditional love and absolute delight. The many ways in which men are cut off from feeling, especially from mature love and the pleasure of delight, constitute one of the tragedies of our culture. Because most of us are shamed for feeling pain, unconditional love, and boyish delight during boyhood and especially as we enter adolescence, we express the Lover. Because most of us associate the Lover with the Feminine rather than with the Masculine, we often turn away from it in our search for manhood. This is the shadow side of separating from Mom—we get the warped idea that because we have the urge to separate from Mom, who was loving, we therefore have to separate from Love to be a man.

As we stand on the threshold of an adventure that promises new insight into loving and new experience with loving, we must understand how we are imprisoned Lovers. In mythology, the imprisoned Lover (usually cursed, turned into an ugly animal, or bound in chains) still needs love. He tries to get it in many ways:

- He relies on fantasy love to help him feel he's not in prison.
- He turns away from love altogether, concentrating on other things till they become obsessions (addictions).
- He waits for the perfect lover to take him out of prison, to kiss him and transform him from frog to prince.
- He forces his mate to change from loving partner to fantasy goddess/whore.
- He makes his Maiden-Lover into his mother (forcing her to wait on him) but punishes her for it with his distance, infidelity, and abuse.

In all of these, he is looking in his lovers' mirrors for his own Lover, because in his prison he has no mirror of his own. As you stand on the earth, at the threshold of your adventure, take time now to trace the history of your Lover.

Spend some time now doing foundational memory work. This work will help you place who you are now on the map of your past and present.

1. Recall whether and how your parents showed physical affection to each other. Use old photos as a way of spurring memories. Look at the photo of your parent or yourself at a younger age at a picnic or sitting around the house or swimming at the lake. Recall incidents and events. Did your parents hug each other, kiss each other?

2. Recall whether and how your parents showed physical affection to you. Again, turn to pictures to trigger memories.

3. Write a list of the lovers you've had up to this point in your life. Briefly note ways in which you used the lover as a substitute for your mother, or to work out things with your mother. Make sure to write down every lover's name (if you remember it—if not, note every one of them somehow).

4. Write how you changed from one lover to the next, if you did change. Concentrate on "deep patterns" of loving. Note how you matured from one lover to the next. Be honest and note what patterns stayed the same between lovers. Use Cutting Off Women's Hair, Holding My Heart in My Hand, and Drinking the Ocean Again and Again (pp. 100–111) as metaphors to help you, attaching to your writing one of these—or some other metaphor of your own that captures your deep relationship patterns and helps you work with your Lover.

> With Naomi I definitely cut off her hair. I was a beer-drinking frat boy at WSU. She was a sorority girl, pretty cute. She really cared about me. I cut her down a lot, verbally cutting off her hair. She just kept taking

it. I feel pretty guilty about it now. Where was my mom in all this? I have to think more about it. College was about the only way I really got away from Mom, even though Mom never was the clingy type. But emotionally I think I always thought of her as the only really trustworthy one. By the time Naomi came along I think I was as much cutting off Mom's hair as Naomi's. I don't know what else to think. I'm really not usually so mean. Father's the one who came down on me about Naomi. What the hell was I doing? he asked me. We were drunk together. I said I wasn't doing anything. He told me to have more respect for women. Soon after that Naomi dumped me. She really cried. I was hurting but didn't admit it. The whole thing affected me later. I've never treated another woman that way. At least I don't think so. My wife thinks I do.

This exercise will take many hours. Include as many details as you can when recording this portion of your Lover's history.

CONSTRUCTING A MORE DETAILED HISTORY
OF YOUR LOVER

I'm now going to assist you to recall an even more detailed history of your Lover, a history that will go back to your earliest days.

In this exercise you will examine four ways in which your Lover may have been negated, wounded, cursed, and imprisoned:

1. *In negative interactions* with immediate family members (parents, spouse, children) and other relatives. How did abuse from, distance from, or other dysfunctional interactions at the hands of these people shame and im-

prison your ability to feel absolute delight and unconditional love?

2. *In negative modeling* from immediate family members and relatives. How did the behaviors you observed in these people, who served as models for your own maturity, frighten, negatively influence, and imprison your own ability to feel absolute delight and unconditional love?

3. *In negative interactions* with and modeling in wider environments (neighborhood and neighbors, school and playground, media, workplace, city and town, war, culture). How did interactions and observations of behavior in these areas shame you, wound you, and force you into imprisoning your own ability to feel love?

4. *In inadequate connection* to the natural world and ecosystem. The Lover in us is fed and freed by deep interaction with the natural world. In what ways did and do others curtail your activities and interest in connecting with nature, and your undistracted self that is so often revealed in the solitude of and activities in nature?

Consider and write on each of these as it may have influenced the various periods of your boyhood, adolescence, and adulthood. If you possibly can, take the time to divide your past into separate years, from birth to the present day. Go back and recall each year and key incidents in that year. If going through your life year to year seems overwhelming, start with the periods listed below. Use a separate sheet for each period or year.

1. Birth to five years old
2. Six years old to early puberty
3. Early puberty to early adulthood (late teens)
4. Early adulthood to marriage (or first "permanent" partnership)

Focus first on these boyhood, adolescent, and young

adulthood periods. They were the most formative and the time in which patterns of intimacy were established. If you wish, move forward into the next periods, in which patterns of intimacy were manifested.

5. Marriage (major loving partnership) to the birth of child(ren)—if you have them

Whether you have children or not, divide your marriage into periods that intuitively feel right to you, using milestone events as markers, and trace the patterns of intimacy through incidents and memories of those periods.

6. Marriage to divorce (if this applies)

7. Relationships between divorces (if this applies)

Be as detailed as possible. Focus on incidents and memories. Use as much of your notebook as you need to. Perhaps a lot of material will come to you about one year or period and nothing about another. Just let come what comes.

Remember that you are looking for incidents and memories that point to moments in which your Lover was imprisoned. Keep focused on the shaming, negative modeling and imprisonment of your own ability to love and feel delight.

For each year or period, focus on how your mother nurtured and imprisoned your Lover. Be honest about the dysfunctional patterns she brought to her love of you. Be honest too about the functional patterns. Call others on the phone—friends of your parents, relatives, your siblings, your father, even your mother, if she's alive—to get clear pictures of how she mothered you. Don't be surprised to discover or recall that her patterns of relating to you changed over the years, and that sometimes you felt lost. Note when you felt abandoned by her, abused, neglected, unprotected. Focus very carefully on your adolescent relationship with her. Look to see if you felt guilty for growing up and away from her. When you have gone through the periods to your satisfaction, answer these questions honestly:

- In what ways do I fear intimacy?
- In what ways do I hold back from deep communication of feeling?
- Is there a particular kind of behavior in my partner that pushes my buttons and shuts me down?
- What were *primary* moments of my father's influence on my fear of intimacy and my Lover's imprisonment?
- In what dysfunctional ways am I loving partners the way my father loved my mother?
- In what dysfunctional ways am I loving partners the way my mother loved my father?
- How am I picking partners who will continue the dysfunction of my childhood, and continue to imprison my Lover?
- What love patterns did I learn from my mother that were positive?
- What love patterns did I learn from my father that were positive?
- What positive love patterns did I learn from one or two primary mentors?
- What must I do to free my Lover?
- What have I already done and what remains to be done?
- What can a partner do to help me free my Lover?
- How is my present partner encouraging my

imprisonment? Or, how did my most recent partner encourage my imprisonment?

When you have answered these questions completely, you'll have a great deal of material. You'll have recalled the chronology of lovers in your life. You'll have noted how you've changed between lovers. You will have traced a great deal of what your mother and father taught you about loving. You'll have a sense of the work you have left to do as a man in regard to the way you love partners and handle other intimacies.

Honor yourself at this point, before you go on to the next piece. Do something to celebrate the hard work you've just done. Show pieces of it to your partner or group or a friend or therapist.

Task 3: A Letter to Your Mother

At the end of each episode of your journey, I will ask you to write a letter to your mother. In that letter, I'll ask you to tell her what happened for you in the episode, what you've felt, what insights you've had, how the journey continues to relate to her, and where you are going. You may never send these letters. For the most part, the writing of them is more important than the sending.

Take your journal and pen to someplace outside the walls of your house, someplace where your feet can touch the earth. Perhaps it will be a place where you can sit beside a river, or the sea. Write this letter while standing (or sitting) on Mother Earth.

In this particular letter, concentrate on four elements—the four key elements of this Goddess-Hero journey: your unresolved issues with your mother, your need to separate fully from her, your relationships with partners, and your exploration of the femininity within you. Write to your mother about where you stand on these four issues as you begin your journey.

Here are pieces of letters from four men.

> When I was four you died and I haven't grieved your dying. I haven't grieved it. I know this is affecting my life, I know it deep down inside, but I've never known how to grieve it, what to do about it. When I was four you died and Aunt Ruth and Pop and everyone said we had to move on and I had to be a big boy. So I was a big boy. About a year ago, when my marriage broke up, a therapist started me on looking at your death. It was too painful for me a year ago. I left the therapist. But I have to deal with it. I have to.

> Let go of me, Mother. You have to let go. How am I going to get you to let go? You bring me food and give me advice and you invite me to live with you. I know you mean well. But you just don't get it. A 30-year-old man doesn't want you telling his girl friend every little thing about him when he was a boy. Don't you see that? I've known Mary Ann three weeks and already you're telling her how I ran around naked in that store in Denver when I was five, and how close you and I have always been, and every other family secret. Maybe if Mary Ann and me had been friends for ten years, or married, maybe then you could say stuff like that, I don't know. I'd have to think about it. Maybe not. Maybe you shouldn't ever tell all those little secrets. I hate it when you do it. Those secrets are like a weapon you use to hold on to me.

> Mom, my relationship with Felice is probably going to break up. I don't seem to last more than a year or so with anyone. For a while you got that I-told-you-

so look when I would break up. But now I think you're worried about me. You, the great "modern" woman, who divorced Dad and preached the sermon that marriage was oppressive to women and wasted on men. Now look at you. You're worried I'll never get married.

. . . I'd like to say Felice and I are kaput because she wasn't good enough for me, or I'd even like to say it's because not she or any other girl can measure up to you, Mom—isn't that what loyal boys in the movies say to their moms?—but the truth is, I really don't know what I want from a woman. I don't know what women are, what they're supposed to be, what we're supposed to get from each other. Once the fighting gets worse than the fucking, I'm basically outta there.

For me the feminine side has always been the Mom-side. Like your love of painting. I always saw that as feminine. And your love of opera, music. The feeling-side, I guess, sure, that's pretty traditional, I guess. Not that Father didn't have any feelings, but he just showed them by buying us things. It's hard for me to work with what the feminine side is unless I think what the masculine is too, at the same time. I don't know if this is a good thing or not. It's real confusing to me too because you bought me all sorts of things, so I should see that as feminine too, but I see it as masculine.

It feels artificial to say "feminine" and "masculine" because shouldn't I be one whole thing, not some duality, but I don't know. Sometimes I say things feel artificial when really what I should be saying is I might get connected to some feelings if I were to think or do that artificial thing, and we wouldn't want that!

Well, anyway, I hope something comes of thinking

about these things. I sure do need to change my life. Maybe the key to it really is in learning about masculinity and femininity. I hope so. I hope one day I'll be able to talk to you about it, Mother, without doing what I always do with you. What do I always do? I guess I could explain it as kind of talking to you about something and then feeling it's not mine anymore.

In writing all this to your mother, you'll find your pen will automatically draw boundaries around the vulnerabilities you reveal. Like some of the men above, you'll reveal yourself to Mom while at the same time saying, "Hey, I only want you to get this close to this vulnerability, no closer. I have my own work to do here." Let this happen, when it happens, and celebrate it.

When you have written what you need to write, move on to the next chapter, in which you discover the male and female mentors who hold wisdom and guidance for your journey.

Chapter 6: The Wise Ones Who Walk with Me

> For those who have not refused the call [to adventure], the first encounter of the hero-journey is with protective figure[s] who provide the adventurer with amulets against the dragon forces he is about to pass.
>
> —JOSEPH CAMPBELL

IF WE ARE LUCKY, some very important people in our lives will tell us that to be Heroes, to take the Hero's journey, we must be conscious of our own heroism. If we are lucky, our parents and our mentors will show us that without a conscious Hero's journey we will soon find ourselves living in a survival mode, in which we fulfill responsibilities, acquire goods, escape into meaningless fantasies, and live in perpetual desire for some other life but our own.

Our parents' job is one of co-creating with us a self-image that enables us to navigate our future with solid emotional boundaries, love to give and receive, a deep sense of interconnectedness with nature, and a passion for life. Our parents help us in this co-creation of self-image in the first ten to fifteen years (approximately) of our lives. The lion's share of the healthy self-image work that occupies our late teens and early twenties is supervised by mentors, transitional "parents" who become, briefly, as important as or more important than our parents.

In the not-too-distant past, these mentors were easily available all around us because *extended families* were intact. Grandparents, aunts, uncles, elder friends of the family took us under their wing and taught us a great deal. Often we relied on them to explain our own confusing nuclear family to us. Often they saw things in us our parents couldn't see, and we let them guide us in the direction of their mentorial vision.

In the distant past (and, still currently, in ethnically insular communities), these mentors came from the tribe. Larger than the extended family, but with a culture, customs, and life-style common with the family, the tribe provided ceremonial elders who helped children make the transition from boyhood and girlhood into the hero's and heroine's journey.

In our own present culture, extended family is virtually gone, elderly people are removed from young people's lives, and the culture of the tribe has been replaced by what we call "popular culture." Diversity is the standard of our adolescence and early adulthood. There are few consistent patterns or persons available to stick with us, mirror us, help us in the transition. If we haven't learned appropriate masculine/feminine boundaries, the male mode of feeling, or even essential life skills and work skills by the time we enter the time of the hero's journey (and few of us have), we find a few overworked teachers, coaches, and friends who try their best to teach us.

And because our culture has within the last few hundred years become so profoundly female-oppressive, adolescents have been getting little female mentoring from elder women, except some meager sexual mentoring. Unaided in the transition by elder women (whether teachers, Grandma, or others), and encouraged by older boys and some men to disrespect these women, adolescent males have been cut off from very important transitional parenting in feminine energy. They need it, however, and later often marry into it, relying on wives to fill the role of transitional female parent, when in fact wives have another role to fill.

In mythology, heroes never make the hero's journey without the aid of mentors. One of the primary goals of Perseus' hero journey is to develop appropriate masculine/feminine balance within himself. Two equally powerful mentors are provided him, one male and one female—Hermes and Athena. Perseus' journey centers around his confrontation with the feminine in the shape of the Medusa. To aid him in that confrontation, Hermes and Athena give him gifts—in the same way that mentors in our lives need to give us gifts. Hermes gives him a sword and Athena gives him a shield. Both are essential to his confrontation. Without the sword, he does not have his assertive energy. Without the shield, he does not have his protective energy.

Along with giving very tangible and physical gifts, Hermes and Athena give their pupil teaching and modeling in the male and female modes of feeling. In ideal male development, this teaching and modeling will be transitional. That is to say, Perseus' father should have taught him the male mode of feeling, but through the male mentor Perseus will have that teaching validated and untaught parts filled in (parts a father can't teach a son because of father-son competition or a father's absence). Perseus' mother should have taught him the female mode of feeling, but through the female mentor he will have that teaching validated and untaught parts filled in (parts a mother can't teach a son because of the sexual tension and boundaries between mother and son, or a mother's absence). In this ideal developmental pattern, the young hero enters his journey ready for life, ready for what comes at him.

Most of us, of course, are not brought up in the ideal pattern. We do not face our Medusa with a sacred sword and shield at ready. Missing one or the other, we compensate for its lack by fearing women, abusing them, letting them control us, avoiding them, avoiding long-term commitment with them, confusing sex for intimacy, and unable to forge a male role that we can enjoy and feel at peace with.

In Native American traditions, like so many indigenous, earth-based spiritual traditions, the Way of the Animal Powers provides young heroes with spirit guides and mentors, both female and male. When the hero of a Plains tribe, for instance, practices the ritual of the medicine cards—developing his Medicine Wheel and Medicine Shield—he will learn his mentor animals, and he will learn his primary male card and his primary female card. Perhaps his male card is the Hawk (far-seer) and his female the Swan (grace). He will learn the positive and the negative lessons of both, and he will feel guided by both these inward powers. In this way he goes into adulthood and moves through life constantly in touch with how he is balancing the masculine and the feminine, how they are getting out of balance, and how he can return to balance.

As you move through this chapter—as you do tasks that guide you in discovering the wise male and wise female who walk with you—you will be recalling the mentors who influenced you, and also discovering within yourself the Hermes and Athena, the Hawk and the Swan, who both guide you and help balance you.

Task 1: Who Has Walked with You?

In this task, you will be asked to recall the lives of people you've looked up to, people who have walked with you. Many of them will be characters from literature or history. While you will be asked to recall both women and men from history and literature, you may find you have trouble recalling women who have walked with you. Women are only recently being written back into history and the foreground of literature. We were all brought up reading and learning mainly about men.

So, as you go through this task, if you find it more difficult to remember women than men, take more time with the women. Look at your bookshelves, go to the library, skim a history book again. You'll need more memory triggers to do the women mentors than the men.

1. *Spiritual Mentors.* Recall the men and women from politics, literature, art, and culture who have been spiritual mentors for you, or role models. Perhaps Gandhi was a spiritual mentor. Often a writer, through his or her work, becomes a spiritual mentor, teaching us for the first time how wonderful it is to have a spiritual vision, helping us move from one stage of our development to another. D. H. Lawrence has been this kind of writer for some men, Hermann Hesse for others, Gertrude Stein for others. Sit for a while and recall these mentors whom you never met but whose work helped you see your own purpose. Concentrate here on the actual women and men.

As you write the entry, focus on your age at the time the man or woman became important to you, the medium through which you gained knowledge of this spiritual mentor, and how that mentor's teachings manifest in your life. You might want to include an important incident that epitomizes your relationship with the particular spiritual mentor.

For me Teddy Roosevelt was a spiritual mentor. The guy was a man's man. He hunted, he wasn't afraid. He was a leader. He suffered hard times and made it through. I still envy the strength he had. I'm short, kind of stocky, kind of like him. I always wanted to be more like him than what I am. In a way I think he was kind of lucky, too. He didn't seem confused about women, relationships, that kind of thing. He just lived.

2. *Mythic and Literary Mentors.* After you've recalled spiritual mentors, recall mythic figures and literary heroes who have been your models and guides. Zeus, Captain Kirk, Pip in Dickens's *Great Expectations,* Athena, Apollo, Rupert in D. H. Lawrence's *Women in Love,* King Arthur, the Good Witch in *The Wizard of Oz,* even Dorothy herself, Steppenwolf, Superman, Shane, any of these or other fictional characters may have had profound effects on your life. All function as heroes we model; reading of them, we feel empowered.

If you have done archetypal work before, you may have identified mythic figures like Zeus or Iron John as archetypes in your own psyche. For most people, heroes from Greek mythology, Grimm's fairy tales, literature, drama, cartoon books, all blend together in a landscape of imaginary heroes. These figures were mentors to us as kids (and can still be, in more sophisticated mediums).

Among these mythic and literary mentors were some unhealthy heroes, fantasy heroes whom we've confused with mythic heroes. A fantasy hero often grows out of meretricious formulas for entertainment, whereas a hero of myth and a mythic hero in a literary medium grow out of a cultural and personal quest for meaning. In our popular culture, a figure like John Wayne was a very limited male model. He taught many of us an unhealthy mode of relating to women, the environment, and other men. We confused his fantasy maleness for mythic masculinity. As you recall your mythic and literary heroes, be honest about which ones were mere fantasy, yet powerfully influential in your life.

Once again, focus on your age at the time the hero became important to you. You might want to include an important incident that epitomizes your relationship with the particular hero, especially an incident where you felt that hero guiding you to a specific kind of action.

> My mother once read a book written a hundred years ago called *The Awakening*. She and I shared a love of reading. I think it was when I was in college, or just after, she sent the book to me. My mother was always a pretty passive person, and this book was about a woman who really finds herself. I've never forgotten it. I don't remember the name of the character right now, but I remember her. I remember wanting in some ways to find a woman like her, a woman who wasn't under my dad's thumb like Mother was.

3. *Living Mentors and Teachers*. Take some time now to recall in your notebook men and women who have been your living mentors and teachers. Recall these men and women who, alive and active in your immediate world during a certain time in your life, influenced your life significantly. Recall even those mentors with whom you have made nasty, painful breaks. Recall grandparents, aunts, uncles, neighbors, teachers, coaches.

Write a small piece in your journal on each of these men and women. Note the person's relationship to you and the time during your life that you related with that person. Note what life skills you learned from that person. Then note which of the mentor's teachings still manifest in your adult life.

Put a star beside the names of each person with whom you had a relationship of intimate trust. For each starred name, recall not only what *skills* you learned but also what *modes of feeling* you learned and modeled. Especially with starred names, recall an incident that epitomizes your experience of learning with this mentor. If one male mentor and one female mentor feel most important to you, don't enter them here. Wait until the next section.

As you recall your male mentors, you may discover that neither they nor your father taught you a healthy and rich male mode of feeling. You have thus become a man disengaged from his male identity who has had to learn, in fragments from spiritual mentors and mythic/literary heroes, what a man should be. The inner mentors you meet later in this episode will be the embodiment of the self-teaching you've done, and they will take you further.

An unstarred entry might look like this:

> Aunt May. She was my father's sister. She lived a few blocks from our house. Her husband had died before I was born. She liked having my sister and me over to her house. She was very physical, a handywoman and gardener. I guess I'd say she was very balanced, feminine and masculine wise. She could help my sister with knitting, which my sister was really into. And she loved to hear me explain car engines to her, whenever my father and I tried to fix her old Chevy. She was a model for me, in terms of balance, in a way I hadn't realized until now.

A starred entry might be a little longer and look like this:

Mr. Ganapoulos. He was my chemistry teacher and football coach. What was amazing about him was how he could teach and coach and raise his kids—one of them was in my class—and never use his left hand. He had been born with some kind of palsy in it, or crippling. I don't really remember what it was, exactly, in medical terms, but I remember it just sort of hung from his shoulder, like a soft, fake paper arm. He coached our football team with that arm! An amazing guy.

I remember once when he took us on a chemistry field trip. His right arm was huge, muscular. He could move more logs and branches with that arm than we could with our two arms. And he had a lot of energy. He was a real example to me. We kids wanted to stop walking and take a break and he kept pushing us to go further, see more. He was really into outdoor life. He was a bird watcher. He would tell us the names of the birds and he could imitate bird sounds.

I learned about passion from Mr. Ganapoulos. He had a passion for life. Some of it came because he was crippled. I'm sure of that. Just like sometimes I feel most passionate when I'm connecting to my wounds, my pain, my hurt. It makes me really want to live, to enjoy life. That might be strange, because I know some people just get depressed when they connect with their pain. I do too, of course. But sometimes I remember Mr. Ganapoulos and I wake up.

YOUR MOST SIGNIFICANT FEMALE MENTOR

After you have recalled your spiritual mentors, mythic and literary mentors, and living mentors, recall the woman who, besides your mother, has had the most profound effect on your life.

Perhaps you can say of this woman, "I learned a lot

from her about women and Woman, and about healthy behavior. In some ways she taught me more than Mom, because Mom was so busy with six kids" (or so passive, dysfunctional, etc.). Or, without any comparison to your mother, you might be able to say, "I learned an incredible amount from her about what women needed and how to be good to them. And I discovered through her parts of myself that would otherwise have stayed hidden or repressed."

Focus on your age at the time she became important to you. Recall the woman's relationship to you in some depth. Remember what life skills you learned from that woman, as well as what you learned about modes of feeling. What did she teach you about how to love yourself and others? What, especially, did she teach you about how to love a mate? How has her teaching and modeling manifested in your life?

Here is a recollection of a man's most significant female mentor:

> I first met her in college, Kathleen Barnes. She taught Drama. I think what she taught me about was how we all wear masks and walk through life in postures and personae. She wanted me to be who I was, not some posture. I tried to get her to tell me what "being myself" meant. I remember she told me a story about when she was my age.
>
> She said there was this teacher, one of her drama teachers. This teacher was an older woman who liked to mimic famous actors, especially male actors. One day Kathleen asked this teacher why she didn't mimic female actors. The teacher said, "Because they're too much like me. I don't like to make fun of myself, I'd rather make fun of others, especially those pompous men."

Kathleen said she really enjoyed this teacher but when she heard that, something clicked in her. She realized she didn't want to be like this teacher. She wanted to be comfortable enough with herself that she could laugh at herself. She said she noticed that in everyone she respected, one day she always saw a big flaw in that person, and when she saw the flaw in that person, she knew she was getting ready to find another teacher, and she also knew she had a kind of window into who she herself was and wanted to be. Because when she saw the flaw in that person it meant it was probably a flaw in herself, and she didn't want to be that flaw anymore.

You don't realize all this till later, she told me. It wasn't till a year or so later that Kathleen realized she was like this teacher, and needed to laugh at herself more, and needed not to hate men so much. She said this had happened for her with other teachers and friends, and through watching them she had seen that she was too rigid with herself, and that she was too picky about people, and that she worked too hard.

From Kathleen I guess I learned her way of seeing who I was. I watch others and learn a lot about myself. It doesn't always work for me, and I still know I don't know who "myself" is, but I have learned an incredible amount.

YOUR MOST SIGNIFICANT MALE MENTOR

After you have recalled a most significant female mentor, go on to identify and recall your most significant male mentor—the man besides your father who has had the most profound effect on your life.

Perhaps you can say of this man, "I learned at least as much from him about how a good man lives, acts, feels, loves, and behaves as I did from my father." Or, without any comparison to your father, you might be able to say, "I learned an incredible amount from him about how to be a good man, how to live, even how to love."

When I think about a mentor I think about my minister, who was also the counselor I went to see when my marriage was breaking up. I didn't want to go to counseling at first, but I went. I guess I felt like it was OK to go once. I'd keep it a secret at any rate, see what happened.

This guy's name was Cooper. He was a black guy. Which I guess threw me off at first. I never really thought of black guys as counselors. I worked with a lot of blacks in my industrial work, but that was about it.

Anyway, his name was Cooper and he had a manner about him. He was steady. He looked right at you, but without making me feel too awkward. He asked me what was going on, what was grating at me. I talked to him. I guess I talked to him more than I talked to any other man in my life, if you count all the time I spent with him. Being with him made me start to feel kind of bad about the way I'd been raised. My dad drank a lot. My mom spent all the money Dad brought in. There were three kids and we all hid a lot because of the fighting.

I guess what I got from Cooper was some kind of hold on life. I was pretty messed up after the separation. I didn't know how messed up until I spent time with Cooper. I never knew I could cry so much or that it could feel so good. Cooper brought things out of me. I hated some of what I saw. I was scared of it. But he helped me. He was pretty gentle but he was pretty hard too.

After you've recalled your most significant male and female mentors, wait a day or two before going on to the next task. Use this time to read over what you've recalled about all your mentors. Form in your mind a composite picture of all the positive attributes of the mentors you've had.

TASK 2: MEETING THE WISE ONES WITHIN

There is within you a male mentor who fits all your personal mythologies of what a wise man ought to be, to whom you can promise cooperation, and whose promises of masculine blessing and support you can absolutely believe. It is this inner mentor—your own inner Hermes— who has formed in you as a composite of all the positive male influences you experienced. He waits in your active imagination to be discovered.

There is also within you a female mentor who in the same way fits all your personal mythologies of what a wise woman ought to be, to whom you can promise cooperation, and whose promises of feminine blessing and support you can absolutely believe. It is that old woman within you that you seek as you seek your own Athena now.

The two wise ones you discover are already in you, already wanting to help you find the balance between feminine and masculine that you need in order to be the man you want to be. As you participate in this guided meditation, they will come from whatever spiritual tradition feels closest to your soul. You may think they should come from the religion of your upbringing, but their attire and faces may actually come from some other spiritual tradition, surprising you.

One of your wise ones may be a Buddhist monk, or a female Chrsitian preacher, or an old Sioux warrior, or a biblical figure, female or male, dreamed up by your imagination. Let your wise ones be who they are—even if they are animal spirits.

Enter now the spirit of meditation. Find a comfortable position. Quiet your breathing. Enter your personal ritual of relaxation. Take three deep breaths, quieting your inner chatter. Concentrate in your third breath on only your own breathing.

When you are relaxed and ready, see yourself standing before a wall-sized mirror. You stand there as a man who is preparing for a long journey. You stand in vulnerability and need; you want instruction and protection. Talk to the mirror a moment, talk about the journey you are on and what you want from it.

(Pause)

Now ask in a strong voice, "Who has walked with me? My journey did not just begin today. I have been on a journey for some time. Who has walked with me?"

Let your spiritual mentors, your mythic heroes, your living mentors all appear behind you. Let them emerge gradually, as if from the air. Let each of them put a hand somewhere on your back, shoulders, head, as they stand behind you and look into the mirror with you. Maybe there will be a huge crowd around you. Maybe Jesus will be in that crowd, and also the old woman from down the street whose name you've long forgotten. Let them all gather and touch you. Enjoy their attention for a moment. Talk to them if you wish. Thank them for their gifts over the years. Tell them the things you learned from them, and learned since you knew them. Do not try to talk to all of them. Pick out one or two.

(Pause)

Now see your most significant female mentor push through the crowd. See her put her hand on your left shoulder. Feel it imprinting there. And see your most

*significant male mentor push through the crowd. See him
put his hand on your right shoulder. Feel it imprinting
there. Let the other mentors step back a little, these two
mentors touching you for a moment. Say anything you
need to say. Thank them if you wish. And tell them things
you learned from them, and learned since you knew them.*

(Pause)

*Then, standing at the mirror, close your eyes. As you
close your eyes, feel your male and female mentors take
their hands off you. They are releasing you. They are
releasing you and allowing you to float to another place,
where you will find your inner mentors.*

*Feel yourself traveling through air. Your eyes still closed,
feel your feet touch the earth and push gently through it.
Feel your whole body push down into the earth. Your body
is floating down through the earth! What does that feel
like? Let yourself be pulled downward through the soil
toward your inner wilderness, which rests down below the
surface of the earth.*

*Feel yourself drop into open space. Open your eyes. No,
you have not gone through the earth and come out the
other side. You have dropped down into a world within the
world. It is a land of magic in here. You are standing in a
forest. Look around you for a moment. Look at the huge
trees and vines. Cries of animals are all around you. Your
call, "Who has walked with me?" still rings in your ears.
Open your mouth in this inner wilderness. Call out,
"Who walks with me?"*

*Walk a few steps toward shadows and light that ema-
nate from behind a mass of trees and vines. Cut through
the vines. The work is hard, and it is difficult for you to
breathe. Feel your perspiration and deep breaths. Your face
and arms are scratched. Your arms and wrists are tired.
Feel the exhaustion that this inward effort causes.*

Push through the mass of vines and see a tiny open

meadow, surrounded by small trees. In the center of the tiny space is a huge carved stone, jutting upward. State-ments about you are carved on it. They are statements that describe how you feel as a man at this point in your life. Some of the statements are statements you want never to change. Some are statements that make you sad, for they reveal your inhibitions, your open wounds.

See some of these statements now. Read them to yourself. Walk up to the monument. Touch the carved statements. Run your fingers on them. As your fingers touch the tiny rivers in the stone, see images of boyhood, images that the statements remind you of. Some images make you happy. Some make you sad. Don't judge the sadness. Celebrate your stamina for having survived your boyhood. Run your fingers along another statement, and then another, until you have run your fingers on them all.

(Pause)

Your sweat is passing, the air is cooling the moisture on your skin. Walk now to the other side of the monument. See there a photograph of your father and mother at the time you were born. You now look a little like them, and they look a little like you. It is only a photograph you see. It does not talk to you.

(Pause)

Turn your back to your parents. Before your eyes is the huge forest around you, and the light grows dimmer now as you leave the meadow. Before your eyes is a darkening place in the forest. Walk slowly toward it. What will you find?

Before you are two huge trees. Their branches form a beautiful archway. Walk toward the archway. Walk under it. Walk forward along the path into a small meadow, a meadow just like the one your monument was in. There are two figures waiting in the meadow for you. Do you see them there? Look at them in the center of the meadow.

They are a piece of yourself. Go closer to them. This woman
and this man, this female animal and male animal, this
goddess and god, come to meet you from the deepest region
of yourself. Note how they are dressed, who they look like, if
anyone, what epoch each of them seems to hail from, how
old they are, what animal.

Come up in front of them and search the eyes of each.
You are meeting the eyes of feminine and masculine mentors you can trust absolutely. Let your vision enter your
crone's and your magician's eyes. See their eyes look deep
into yours. For a moment be in total connection with both
sets of eyes, both souls.

Hear your magician's voice, old and loving, wise and
strong. "I walk with you," he says. "You are the man I
have been waiting for."

Hear your crone's voice, old and loving, wise and strong.
"I walk with you," she says. "You are the man I have been
waiting for."

Celebrate this moment. Feel how absolutely these wise
ones believe in your worthiness. Feel their affection for you.
You are worthy of this affection.

Hear your crone ask you, "What do you most fear as
you journey toward balance?"

Answer her with honesty. If she or your magician have
responses to your answer, hear those responses.

(Pause)

Continue your conversation with these wise ones in
whatever way you need to continue it. Let your magician
say to you what you need a caring elder male to tell you at
this moment in your life. Let your crone say to you what
you need a caring elder female to tell you at this moment
in your life. Let these wise ones give you advice and
emotional sustenance as you seek to become the hero you
wish to be. Let them tell you especially what you need to
know about yourself—your strengths and your weaknesses,

as you move forward to face the feminine energy, the
Medusa, that most frightens you.

Each of us men has a Medusa locked deep inside us, a
mask of the feminine that we fear will turn us to stone.
That mask is our mother's face, or a former lover's, or a
feminine illusion we carry around with us, or all of these.
We must confront it if we are to find the relationships we
want. We must confront our deepest fear of the feminine.
Let your crone and magician talk to you about your life,
and tell you what you must do to confront your Medusa.
(Pause)

When you have heard and said what you need, ask your
crone and your magician for the gifts you need to continue
on your journey. Say to them, "What shield will you give
me, Crone? What sword will you give me, Magician?" Do
not be afraid to be bold. You are a hero. You have a right
to your mentors' gifts. As Hermes gave to Perseus a sword
with which to cut off Medusa's head, so too will your
magician give you a sword. Let him explain to you what
inner strength of your own that sword signifies. Let him
show you a strength you have, that you perhaps do not
honor enough, with which you can challenge the shadow
powers of the feminine in your life.
(Pause)

After he has explained it to you, reach for the sword he
holds out to you. Hold it in your hand. Feel its power.

As Athena gave to Perseus a shield-mirror with which to
protect himself from Medusa's stone-cold glare, so too will
your crone give you a shield. Let her explain to you what
inner defense of your own that shield signifies. Let her
show you a defense you have, that perhaps you do not
honor enough, by which you can protect yourself from the
shadow powers of the feminine in your life.
(Pause)

After she has explained it to you, reach for the shield she holds out to you. Hold it, your fist wrapped in the leather strap, your elbow crooked, the sword pulled against your body. Feel the power of this shield.

Thank your crone and magician for the gifts they have given you. These are gifts you can notice throughout your life and relationships—strength and protection that is yours, and will always be yours.

When the time is right, hear one of your wise ones say, "Go back. We will see you again when you need us."

Take a moment to express to these wise ones how being with them has made you feel. Ask them how you can be put in immediate intuitive touch with them again when you need to be, perhaps in a day, a week, a year from now.

(Pause)

Close your eyes. Feel yourself moving on air. Feel yourself returning to your body and place. Return to ordinary reality. Take three deep breaths. Open your eyes. As you open them, cover them for a moment with your palms.

When you have returned, write what you need to write in your journal. Describe your experience as you stood with your wise ones. Describe their faces, dress. Describe the sword and shield. Describe the monument and its carvings. Describe your parents' photo and faces. What feelings arose for you? What memories?

Describe your experiences as you met and talked with your wise ones. Write what you need to write. If at this time or other times in these rituals your pen can't move fast enough, speak your experience into a tape recorder.

If this first guided meditation experience did not reveal to you either your magician or your crone, or both, do it again. Do it until you find the male and female mentors who feel right to guide you forward. You are on a vision quest. There is no competition and no judgment. You don't have to "get it" the first time. Do this meditation ritual as many times as you need to without self-criticism. Do it as many times as you want throughout your life, as it is a direct pathway to your inner wisdom. As you continue to do it, you will get new messages from the wise ones who walk with you.

TASK 3: HOLDING YOUR SWORD AND YOUR SHIELD

It is time again to write a letter to your mother. Again, you may decide not to send this letter. Just writing it will mark this point in your journey and give you the opportunity to solidly grasp *your* sword and your shield.

Begin by telling your mother the highlights of this episode of your journey. As you are writing, make sure to bring your life with her into the picture whenever you can. Be specific about when you met certain mentors and what they gave you that she did not, or which of her teachings they validated. Draw clear boundaries between your mentors, especially your female mentors, and your mother.

When you have talked about your mentors, then describe your inner mentors to her. What was your guided meditation experience like? Who did you meet? As you write, remember that you are writing her without need of her approval.

When you have finished writing these things, concentrate on two topics: (1) your sword—your strengths as a man; and (2) your shield—your boundaries as a man.

Tell your mother what your strengths and boundaries are. If you have trouble starting or completing this exploration, answer some of these guiding questions. If this letter just does not feel appropriate addressed to your mother but does feel appropriate addressed to your father, then address it to him. You may want to write one letter to your mother and one to your father, addressing to both of them issues of sword and shield.

The Sword

- What are my strengths as a man? What am I good at? What feelings and activities exude my personal power?
- In what circumstances and with whom do I feel most strong, most together?
- In what circumstances and with whom do I feel most weak, most indecisive and ashamed?
- In what ways did Mother help me feel strong and integrated?
- In what ways did Mother help me feel fragmented and weak?
- What are some examples of times she helped me find my strength?
- What are some examples of times she has taken my strength away, made me feel guilty for being strong, or didn't know how to nurture my swordplay, or taught me dangerous swordplay?
- What role did Father play in helping me gain my strengths?
- What role did Father play in keeping me from gaining my sword, and/or in teaching me swordplay that was dangerous?
- What strengths do I need to start developing in my life, especially in my close relationship(s)?

The Shield

- Where are my boundaries? Are they walls that let little love in? Are they thin gauze that let too much in?
- What does it mean to me to "hold healthy boundaries"? What does this feel like?
- What are some examples of times I've held boundaries well?
- What are some examples of times I've held them badly?
- Are there certain people with whom I'm better at holding healthy boundaries? Am I better with men? Better with women?
- Do I often worry about what others think of me? When, especially, does this occur? When I get angry? When I get sad? When I'm happy?
- What did I learn from Mother were healthy boundaries?
- What did I learn from Mother were unhealthy boundaries? What kinds of people or things would dissolve her boundaries?
- What did I learn from Father were healthy boundaries?
- What did I learn from him were unhealthy boundaries? What kinds of people or things would dissolve his boundaries?

As you write this letter, challenge yourself to look honestly at your fears, the ways your self-image is most easily sent into crisis, and the kinds of personalities who send it into crisis. Also look honestly at, and celebrate, your strengths, what you do well. Finally, view the positive direction in which you are going as you become conscious of and activate the hero's journey your life is taking—with mythological support but in your own unique way.

My boundaries. What should I say about them? I'm not sure I know what appropriate boundaries are. This is the biggest question for me, still, Mom. Even after all these years. When you used to be so good to me, making me feel better, I really needed that. And I really really thank you for it. But I guess I still expect it somehow. Before I'll feel good I think I need other people to feel good too. I feel responsible for their feeling good. I feel like it's my job to make them feel good. Part of my job with you was to do this. I know it was. It's so hard to figure out, but when I was doing this exercise where I was remembering mentors and heroes I remembered Mrs. Kauffman. Remember her? She was married to Mr. Kauffman who managed the IGA store I worked at the summer of my senior year in high school. I got to know her pretty well, you could say. Let's just leave it at that. I got to know her and she taught me a lot.

The point is, when I think back I remember she was one of the only women I've ever known who just let me be happy. She didn't seem to need me to make her happy before I could be happy. It was like her life said to me, "You're young, be happy, we'll sleep together a few times and have some great times and I'll teach you a thing or two and you teach me a thing or two and that's enough." But the thing is, my relationship with her wasn't permanent. Right? That's where the problem is. When I get in a long-term relationship. That's when I feel like I'm responsible for the other person's happiness.

What's so confusing to me is sometimes Anne [his wife of 14 years] accuses me of being selfish and "narcissistic," that's what she calls it. Sometimes I can see what she means. I'm pretty tired, I'm pretty dissatisfied a lot of the time. I kind of go into myself. But at the same time I wish I could tell her that I don't usually feel that kind of self-centeredness she accuses me of. Usually I feel like I've got to do everything I can to make her happy. It's real confusing.

When I was growing up with you, Mom, I'll tell you I really felt like I had to make sure you were happy. You always seemed so . . . well, not unhappy, but just not satisfied. I know Dad was pretty self-centered. That's probably where I get my self-centered streak. I know you suffered in your relationship with him. You always said your marriage was fine but Jim and I must have known as kids that it wasn't. And what's so hard for me, what I still have to explore as I make my journey, is to try and remember how you got us pulled into your problems. My memories of you are of all your love of us, but then I have these flashes of you playing us against Dad, and telling us he was inadequate. And I remember that he was in so many ways. And I remember that your standards were high too, real high. And I'm confused. I'm wanting to stop making others happy and I'm wanting to stop hiding in my own distance. I want to get out of the patterns you all were in. I want to find something like I had with Mrs. Kauffman but on a permanent basis, something where I'm a person and she's a person and we come together to love each other, not to save each other.

When you have completed your letter to your mother, take a day or two to journal anything else that comes up for you, and then go on to the next episode.

Chapter 7: Stealing The Gray Woman's Eye

Soon after Stone Boy left his mother, he came to
an old woman in a tepee. The old woman invited
him in for food and rest. After they ate, the old
woman asked him to walk on her back, for it
ached. He did this, but as he did it he felt a knife
jutting from her buckskin. This was the old
woman, he realized, who had trapped and killed his
uncles. She would do it to him too. He jumped up
high and came down hard on the old woman's
back, killing her. In the five bundles in her tepee he
later found his dead uncles. It became his job to
revive them.

—FROM *The Stone Boy*

As PERSEUS MOVES TO confront the Medusa and initiate the
archetypes he must initiate if he is to become a man, rule
a kingdom (his own psyche), and live a safe and mutually
nurturing life with the feminine, he is told by his mentors,
Athena and Hermes, that he cannot accomplish his goal
without accepting certain gifts from the Maidens; he cannot find the Maidens unless he goes to the Gray Women
and gets directions from them; and he cannot exhort
directions from them unless he steals their eye (they only
have one, which they pass between them) and frightens
them, thus, into relinquishing the proper directions, after

which he will return their eye. And so, Perseus' first major test is his encounter with the Gray Women.

In mythology, a first test of young man's Warrior is often an encounter with an old woman or a group of old women so withered they look not like inhabitants of the earth. Maybe the old woman is a "bad" witch as in the story of Hansel and Gretel, a hag as in The Stone Boy, or a group of haglike figures—some of whom, as in the witches of *Macbeth* or the Gray Women of the Perseus story, probably represent the three Fates themselves.

By challenging the Gray Woman, the young initiate tests his ability to challenge *passive fate* and engage *active fate*. He takes his first major step in the journey of becoming a Hero—he chooses sacred action rather than remaining a passive victim of destiny. While every Hero has a "fate," every initiated Hero also knows that his spiritual growth within that fate depends very much on how he challenges it, endures it, and grows within it. In challenging that fate, especially as he is well advised by mentors and Magicians, he learns how to distinguish between sacred thefts and shadow thefts. He learns where his Warriors are to stand and whom they are to fight. Thus, sometimes the Warrior's work begins with killing the old hag, as in the tale of The Stone Boy; or sometimes in taking something of value from her, in Perseus' case her eye, her vision.

Every child, without even realizing it, learns warrior skills as a boy. But these do not make him an initiated warrior. It is precisely because he learns the skills but is not initiated in a balance of spiritual/physical/psychological warrior energy that he becomes a shadow warrior, misusing his skills or turning away from them. If, however, he is initiated, in the same way Perseus is in receiving his sword and shield, he becomes a warrior, and immediately faces a first set of warrior tasks. In mother-son archetypes, in the Goddess-Hero journey, this first set of tasks involves the hag, the witch, the Gray Woman.

What kind of warrior are you? What kind of warrior do you need to be? How do you need to steal the Gray Woman's eye? By killing the hag? By tricking her? These are what we want and need to know in this episode of your journey. As we move through the tasks of this chapter, remember that a warrior is not a single-dimensional stereotype. The Warrior archetype is more than a war-maker. In fact, the etymology of the word probably goes back before the word *war*.

TASK 1: THE SACRED THEFT
YOUR SEPARATION FROM YOUR MOTHER

The Sacred Warrior cannot complete his initiation in the mother's world—he needs to be initiated by the father and mentors. Mom's job tends to be the domestication of the Warrior, the holding in check of that energy. Mom tends to fear the son's Warrior for a number of reasons. Primary among these are her fears for her son's safety and her fear of losing him to far-away, masculine worlds that seem alien to her.

One of the Warrior's first acts of initiation is his separation from Mom—his use of the sword and shield to cut himself away from and protect himself from the part of Mom that continues to want the man to remain a boy. This is what poet Robert Bly means when he talks about the boy needing to steal the key to the wild man's cage from under his mother's pillow. The boy can't ask his mom for the key. He cannot ask his father or older brother to steal it for him. This is not the way mother-son psychology works. He must steal the key if he really wants to discover what his own healthy masculinity is and will be; it is a sacred theft found in mother-son mythology throughout the world.

In chapter 1 we explored how our culture provides very little ritualized separation from Mother. We have forgotten that the key, the Gray Woman's eye, must be stolen. We teach separation by default—by a son moving out of the house; or by disrespect—by a son verbally abusing his mother for being a mother and a woman.

Recall your separation from your mother. Begin by looking at pictures of yourself as a boy and adolescent, especially between the ages of nine and nineteen. What memories are triggered by the pictures, memories that come because you are so focused on mother separation? Journal the memories and the feelings that arise.

Continue your recollection of your separation by calling and writing siblings, boyhood friends, relatives, former teachers and mentors, your father, and, finally, your mother. In this call to your mother, ask her only about how you separated, when she felt the pain of your pulling away, what exactly you did to cause that pain. Don't pursue other issues with her at this point.

Pursue all these calls and letters with passion. There's a lot to be learned by contacting teachers, brothers, parents with a focused and sacred mission at stake. And *sacred* is a very appropriate word for the work we're doing here. If we were boys in a culture that knew how to initiate its sons in healthy ways, we would hear the word *sacred* used continually concerning our development, our needs, our desires, our lives. As we get connected with some of the healthy tribal traditions related to sacred manhood, initiation, and vision, we can raise our children to know and recognize the sacred in themselves and around them.

In your journal, list incidents and conversations in which you recall feeling or pursuing separation from your mother. Was it something you said to her, perhaps very rudely? Was it a time you ran away from home? As you recall these incidents, answer these questions generously.

- What did my father tell me a man was?
- How did he tell me to act, as a man, around my mother?
- How did my mentors advise me concerning these two questions?
- What did girls tell me a man was?
- What did I want to do with girls that helped me separate from Mom?
- How did I hurt my mother to push away from her?
- How did my mother push me away?
- How did she hang onto me?
- What did other boys tell me a man was?
- How did they encourage me to separate from Mom?

If you don't remember much of this or can't see it clearly, don't be hard on yourself. Most of us don't. Most of us just weren't initiated enough to have a lot of memory of this material. And, as in Sam's example here, many of us were initiated away from our mothers in unhealthy, confusing ways—ways that didn't speak directly, as tribal cultures tend to, to what appropriate psychological boundaries with Mom need to be.

The war is probably where I learned about being a man. I was eighteen and went to Nam. Mom was someone we were supposed to worship. But I wasn't supposed to be a momma's boy either. No way.

I was one of the tough ones. I had the body for it. I played football in high school. I was kind of a bully. The Marines tempered me some, but not much. Just redirected the energy, I guess.

Mom was kind of a passive person, liked to be bullied, liked to be taken care of. At least that's what I thought. That's what Dad did with her. Told her what to do. Made sure she had what she wanted.

Boundaries. I don't know if I know what that means. Sure I had good boundaries with Mom. I went away to war, she stayed home. I was ten thousand miles away from her. I guess I had good boundaries. I don't really know, though. She's dead now and all I feel when I remember her is kind of a guilt, like I never did right by her. I never really said goodbye to her. I never have and don't know how to.

I don't feel like I ever did enough for her. That's what it is. Being a man meant bullying her, but I didn't want to do that stuff like Dad did. But I didn't know any other way. Until she died I didn't know what to do with my feelings toward Mom. I still don't.

Task 2: Tracing Your Warrior's Personal History

The two primary archetypes your unconscious was trying to initiate into maturity as you were separating from your mother were your Warrior and your Lover. As Perseus meets the Gray Woman, he initiates (with mentorial help) his Warrior. Let us now focus on what that Warrior is in you.

The many ways in which men are cut off from feeling and the Lover, we have said, constitute one of the tragedies of our culture. It is precisely the uninitiated or badly initiated Warrior who cuts off much of this feeling and this Lover within himself. It is this Shadow Warrior in us who draws hypervigilant walls around our feelings, letting no one in; or protects us by oppressing and abusing others we live with, raise, supervise, teach, and love; or protects us not at all from the onslaught of others' feelings.

An uninitiated Warrior raises terrible havoc in personal relationships, especially in an age when women are becoming empowered, are discovering the Warrior within them, and need men who are similarly, and sacredly, empowered. We tend to see two extreme male responses to the new female empowerment of the Woman Warrior: on the one hand, we see an increase of violence against women; on the other hand, we see an increase of passivity among men and domination by women. We are in a transition period in our culture which has a lot to do with how the Warrior in both men and women is being initiated, communicated, and honored.

In this task, you will be asked to trace your Warrior's development. You will find the pattern of this task similar to your tracing of your Lover's history in chapter 5. That is no accident. As you will discover during this task, many of the same events, experiences, and feelings that affected your Lover positively or negatively also directly affected your Warrior, and at nearly the same time. That is how closely linked the Lover and Warrior are in the male psyche, especially in the psyche's development in relation to the mother.

Spend some time now doing foundational memory work. This work will help you place who you are now on the map of your past and present.

1. Recall whether and how your parents showed their Warrior archetype to each other. Use old photos as a way of spurring memories. Look at the photo of your parent or yourself at a younger age at a picnic or sitting around the house or swimming at the lake. Recall incidents and events. Did your parents fight with each other? How? All the time? Never? Did they hit each other?

2. Recall whether and how your parents used their respective Warrior archetypes in direct confrontation with you. Again, turn to pictures and films to trigger memories.

3. Recall the people who initiated (or tried to initiate) your Warrior. Recall the positives and negatives in the ways they initiated it. Memories will take you everywhere from older brothers, to parents, to teachers, to friends, to supervisors and military superiors.

4. Write a list of relationships you've had in which your *uninitiated* Warrior caused deep problems in the relationship. Briefly note ways you used your Warrior to punish others for things you really wanted to punish your mother for.

5. Write how you changed and perhaps initiated your Warrior from one relationship to the next. What did your Warrior learn to do better with each relationship?

6. Write a list of relationships you've had in which your *initiated* Warrior helped you make the relationships what you needed them to be. Briefly note ways you used your Warrior to keep you from punishing others for things you really wanted to punish your mother for.

This exercise will take many hours or even days. Include as many details as you can when recording this portion of your Warrior's history.

CONSTRUCTING A MORE DETAILED HISTORY OF YOUR WARRIOR

When you have the list of brief memories and the review of your Warrior's changes, move forward. I'm now going to assist you to recall an even more detailed history of your Warrior, a history that will go back to your earliest days.

As you are moving chronologically through your life, you might have memories of times you have forgotten, perhaps times of sexual abuse you didn't know were there. If one of these moments arises, and if it shocks and overwhelms you, don't be afraid to seek counsel or therapy.

Consider these four ways in which your Warrior may have been initiated or negated:

1. In interactions with immediate family members (parents, spouse, children) and other relatives. How did example and teaching from abuse, distance, or other dysfunctional interactions at the hands of these people initiate your Warrior into negative patterns of shame, hypervigilance, and abuse?

2. In modeling from immediate family members and relatives. How did the behaviors you observed in these people, who served as models for your own maturity, enhance, build or negatively shape your ability to assert your needs and protect your boundaries?

3. In interactions with and modeling in wider environments (neighborhood and neighbors, school and playground, media, workplace, city and town, war, culture). How did interactions and observations of behavior in these

areas initiate your Warrior? How did they teach it patterns that are more dangerous than your life needs?

4. In connection to spiritual mysteries. The Warrior in us must be initiated into a spiritual framework or it will not know how to be grounded in the sacred. It will not have a sacred "cause." In what ways did and do religions and spiritual teachings initiate your Warrior to valued behavior, and how did they force your Warrior into patterns of destructiveness against others and the environment?

Consider and write on each of these as it may have influenced the various periods of your boyhood, adolescence, and adulthood. If you possibly can, take the time to divide your past into separate years, from birth to the present day. Go back and recall each year and key incidents in that year. If going through your life year to year seems overwhelming, start with the periods listed below. Use a separate sheet for each period or year.

1. Birth to five years old
2. Six years old to early puberty
3. Early puberty to early adulthood (late teens)
4. Early adulthood to marriage (or first "permanent" partnership)

Focus first on these boyhood, adolescent, and young adulthood periods. They were the most formative and the time in which patterns of intimacy were established. If you wish, move forward into the next periods, in which patterns of self-assertion and conflict in intimacy were manifested.

5. Marriage (or major loving partnership) to the birth of children—if you have them

Whether you have children or not, divide your marriage into periods that intuitively feel right to you, using milestone events as markers, and trace the patterns of self-assertion and conflict through incidents and memories of those periods.

6. Marriage to divorce (if this applies)

7. Relationships between divorces (if this applies)

Continue life divisions, if necessary, until you come to your present age. Modify these life divisions as necessary to accommodate the periods and major events of your Warrior's journey.

Spend a lot of time with these passages in your life. At first, the list may seem too daunting to pursue, or too simplistic. If you settle into each period, however, even dividing each period by single years in your notebook, if you really search your memory, focusing on the four ways the Warrior is initiated into Sacred and Shadow, a lot of material will rise up in you, and a lot of feelings.

For each state, spend some time focusing on how your mother nurtured and hindered your Warrior. Be honest about the dysfunctional patterns she imposed on you. Be honest about the functional patterns as well. Call others on the phone—friends of your parents, relatives, your siblings, your father, even your mother, if she's alive—to get clear pictures of how she mothered you. Don't be surprised to discover or recall that her patterns of relating to you changed over the years, and sometimes you felt lost. Note when you felt abandoned by her, abused, neglected, unprotected, held back. Focus very carefully on your adolescent relationship with her. Focus on the confusion you felt as she was holding on to you and others were telling you to pull away or disrespect her. Look to see if you felt guilty for growing up and away from her.

The more deeply you go into these recollections, the

more potential healing and transformation can occur for you as you continue your journey.

OWNING DYSFUNCTIONS IN YOUR WARRIOR

When you have gone through the periods to your satisfaction, answer these questions honestly:

- In what ways do I seek to escape or deny fear rather than feeling it and moving through it?
- In what ways do I sacrifice asserting what I need in order to satisfy my perceptions of what I think others need?
- Is there a particular kind of behavior in my partner that enrages me? How does it connect with my mother's behavior?
- Is there a particular kind of behavior in my partner that frightens me into paralysis? How does it connect with my mother's behavior?
- What were the primary positive moments of my father's influence on my Warrior?
- In what dysfunctional ways is my Warrior treating partners the way my father treated my mother?
- In what dysfunctional ways is my Warrior treating partners the way my mother treated my father?
- How am I picking partners who will continue the Warrior dysfunctions of my boyhood, adolescence, and early adulthood?
- What Warrior patterns did I learn from my mother that were positive?
- What positive Warrior patterns did I learn from one or two primary mentors?
- What must I do to fully initiate my Warrior?

When you have answered these questions completely, you'll have a great deal of material. You'll have recalled the historical development of your Warrior. You'll have noted how you've changed from one kind of Warrior to another (and sometimes back again). You will have traced a great deal of what your mother and father taught you about the Warrior. You'll have a sense of the work you have left to do as a man in regard to the way you live as a Sacred Warrior.

Honor yourself at this point, before you go on to the next piece. Do something to celebrate the hard work you've just done. Show pieces of it to your partner or group or a friend or therapist.

TASK 3: THE GRAY WOMAN'S EYE: ACCEPTING YOUR MOTHER'S VISION

In the Perseus tale, as you'll remember, in order to find the world of the Maidens, Perseus must first get directions from the Gray Women. To find the nymph, Perseus must first pass through the hag. This is an interesting archetypal pattern in mythology about which a great deal has been written over the centuries.

In regard to the mother-son journey, is there a connection? There certainly is. A young Hero, initiating his Warrior as well as other archetypes, and initiating them in first stages in preparation for the central initiatory conflict of his journey—his confrontation with the monster, Minotaur, or, in Perseus' case, the Medusa—will most certainly have an encounter with the fantasy and nymphlike feminine. But if he is not given directions toward it, will he perhaps find nymphs whose gifts are not the right ones for him? Yes. And will he perhaps not find the nymphs at all? Yes.

The integration of the old and the young, in the context of a man's encounter with the feminine, is essential for the hero's journey and for the initiate's quest for his vision. Not all our vision of what femininity is should come from the nymph. Some must come from the hag.

In the context of the mother-son relationship, this is about (1) our vision of our mother—whom we see sometimes in deep confusion, during our boyhood, as both nymph and hag; and (2) our acceptance of pieces of her vision of the world and cosmos that give us directions for our own healthy future life.

In this task, you will be led to explore your mother's eye, her "vision." Whether you realized it or not as you were growing up, you "stole" a lot of your mother's vision during your boyhood and act on the basis of that vision now. Because you were not well initiated, you probably were not led, during your adolescence, to consciously explore her vision and what parts of it you accepted (and what parts you rejected). Also, because you were not led through ritualized separation and initiation, you were probably not led through experiences that helped you resolve your hag/nymph confusion into a clear adult vision of your mother. The journey you are on works to resolve this confusion, so in this task let us concentrate on the issue of what is in your mother's "eye."

In your journal, set aside space to explore what values and vision you received through your mother. Some values you will notice to be unhealthy and repressive. Don Juan, in Byron's poem, had a mother who so completely imposed her moral values and vision on her son that later he fled her and went in the exact opposition direction, into an out-of-control period of debauchery. Perhaps you will notice that your mother's eye sent you in that direction. Whatever you notice, be prepared at the end of this task to write a long letter to your mother in which you detail for her the directions she sent you in.

Answer these questions in detail, recalling incidents, places, conversations.

- What moral values did my mother teach me?
- Did they come from a source that ruled her, or was she the most powerful source of the moral structure? (I.e., was there a religion that ruled her values, or did my father rule her values, or did she seem to be the queen of her values?)
- What forms of encouragement/punishment did she use to teach/force me to accept her moral values?
- How did she respond when I began to develop moral values of my own?
- Were she and my father in conflict over the teaching of moral values to their children? Which values especially created conflict between them?
- What did my mother teach me young women needed and wanted from a man?
- What values did my mother teach me that were different for men and women?
- Did my mother teach me that the values appropriate for men were superior to those appropriate for women, or vice versa?
- Did my mother value either sex more than the other?
- Did my mother absolve boys and men of cer-

tain things, sins, and crimes about which she was harder on girls?

- What worldview did my mother teach me?
- Did her vision of the world come from a source that ruled her, or was she the most powerful source of her vision?
- In what ways did she cajole or force me to accept her vision of the world, the way things should go in the world, the way it should be ordered?
- How did she respond when I began to develop a worldview of my own?
- Were she and Father in conflict over their worldviews? Which pieces of their visions created the most conflict between them?
- Did my mother teach me that the world should look significantly different to a man's eyes than to a woman's?
- Was my mother able to actualize in her world all or most of the potential her worldview called on her as a woman to actualize?
- If not, how did she bring her failures into my relationship with her?
- If so, how did she bring her success into my relationship with her?
- Do I like the world my mother saw?

After you have answered these questions, turn to a different page in your notebook and write down every proverb or saying of your mother's that you can remember. Call your siblings, father, boyhood friends, relatives, even your mother to recall her "little teachings." Especially note those pieces of her values and vision that affected you as a boy. Some of these you may now teach to your own children.

Be especially conscious of what she taught you a man and woman should do and be like together. What did she teach you to do when you became intimate with a mate? Note carefully how what she taught you worked in concert or conflicted with what your father was teaching you about women. Perhaps what she was teaching you was best for you but got overwhelmed, especially in your adolescence, by what your father or other older boys were teaching you. Perhaps you need to recall the jewels in what she taught you. Or perhaps what she was teaching you was incestuous, abusive, too passive, or otherwise dysfunctional—perhaps it overwhelmed the healthier qualities in your father's vision—and because you and she never separated very well, you still live a lot of her dysfunctional vision, neglecting healthy visions of your father or others. Explore these key themes in your writing now. Lay the foundation now for these pieces of your vision quest, pieces that will get explored in even more depth as we move forward.

When you have written what comes to you about the directions your mother gave you, her values and her vision, take a day or two off, then write another letter to your mother. Spend time writing about your Warrior, how it developed, how it is undeveloped, how she enhanced it and how she hindered it. The time you spend with your mother on the Warrior is time spent separating from her. The more feeling you put into this material, the more powerfully you will feel your sacred Warrior developing. The act of communicating with Warrior energy to your mother about the development of your Warrior is an act of initiation. It is an act of separation. Use it as such.

Spend significant time, also, on how you feel (and felt growing up) about your mother's values and her vision. Use your Warrior energy here too. Accept those values of hers you are now consciously familiar with and able to feel comfortable accepting. Specifically do not accept those values you do not wish to accept. Make a list in the letter of each, if you wish. Do the same with your mother's worldview. Which parts of it feel now like wise crone material? Which parts of it feel like hag material that you must kill?

Let feelings of anger, pride, shame, grief, joy, and pain rise and fall as you move through your Warrior's history and attach that history to your relationship with your mother. You will recall moments in your youth and adulthood when you "killed" pieces of her values and vision. If your Warrior has done his job well, you'll no longer feel unresolved emotion about those times. But especially when you feel you still must kill pieces of her values and vision, do not be surprised to feel protective of her. If you were doing the same exercise with your father, you would probably feel that he is a man and therefore capable of taking care of himself. In doing this with your mother, you might tend to feel that she is a woman, your sweet, sacred mother, and your Warrior must not be too empowered with her.

Be careful of this feeling. Your mother is stronger than you know. And your Warrior needs to move beyond its hyperprotectiveness of Mother if it is to find its own way. Because this is a letter you probably will not send your mother, let your feelings flow powerfully, unprotectively, and learn from what happens:

You were the source of my greatest blessings and my greatest fear. Your strength as a woman and commitment to your values was something I've gotten strength from, but at the same time it was the very thing that ate me up. I'll never forget how you stood up in front of about 200 people and gave that anti-Vietnam speech in Washington Square Park. You were a Woman, a Leader, a Queen. You had such strong, complete values. And they were *yours,* not Dad's or God's or someone else's. You had really matured into them. You had formed them by *living* your vision, really *living* it. I was so proud of you.

That's the part of you I miss most. It's hard to see that woman now. It's like when I see you speaking there in the park, I always get this sudden imprint of you dying, and being so skinny. When I sit at your grave now, once a year at yahrzeit, and I light the candles, I try to remember back to the park. I try not to see you all shriveled.

I'm angry with you for being so nice at the end. That's part of it. You left us. I know Dad didn't satisfy you. I understand that. But you just left us. I didn't hardly see you for most of my teenage years and I spent all those years yearning for you, trying to understand why I had driven you away. In group about a month ago we were doing this stuff around separation from mothers and I said how I was forced to separate, because you left, and all the men just looked at me like I was crazy. "It's just the opposite," one of the men said, "don't you see, Chuck, you weren't separated at all. You spent your whole adolescence connected to her with an umbilical cord of guilt and shame and longing for her."

He was right. He was so right. That's how I spent those years. I yearned for you so much. Then you and I had a few talks and you turned apologetic. And I thought that would be enough. Then you started dying. How was I going to blame you for anything? You were a woman shriveling up with lung cancer. And then you died. All through my life I've waited for other people to abandon me or do something to prove they're not trustworthy and sure enough they always do. How convenient for me that I can always get mad at them but I can never seem to get mad at you. That's the task that's ahead of me. That's what I need.

I need to find some goddamn way to get enraged at you! Until I do, I know I'm doomed to not trust anybody else.

When you have completed your letter, take a day or two to journal anything else that comes up for you, then go on to the next episode of your journey.

Chapter 8: Accepting Gifts from the Maidens

Come with bows bent and with emptying of
  quivers
Maiden most perfect, lady of light.
                              —CHARLES SWINBURNE

Let not my love be called idolatry.
                              —WILLIAM SHAKESPEARE

WE ALL KNOW WHO they are, these maidens. They move
all around us with youthful vitality and sexual power.
They seduce us, tempt us, are seduced by us, are tempted
by us. Our relationship with them is as much about
competition and power as about companionship. The
maidens are not the kind of girls we imagine feeling
contentment with. Just the opposite—the maidens represent constant passion, and passion means constant risk and
change.

  In our beds, in our workplaces, in our schools, in our
dreams, they are the bodies/hearts/minds on whom we
project our fantasies of female beauty, female loyalty,
female sexuality, and, sometimes, female servitude. During our adolescence, we would do anything to get into bed
with them, or get them to pay attention to us. We would
lie to our brothers and friends to prove we had received
gifts from the maidens. We would lie, cheat, and steal to
get the Maiden's love. Many of us still do.

In the Goddess-Hero journey, the Hero comes to the world of the Maidens (sometimes called nymphs) *after* he has been to the world of the hags and stolen (and given back) their eye. He is accompanied by his father or, in the absence of his father (as in Perseus' case), his primary male mentor (Hermes). Having separated from his mother, learned his father's arts and mode of feeling, gotten directions from the grandmothers, and relying on his male mentor to keep him directed, he comes to the maidens, who will most challenge his boundaries, with a balance of elder female and male influence. From the maidens he gains certain gifts, gifts essential to his masculine development (youthful female attentions, sexual and otherwise, that help him feel worthy as a male lover), and gifts essential to his sense of boundaries with the feminine. The maidens are only a step in his journey of maturity. They are not the end of his journey toward the feminine, even though many of us get stuck in the Maidens' world, wanting to mate only with a woman ever-young.

There is great wisdom in the archetypal scheme. If the hero comes to the maiden before he is adequately parented, mentored, and grandparented, he will tend to want to stay with the maidens forever, and, unconsciously, he will face the loss of himself in the Maidens' world. He will still be a boy, hungry for love and attention, deeply unsure of himself. In all his doings, especially his doings with the Maidens, whom he seems to love so purely and who often seem to love him so purely, he will be willing to give up Self for attention, love, and self-image development. And, especially if he's encouraged to do so by the culture around him, he will think the world of the Maidens, where he feels secure (or even just fantasizes security), is the *end* of his romantic journey. He will come to believe that gaining the love of a beautiful princess *is* manhood. If, for whatever reasons, he has little luck sustaining the Maiden's rapt attention, he will create ongoing fantasies, often throughout the rest of his life, through which to assure himself that he can possess the maiden, be loved by her, dominate her, "have her."

If the hero has not been through a great deal of initiation before he lands on the Maidens' shores, if the hero has not "grown up" through his tasks, conflicts, separation from mother, learning from father and elders, responsibility-taking, and personal actions of conscience during his early to mid-adolescence, he will come to the time of the Maidens with a consciousness that is still unseparated from Mother, still only minutely initiated. The maidens will become for him what his mother was when he was born—beautiful, young, sensual, the feminine life-force. He will cleave to the maidens like a baby cleaving to his mother for self-image.

And while all of us use the maidens as part of our separation from Mother, our growing up—our "I'll go out with whoever I want, Mom!" "I'll have sex with her if I want, Mom!"—when a hero comes to the maidens unseparated from his mother, he will tend to use the maidens *primarily* for separation. He will not discover in the maidens the other gifts he needs to receive from them. Because he does not recognize and receive these gifts, and is unable to accomplish complete separation from Mother through the maidens, he will often remain locked in the maidens' world for decades. He is locked there in part because he cannot get out of his confusion, confusion mentors, parents, and support systems are supposed to help him with, confusions about women, the feminine, mother, girls, mates, sex, boundaries, and feelings—confusions that the time of the maidens, overseen by elder mentors, is supposed to help young men emerge from with wisdom and direction.

In mythology, a young man's arrested state of development is often represented by a hero's prolonged sleep on the maidens' shore, or in their castle, or in their servitude, or in their flower garden—a sleep from which the man may never wake, a sleep in which he may never realize he has given himself up to an idolatry of feminine physical beauty and his own sexual/social performance in the face of that beauty. Whether in a young man's jealousy and possessiveness of his young sexual partner, girl friend, or wife, or whether in romantic and sexual fantasies that rarely come to fruition, the uninitiated hero, who comes to the Maidens' shore before he is ready, will gain their love and from then on find himself feeling lost without it.

As so many of us do. Our culture has strayed very far from the archetypal paradigm, recorded in mythology, that helps boys, adolescents, and young men (1) understand what the world of the maidens exists to teach them, (2) accept and look closely at the maidens' gifts, and then (3) move on, integrating the lessons/gifts into the next stages of mature love. Our culture fantasizes and stereotypes the maiden and condemns men to worship the maiden above all other partners in love.

The popular culture of television, Madison Avenue advertising, and Hollywood are the most obvious culprits in pedestalizing the maiden. And they reflect the cult of youth we all live in. They give us the images of the maiden we ask for. Men buy into these images, and so do women. Women try to *be* those images as hard as the men try to *do* enough to earn those images' affections.

The Maidens' World and Power with the Feminine

When you were in your adolescence, you were in the Maidens' world (or hungered, above all else, to be in their world). Your hormones drove you to that hunger sexually. Your desire to experiment with love's feelings drove you to it emotionally. Your need to feel loved by females other than your mother drove you to it psychologically. All parts of your being at various times during those years felt utterly lost and utterly found in the Maidens' world. (And this applies, with a different complexity, if you were homosexual and your "maiden" was male. Gay men might refer to Robert Hopcke's *Jung, Jungians, and Homosexuality*.) In feeling extremes of despair and salvation in the Maidens' world, you were archetypally challenged to learn boundaries with that world.

The Maidens' world was the place you would *earn* affection from a woman. In your mother's world you got affection relatively unconditionally.

The Maidens' world was the place you would experiment with a way of loving in which you could be equal partner. In your mother's world, you were "son."

The Maidens' world was the place you could glimpse what your mother must have been like in her youth, and/or when she gave birth to you. In your mother's world, especially as you began separating from it, Mom had become more hag than youthful. In the stages of male development, adolescence is a second birth. At biological birth, the infant is born into boyhood. In his second birth, the boy is born into manhood. A boy/adolescent cannot help but feel that a Maiden (and/or sometimes a female mentor with whom he has sex or another intimacy) is mothering him into manhood.

The Maidens' world was the place where you would learn whether the female could be possessed. Your mother was either possessible by your manipulations or too devouring to be possessed, or both—with her, you could not discover your own authentic male power over/under/with the female. In the Maidens' world, you are forced to deal with cross-gender power issues in adult coupled situations.

This latter issue of power is archetypally essential to the growing adolescent. During our boyhoods, our mothers have incredible power over us. As we try to separate from Mother, and especially if we are underfathered and undermentored during that separation, we try to separate by gaining power over Mother. In separating from Mom, we experiment with Warrior power, often make wrong choices in its use, and often don't get enough guidance from fathers and elder men to know another course.

When we come to the maidens, we bring our confusions about "power with" and "power over" the feminine. We bring them whether we've had guided and ritualized separation or not. But especially if we haven't had good separation, we experiment with the Maidens to extremes. Many of you will remember how much you feared an adolescent girl friend having too much power over you—sometimes you left her or otherwise hurt her when she threatened your very fragile, undeveloped, and basically uninitiated sense of masculinity. Many of you also remember giving the girl friend complete power over you—serving her, doing anything she wanted, to get her to love you. These extremes are very much issues of power. Our time with the Maiden is a time when we need to learn "power with" the feminine, not only so we can live in passionate contentment with a mate, but also so we are not in constant inner battle between our masculine and feminine elements.

In tribal cultures, the importance of our learning how to get along with the feminine, and how to feel balanced within ourselves, was well known. Elders guided young men in developing power with the feminine. Elders taught sexuality, cross-gender relational skills, and basic differences between genders. Many ancestral cultures taught "power with" the feminine, mainly through agreed-upon family roles. For many reasons, including female disempowerment, economic and social systems, and our neglect of healthy adolescence, we teach our adolescent boys to seek power *over* women, not gender equality, and/or we vaguely teach them power with the feminine but leave them so destitute and alone during adolescence, so unguided and uninitiated and so unseparated from Mother, that they have no choice but to choose power over a woman or a woman's power over them.

In the tasks that follow, you will be asked to meet the Maidens, accept their gifts, and, if you are a man who even in middle age still seeks Maidens as primary lovers, you will be led in tasks that will help you separate from this addiction, and move on to more mature modes of intimacy.

Task 1. Who Were Your Maidens?

Because your archetypal relationship with the Maiden and much of your present mode of relating in your present love relationships are founded in your adolescent and young adult relationships with maidens, it's important for you to go back to that time, recall who you knew there, and look carefully at how you loved those girls and young women.

To do this, return to your Lover's history, which you did in chapter 5 (p. 144). Reread the material you wrote about the lovers/girl friends you had during your adolescence and early adulthood. Even if one or more of those lovers was an older woman, a sexual or romantic female mentor, reread what you wrote about her. Although she was an elder, she was also a maiden to your young and hungry consciousness.

After you have reread this material, write down the names of the lovers on a blank page and answer the following questions for each. In listing these questions I will use the word *girl*. Although biologically most of your lovers/girl friends were probably women, they were most likely psychologically still girls. As you got into your late teens and early adulthood, they were probably more "women" than "girls." For those later maidens, you might note what piece of maturity in them seemed to make them women. And you might note how you responded to that maturity as a boy, adolescent, or young man.

1. What did I do to earn this girl's affection? What expectations/needs of me did she seem to have? What expectations did I just project onto her?

2. What experimenting did we do, sexual or otherwise? What experiments did I lead? Which did she lead? Did I force experiments on her? Did she force experiments on me?

3. How did I let this girl mother me? What things did I let her do for me or force me to do which I would have let Mother do or force during my boyhood?

4. Did I give up my life to this girl? Did I dominate

her and force her to serve me? Did I develop a compromise with her that allowed both of us to share power?

5. How much was I consumed with needing to perform with her, sexually and otherwise?

6. What was the best part of our time together? What was the worst part?

7. During my time with her, what was my mother saying about her and my relationship with her?

8. During my time with her, what was my father saying about her and my relationship with her?

9. During my time with her, what were elders, grand-parents, mentors, or teachers saying about her and my relationship with her?

10. During my time with her, what things did I say to her about what I liked and disliked in her and in women?

After you have answered these questions, write about these ancillary issues. If you were ever impotent with one of these girls, note it and recall it. Recall your feelings. Recall fights you had with the girls. What were they about? How did you feel? Recall those things you did with girls about which you still feel a pang of shame today. Recall those things you did with girls about which you still feel very proud today.

Last of all, write down why and how you two broke up. Who caused the breakup? What did you feel? When did you finally let go of this maiden? Do you still hang onto her in any way?

Here is a piece of what one man wrote about a fifteen-year-old girl, LeAnn, with whom he fell in love when he was sixteen. This piece concerns #7.

Mama was pretty straight, pretty prudish. LeAnn dressed up pretty well—she wore lipstick, a lot of makeup. She wore tight pants. Mama was a Catholic's Catholic, if you know what I mean. She constantly railed at me about LeAnn. God was watching me, she said. The angels were watching. Mama tried to get Papa involved. "Can't you see the girl's bad for him? Do something!" That kind of thing. When I would come home from a date, Mama wouldn't talk to me. Sometimes she wouldn't talk most of the next day.

In the work I'm doing now I can see how confused and upset she was that I was leaving the nest. I couldn't really see it at the time. Neither could she, or Papa or anybody. At least no one acted like they could. All that happened is Mama got more and more upset and got me more and angry and I did more and more to spite her. LeAnn and I never slept together. I was too afraid of hell, I guess. But things were never the same between Mama and me.

Here is a piece of what one man wrote about Sally, his college sweetheart.

One of the scariest times in my life was when I was impotent with Sally. I thought all sorts of terrible things about myself. I thought I was a piece of dirt. I thought I would never be able to have sex again. Sally and I had an incredibly intense relationship but I was impotent with her. I didn't have anyone else to talk to about it. I couldn't really tell my friends, even my best friend. It was too embarrassing. The weird thing is the only person I really thought seriously about telling was my mother. I almost brought it up to her on the phone, more than once in fact. Now that I look back on it I see that as sort of weird. The main reason it's weird is because my mother probably would have been embarrassed, even mortified. She definitely wasn't the one to talk to about it. But I didn't feel I had anyone else. Or maybe I just wanted to mortify her. I don't know.

As you are recalling your maidens, telling your story and answering the questions, focus as much as possible on similarities between the maidens and your mother, or differences, or tensions between them. See the maidens as maidens, as young goddesses, but whenever your story takes you toward your mother, see the maidens in the context of your relationship with that first Goddess.

After you have finished answering the questions and writing about each maiden, go back over what you've written and look for particular details and patterns that match in all or most of your love relationships, including the one you may be in now. Put a star in the margin beside these details or patterns. Perhaps it is about your sex life, your allowing your lover to mother you, your domination of her, your wanting from your present lover or mate something you had with the maidens in your adolescence. Pay special attention to just how much your expectations in your present or most recent love relationship have grown beyond what you expected of the maidens during your adolescence. Pay attention, too, to expectations that have not. This information can be crucial to your adult love relationships.

TASK 2: ACCEPTING THE MAIDENS' GIFTS

Hermes guides Perseus to the world of the maidens. In that world, he receives and accepts three gifts, each magical: winged sandals, with which he will be able to hover over his future antagonist; a magic wallet or bag in which to put dangerous objects; and a cap that will protect him by making him invisible. The Greek hero Odysseus, on his journey back from Troy to his home in Ithaca, spends time on Calypso's island. A young and beautiful goddess, Calypso represents the Maiden archetype. On her shore he receives gifts, including trees to build a raft, lessons about who he is and what he wants out of life, and guidance on how he can navigate his confrontation with his antagonist (Poseidon, the God of the Sea). As Odysseus is preparing to leave Calypso's shore, he says:

"Gracious goddess . . . my wife is nothing compared to you for beauty, I can see that for myself. She is mortal, you are immortal and never grow old. But even so I long for the day of my homecoming. And if some god wrecks me again on the deep, I will endure it, for I have a patient mind. I have suffered many troubles and hardships in battle and tempest; this will be only one more." With that, and after one last night together, Calypso lets Odysseus go to his destiny.

The gifts maidens give to young heroes are gifts that help the heroes mature, help the heroes see how they've matured, and prepare the heroes for further trials in the journey of maturity. What gifts did girls and young women give you during your time with the Maidens?

Go back to Task 1 and reacquaint yourself with the maidens you worked with in that task. If there are some maidens from chapter 5 you didn't work with in Task 1, go back to chapter 5 and reacquaint yourself with them. If you still have pictures of these girls and young women, even in a yearbook, look through the pictures; let memories come to you of your time with these girls and young women.

In your journal, write down each name as you did

previously, this time answering these questions but leaving room for ten more questions to come later:

1. What did she teach me about sexuality and sensuality?
2. What did she let me teach her about sexuality and sensuality?
3. What did I learn from her about how to do boundaries?
4. What did she let me teach her about how to do boundaries?
5. What memorable and wonderful gifts (actual objects like rings, etc.) did she give me, and what significance did these gifts have for me in my adolescence and early adulthood?
6. What intellectual gifts did she give me and let me give her?
7. In what ways did she nudge me toward becoming more sensitive to women's needs, and to my own?
8. What wonderful lessons of hers will I never forget?
9. How did she help me to feel I was becoming a worthy young man?
10. What feelings did I have with her? When did I cry with her and/or nurture her tears of pain and joy?

Having answered these ten questions, answer these next ten questions:

1. What was I afraid to learn during my time with her about sexuality and sensuality?
2. What was I afraid to teach her about sexuality and sensuality?
3. What was I too immature to learn from my time with her about boundaries?
4. What was I too immature to teach her about boundaries?

5. What painful and hurtful gifts did she give me and/or hold back from giving me?
6. What of her intuitive and intellectual gifts did I turn away from, spurn or put down?
7. Which of her lessons about becoming more sensitive to the feminine did I spurn?
8. What wonderful lessons of hers have I forgotten, lessons I should have learned better?
9. How did she hurt and negate my feelings of worthiness as a young man?
10. What feelings did I repress with her? When did I hold back feelings and force her to hold back hers?

After you have finished answering the questions and writing about each maiden, go back over what you've written and look for particular details or patterns that have been typical of your love relationships. Put a star in the margin beside these details and patterns. In fulfilling this last part of this task, pay special attention to what things you did with and expected of the maidens that you are now doing and expecting in your present love relationship. Are these actions and expectations healthy, useful in your present relationships, and growthful? Which of your actions, actions that seemed healthy in your adolescence, actions that may even have worked then with those maidens, do not work now?

TASK 3: WORKING WITH YOUR FANTASIES

Much of our fantasy projection about the Maiden is projection having to do with physical beauty. In this task, I'll ask you to focus on a number of aspects of your fantasy life, with that particular aspect in the forefront. Our culture teaches us to be locked into love fantasies about the maiden throughout our lives. Love of the Maiden and fantasies about maidens are often worship of external beauty.

Deep inside us, we tend to hold up the Maiden, especially the beautiful and young one, as more perfect than ourselves, getting from her love our own sense of worthiness—"that that gorgeous girl (a.k.a. fantasy projection) could love me must mean I'm OK." When in midlife we return to very young women, divorcing our wife, who is becoming Medusa or hag, and marrying a new maiden, we are often in midlife shock and fear, fear of our own aging and death. Having been taught that the Maiden is the ultimate perfect feminine, we go back to her for love, for our self-image and worthiness—to convince us we're OK, we're fine, we're flourishing, we're not going to die, we still have it in us to be the great lover.

By looking at your fantasies, you will be able to see to what extent you base your self-image in how you are seen by and seen with the Maidens.

To begin this task, turn to a blank page in your notebook and answer these questions.

- Do I need young, beautiful women around me to feel whole? Do I need others, male or female, to admire my mate's physical beauty and youth?
- Am I unable to see any maiden-like beauty in my partner as she gets older and her body ages?
- Do I prefer sexual and other fantasies, involving adolescent girls and very young women, to actual relationships with women who are my peers?
- Does my eye stray a lot from my partner to beautiful girls and young women around me,

so much so that my affection is distracted from my partner, especially at times when she really needs my attention and positive mirroring?

- Am I sex addicted—do I need to be having sex constantly, often with many partners, including constant masturbation with pornographic stimulants?
- Do I fantasize about other women, generally younger ones, while at home or out with my partner or wife?
- Am I love addicted—do I need constantly to be in a relationship, usually with someone younger than me?
- Am I violent to women in my fantasies—do I yearn to bring that violence to my partner and our sex life? Have I brought it into our sex life?
- Am I afraid of solitude—do I escape that fear by a very active fantasy life or constant relationships with younger women?
- Am I unable to have an orgasm or enjoy sex without concomitant sexual fantasies during sex?

As you answer these questions, remember that while you may have sexual and other fantasies involving young, beautiful maidens, you may still be living a very functional, intimate life with your mate. An active fantasy life, which involves the maiden, is not a "sin" or a reason for alarm; in fact, it can be a healthy and wonderful part of intimacy. If, however, that fantasy life is impinging on your intimacy with your partner(s), then it is important you explore it further, in your men's group or with a therapist or other trusted friend.

If your intuitive answer to any of the questions about

maiden-fantasy was "yes," then you will most likely find a great deal of personal growth in working with a therapist or group on issues involving your relationship with your mother, your lack of separation from her, your lack of initiation, and your hunger for healthy fathering and mentoring.

TASK 4: SAYING GOODBYE TO THE MAIDEN

When Odysseus left Calypso, as when Perseus left the Maidens, he said goodbye, knew he had gotten from her what he needed, and knew that now he must move on. Throughout world mythology, heroes came to that time when they must say goodbye to the maidens, whether the hero is Gilgamesh, Indra, one of the Grimm brothers' young princes, or an African initiate. So too in your life there will have been a time when you needed to say goodbye to the maidens in your life, a time when you needed to stand on the maiden shore, like Odysseus and Perseus, pocket the gifts you had received, then sail or fly away to the next stage of intimacy and adventure in your journey.

In the guided meditation that follows, you will be invited to recreate that moment archetypally, if in fact you had it in your life, and to create it anew now, in your imagination. Use this meditation as a place to move forward from, a place to leave behind dysfunctional patterns relating to the Maiden and move forward to greater growth and maturity.

Enter now the spirit of meditation. Loosen any tight clothing. Sit or lie comfortably. Enter your personal ritual of relaxation. Take three deep breaths.

When you are relaxed and ready, see yourself standing before a wall-sized mirror. You stand there as a man your present age, a man looking back at his youth. Close your eyes at that mirror, asking aloud, "Who were my maidens?" Pause a moment then open your eyes. See the maidens from your own life beginning to encircle you.

Let the maidens of your boyhood, adolescence, and young adulthood emerge gradually, as if from the air. Let each of them put a hand somewhere on your back, chest, stomach, shoulders, head, torso, legs, thighs, groin, everywhere on your body where that particular maiden seemed to have been most focused in your youth. As the maidens encircle you, maybe there will be a huge crowd around you. Maybe there will only be a few maidens. Let them all gather and touch you, no matter how many. Enjoy their attention for a moment. Talk to them if you wish. Thank them for their gifts, for the good times you had with them. Grieve the bad times for a moment with them. Do not try to talk to all of them. Pick out one or two.

(Pause)

Now see your most significant maiden in the mirror before you. See her take her hand off your body and stand beside you. As she does this, let the other maidens disappear. Talk to this one significant maiden. Say whatever you feel the powerful urge to say to her. Hold this maiden's hand.

(Pause)

Standing at the mirror, close your eyes. As you close your eyes, feel the maiden release your hand. She is releasing you and allowing you to float to another place, where you will find your archetypal Maiden, the one who lives in you even now.

Feel yourself traveling through air. Your eyes still closed, feel your feet touch the earth and push gently through it. Feel your body push down into the earth. Your body is floating down through the earth! What does that feel like? Let yourself be pulled downward through the soil toward your inner wilderness, which rests down below the surface of the earth.

Feel yourself drop into the center of the earth. Open your eyes. You have dropped down into a world within the world. It is a land of magic in here. You are standing in a forest. Look around you for a moment. Look at the huge trees and vines. Cries of animals are all around you.

Walk a few steps toward shadows and light that emanate from behind a mass of trees and vines. Cut through the vines. The work is hard, and it is difficult for you to breathe. Feel your perspiration and deep breaths. Your face and arms are scratched. Your arms and wrists are tired. Feel the exhaustion that this inward effort causes.

Push through the mass of vines and see a small river and a small bridge. What lies on the other side of the bridge? There's something there, a figure there. It is female, and naked. Run toward that figure, watch that figure running playfully away. Chase that young woman. Run fast after her. What glimpses are you getting? What color is her hair? How long is it? What does she look like as she runs? What do her buttocks, legs, back look like? You wish you could see her face, but she's running fast.

Run further into the forest, deeper into the trees. Turn a corner and see no running girl in front of you. Where did she go? Stop, listen carefully. Look around. Where is she?

Continue down the path. Will you run or will you walk? Does it matter if you've lost her, or do you know with certainty you will find her when you need to?

See, many yards in front of you, two huge trees. Their branches form a beautiful archway. Walk toward the archway. Walk under it. Walk forward along the path into a small meadow. Now do you see her again, facing you, in

the center of the meadow? Look into the center of the
meadow until she reappears.

Walk up to her. Look at her face, breasts, her stomach,
her patch of hair at the groin, her legs and feet. Does she
look like any man or woman you know? Is she someone
altogether new to you?

Look deep into her eyes. You are meeting the eyes of the
Maiden who, in your youth, made you so nervous. See her
eyes look deep into yours. For a moment be in total connection with her eyes, her soul.

Hear and watch the Maiden say, "It's good to finally
meet you face to face." Let her reach her hand out to you.
Say whatever comes to you in response. Then hold her
hand for as long as you need to, in silence.

When you are ready, ask the Maiden two questions and
let her answer. First, ask her: "What adversity must I face
soon if I am to find the love I need?" Wait for her answer.
(Pause)

Ask her: "What gifts can you give me to help me face
that adversity?" Wait for her answer. She may actually
give you something, which she magically brings in to the
meadow. Or she may have words of meaning for you.
(Pause)

Thank the Maiden for the gifts she has given you.

Celebrate this moment. Feel this Maiden's affection for
you. You are worthy of this affection. Feel, too, that this
Maiden is a spritely, temporary presence, a runner, a
floater who will disappear soon.

Hear her ask you, "What do you most fear as you live
intimately with women?"

Answer her with honesty. If she has a response to your
answer, hear that response.
(Pause)

Continue your conversation with her in whatever way
you need to continue it. Let her say to you what you need

a caring former lover, a girl with whom you have history, to tell you at this moment in your life.

(Pause)

When you have heard and said what you need, explain to the Maiden how you still feel about her. Tell her honestly about feelings you have toward her, feelings that cling to her and make trouble in your present partnership. Tell her honestly, too, about ways in which you see her in your present partner and that seeing feels wonderful.

(Pause)

When the time is right, hear and watch the maiden say, "Go away now. It is time for you to leave me for good."

What do you feel as she says it? Open your feelings to her. Let her help you.

And hear her say again, "It is time for you to leave me for good."

Let her take your hand. Hear her say, "Take us to an ocean shore. You have the magic to do it." Even if you *think* she *should* be the one to take you there, even if you feel she *is* the one with the magic, celebrate for a moment your own magical abilities. Feel how light she is, how capable you are of lifting the two of you through the air. Close your eyes if it helps. Do nothing else until you are able to feel the two of you floating.

(Pause)

Celebrate the power you have. Celebrate the magic. Float toward an ocean shore and land the two of you on it. See a ship waiting for you there. Feel the sand under your feet. Turn to the Maiden. Talk to her if you need to. Tell her last thoughts, ask her last questions. Feel her gifts still in you or clasped in your hands or in your pockets. Let your nervousness flow. You are about to leave the Maiden behind forever. You have only a few gifts and a few memories.

(Pause)
When you are ready, embrace her.
Say goodbye.
(Pause)
Watch the Maiden run away, up the beach, back into the woods. Do not chase her. Grieve her loss. Make whatever resolutions you need to make to help yourself, in the future, leave her behind, leave the shore, move forward, across the ocean, into your journey.
(Pause)
Close your eyes. Feel yourself returning to your body and place. Return to ordinary reality. Take three deep breaths. Open your eyes. As you open them, cover them for a moment with your palms.

When you have returned, write what you need to write in your journal. Describe your experience as you stood with the Maiden. Describe her. Describe the gifts. What feelings arose for you? What memories?

If this guided meditation experience did not reveal a Maiden, do it again. Do it until you find the Maiden who feels right to you. You are on a vision quest. There is no competition and no judgment. You don't have to "get it" the first time. Do this meditation ritual as many times as you need to without self-criticism.

TASK 5: A LETTER TO YOUR MOTHER

As you finish this episode of your journey, mark your time with the Maidens in a letter to your mother. In it, write what you need to write, focusing on the time in your adolescence and young adulthood when you experimented with the maidens. Focus, too, on how the maidens and your mother were interwoven in your life during those years. Tell your mother what it was like to be trying to separate from her by loving girls and women. Tell your mother what you were going through during this difficult time in your life.

You probably will not send this letter, but that does not matter. You write it to mark *your* journey. As you write it, you might focus on one primary maiden, your relationship with her, and what it had to do with your mother. This is what Ben did.

It was Marie who was most important to me back then. She gave me a lot of gifts. I gave her a lot. We hurt each other a lot, a hell of a lot. As I went through these exercises and meditations I realized how much of that hurting was about hurting you, Mom. I realize how much of my hurting Ginny (first wife, married at 21, divorced at 24) was about hurting you too, controlling you. I think Ginny was a maiden, not a life partner, not a queen. I shouldn't have married her.

Do you remember how I hated adolescence, Mom? I wonder if you remember? I wonder if you ever really knew. I hated it. I never felt like girls would like me, even though you always told me I was good-looking and all that stuff. You were trying to be nice, right? But it was just another example of how controlling you were, so domineering. I can't even begin to describe how it felt to have you always waiting up for me, always worrying over me, always telling me everything would be fine. You wanted to know everything about my life.

Jennifer—remember her? She really liked me. I remember that. I couldn't believe she liked me. I think that was my problem, in retrospect. I couldn't believe it. I treated her like dirt, never paying attention to her. Then there was that girl, I can't even remember her name, who I and Brad and the rest of us had the damn hots for all the time. I used to jerk off with her in mind. I gave up Jennifer because I had the hots for that other girl. I was so hard on Jennifer, telling her she wasn't good enough.

It was so confusing to be your son. It was hard because it wasn't like you were one of these domineering mother types. You didn't yell and scream. But there was something going on. Somehow I thought by keeping Jennifer and anyone else at arm's length from me I was doing what you wanted. I was staying loyal to you. And at the same time you were encouraging me to go out with Jennifer all the time. Was I stupid? Was I missing something? Did you or didn't you want me to fall in love with a girl? . . .

Then came Ginny. She was perfect. Absolutely perfect. You thought she was great. This time I agreed with you. I married her. But soon I was hurting her and she was hurting me. And until Alison that's been the pattern. I've got to do everything I can to see Alison as a mature woman of her own, not a mother and not a maiden. Having Justin has really helped. But it's also brought up a lot of stuff too. It's the saying goodbye to the maiden that I've got to do. But it has to do with you, too, Mom, with saying goodbye to you.

When you have written what you need to write, take some time off. Discuss appropriate pieces of this chapter with your partner and others. Gather energy to confront your Medusa. This confrontation will include a confrontation with your mother, living or dead. Start the next chapter when you have your energy back.

Chapter 9: Confronting Your Medusa

> The real accomplishment [in life] is the art of being a warrior, which is the only way to balance the terror of being a man with the wonder of being a man.
>
> —CARLOS CASTANEDA

> In [Buddhist Shamanic] teachings there is a great emphasis on working with fear—especially the fear of death—by transforming it into an *ally* (a particularly shamanic notion). The method used in this practice is that of gentle confrontation; that is, the absence of courage is viewed as a refusal to acknowledge reality, resulting in the invention of endless strategies to avoid facing fear or to deny its presence; whereas the presence of courage comes from facing fear with an open heart and keen awareness.
>
> —JOAN HALIFAX, *Shamanism*

THERE ARE FEW THINGS in life more terrible than to live in fear. At one time or another, it has been the case for almost everyone. For many of us, the time of fear took place during our boyhoods, when one of our parents beat us continually, or abandoned us, or, unable to be intimate with us, did not seem to love us. Our fear felt like mortal fear and took over our bodies and our souls without our realizing how devastating it was. For many of us, the time of fear took place during our adolescences, when we had little fathering and mentoring and lived in mortal fear of not becoming a man, or not becoming the right kind of man. For many of us, the time of fear took place in the military, when we were getting shot at and killing others.

The times of fear we have lived through, coupled with our cultural socialization, lead most of us to repress our feelings, so much so that we can't admit fear, can't feel catharsis and move through fear. The times of fear have led some of us to destructive violence against whoever was nearby—women, men, children, the environment. The times of fear have led some of us to life-destroying addictions and suicide.

For men, perhaps the most complicated and least admitted fear is the fear of women. As Sam Keen has put it in *Fire in the Belly,* "the essence of the threat [a man] feels from WOMAN lies in its vagueness. She is the soft darkness at the core of his psyche, part of him, not a stranger. We are linked to her in our deepest being, but she remains hidden in a haze just beyond the horizon of our reason and never comes out of the shadows to meet us face to face."

In the Goddess-Hero journey, the hero must confront the Shadow Feminine. Mythology is very wise about this. The Stone Boy must confront the hag in the tepee. The frightened husband must confront the leopard woman in the African tale of the same name. Perseus must confront the Medusa. Without that particular confrontation (confrontation that can last months or years in real time), the Warrior within the man will live in fear of the devouring Feminine. He will become intimate with a mate but not know what masculine boundaries should be, ultimately withholding affection and punishing the woman, in myriad ways of silence, abuse, and distance, for moving across those unnamed boundaries.

In the man's confrontation with the Feminine is a confrontation with his mother. Each of us knows this in our gut when we have certain huge conflicts with our partners. We may not have the words, but part of what we are yelling at our mate is, "You're trying to mother me, leave me alone! You're just like my mother, leave me alone! I'm a man, not your boy to tell what to do all the time. Leave me alone, leave me alone, leave me alone!" A son must confront his mother during the transition time between his dance in her mirror and the finding of his own life. Most of us in our adolescence do not fully confront our mothers. Most of us do not even begin to do the deep psychic work of confronting Mom. Without that confrontation through ritualized and guided initiation ceremonies, our later confrontations with women, with the Feminine, and especially with the devouring Shadow Feminine, are frightening unto death.

In mythological tales and tribal cultures, the transitional confrontation is ritualized. A requisite part of separation from Mother and development of healthy masculine identity, it occurs after the adolescent son has been adequately fathered/mentored, and before he meets his Beloved Feminine, the Andromeda of the Perseus story, the wife, partner, or mate of our own stories. Even in cultures in India in which marriages are arranged and partners married at puberty, the children are not considered psychologically mature. They still live in dependency patterns at home. They still need to be initiated, and confrontation with the Mother is still pending. Toward later adolescence and early adulthood, after the adolescent journey of individuation, the partners often find they begin to "love each other." Even in parts of India where life and death depend on fulfilling the biological imperative to reproduce quickly, the psychological imperatives are carefully ritualized. The young man learns, by fighting the Medusa in his mother, how to navigate later relationships with women. That navigation is always fearful—but not terrifying, because he has been initiated into it.

Thus, in this chapter, you will be led in a confrontation with two Medusas—your mother, and your partner. Even if you are not presently in a love relationship, you hold an image of an ideal primary partner. Your confrontation with her will teach you a great deal about how you handle confrontation in intimate relationships.

Because of our fear of women, we men make a number of mistakes in our relationships with women, and especially in our confrontations with them. As you move through the material that follows, recall Part One of this book. Recall the mother-son dysfunctions you identified in your life. Recall how you still feel yourself dancing in your mother's mirror, and feel yourself dancing in your lover's mirror, without much of a mirror of your own. Know that it is the Warrior in you who must do the work before you now.

As you do this work, be prepared for powerful feelings to rise up. In both your confrontation with your mother and your confrontation with your partner, you may feel anger, fear, guilt, and shame you have been repressing. Seek help as you need it, in your group or with a therapist or friend. This is absolutely crucial. Sacred Warriors rarely fight alone. They have been befriended by gods and mentors, and they often fight together as brothers. Seek out your brothers and friends.

Should you find that the work leads you to take some

time off from your mother or even your lover, don't be afraid to take that time off. Many men I've worked with, who did not have the transitional confrontation with Mother during adolescence, have it as adults by following a process of confrontation, as suggested in this chapter, and then by forcibly separating from their mothers for a few months or more. Some have even taken time off from partners, especially partners whom they discover, through their own work, to be in unhealthy and constant Medusa roles of punishing men, their male partner or their own father through that male partner.

As you go through the process, shadows will probably emerge in your mother and partner. Be ready for them; take care of yourself as you need to. Remember one thing very clearly: shadows in her do not mean she doesn't love you. Shadows that emerge within yourself do not mean you don't love her. They are shadows, simply that. They need to be felt, honored, and moved through. Often a man finds that he loves his mother or partner even more after moving through the shadows, taking the time off, and coming back with his own (and hopefully her) Warrior stronger and wiser.

TASK 1: CONFRONTING YOUR LIVING MOTHER

If your mother is dead, answer the questions in this task as you think she might have answered them at your age. Imagine her sitting in the room with you. Talk to her. If your mother is alive, try to talk to her personally.

Call your mother or write her. Don't be surprised if this task requires a series of conversations and encounters. If at all possible, go see her. Ask her questions—like those

---

suggested below—about herself, about her role as your mother, and about how she treated you. Ask her specific questions about the messages she may have given you, messages we explored in chapters 2 and 3. Focus her memory on the years during which you lived with her. It is more important for you, at this point, to learn her point of view during your first two decades of life than her point of view now, decades later.

Within your present family system and your relationship with her, certain questions may be too painful, too likely to cause upheaval in the relationship. Pick and choose your questions carefully. Be as nonthreatening as you can. Talk to her with as much steady emotion as you can, keeping your shield up and letting it protect you from the bad or confusing memories that will arise as you talk to her. Tell your mother about the journey you are on. Help her understand that it is not a journey of blame. Begin your conversation with positive statements about her, her influence on you, and her mothering. With that positive connection made, proceed to the more painful. If you have to protect her from feelings that rise in you as you talk to her, control those feelings only until you can find a safe friend, group, or therapist with whom to let the feelings flow.

Questions about How Your Mother Saw Her Own Womanhood

- How did you feel about yourself as a woman?
- What were you taught were your duties as a woman?
- Who taught you these duties?
- What sense of the divine did you have?
- When you were hurting, what did you do?

- What was the most painful time in your life?
- What was the most pleasurable time in your life?
- How did you feel about my father?
- If you could do things over again, what would you change in your life?
- Did you like being a mother?

Questions about How Your Mother Saw Her Relationship with You

- Mom, in your mind, what are the characteristics of a good mother?
- Do you feel you possessed these characteristics?
- Why did you . . . ? [Recall incidents from childhood in which she hurt you.]
- What expectations did you have of me as I was growing up?
- In what ways did you try to get me to fulfill your own unfulfilled dreams?
- How did you help me separate from you? How did you cling to me and not let go?
- How did your attitude toward my father affect the way you treated me?
- What did you see men around you doing to initiate me into manhood during my boyhood and adolescence?
- How did your attitude toward yourself affect the way you treated me?
- What did it feel like for you when I left home?

Questions about How Your Mother Saw You

- Were you proud of me? What about me made you proud?
- What most angered you about me?

- What about me gave you the most pleasure?
- What was I like as an adolescent?
- I remember a time . . . [Recall a negative time still vivid in your memory, a time of great fear for you as a boy.] What did you see during this time as you looked at me?
- I remember a time . . . [Recall a positive time, still vivid, of great triumph for you as a boy.] What did you see during this time as you looked at me?
- I remember a time . . . [Recall a negative time during your adolescence.] What did you see as you looked at me?
- I remember a time . . . [Recall a positive time during your adolescence.] What did you see as you looked at me?
- What was a "good son" in your mind?
- Was I a good son?

Handle this confrontation in whatever way you can. Write out questions ahead of time that you want and need to ask her. Perhaps the confrontation will get out of hand. Go into it knowing that potential exists. Go into it knowing the consequences of that, whatever they will be for your family. Remember that you are confronting her not to change her and not for her sake. You are confronting her, at this point in your life, for your own benefit. Try not to let her push the buttons in you that will strip and gouge you in order to fill her needs. Stay focused on what *you* need.

You may feel guilty about being hard on your mother after talking to her. You may realize she suffered in ways you didn't know about and had "good reasons" for being abusive, neglectful, impinging, unprotective. Sit with that knowledge and those feelings. But don't let your guilt rule you. It's an important and honorable feeling. It is easier to see her point of view and sympathize with her defects as a mother if you have children of your own. To heal yourself, however, you must move back into your own pain and your own wounds.

Whether the confrontation with your living mother leads to little growth but merely silence, or goes very well and leads to some healing and making peace, proceed when you are ready to the inner work that follows. The journey you are on asks you to confront the Medusa-Mother—the shadow feminine in your mother—outwardly when she is available. And the journey recognizes that she is also, always, waiting within.

TASK 2: CONFRONTING THE SHADOW FEMININE IN YOUR MOTHER

Two rituals of confrontation follow. Do the first, then wait a few days before doing the second. Your memory and your emotions need time to regroup. You'll also need time to write after each one. In the writing will be a lot of healing. To rush the rituals is to deny yourself their deepest content.

In doing these rituals, your memory needs to be open and active. You will be asked to recall painful incidents, when your mother kept you locked into being "her little boy," when she shamed you in front of others, when she debased your father and manhood, when she abandoned you in a strange place and you were terrified, when she beat you, when she self-destructed, or committed suicide. Let your memories flow.

If your mother is dead, imagine in these rituals that she

is alive. If you had a mother and then a stepmother, do each of these rituals for each of these mothers. If your mother left and you had no mother for many years, let your imagination do what it wants as it confronts that time in your life. If you are adopted, do the rituals for your adoptive mother and, if you wish, for your biological mother, even if you never knew her. You still have mythology in your imagination about her.

MEETING YOUR MOTHER AGAIN

Get comfortable in your chair. Undo tight clothing. Close your eyes. Stiffen all your muscles, then relax them.

Take three deep breaths. Continue through your rituals of meditation and relaxation.

> *When you are relaxed, imagine yourself in a hospital room. Your mother is pale, lying on the bed. Tubes are attached to her wrists. There is the hum of machines. The door is closed, but you hear a phone ring, muffled, down the hall. The wing is relatively quiet. In the room is the smell of hospital sheets and antiseptic.*
>
> *You are sitting at your mother's bed, holding her hand. She has been in a coma for weeks, her condition getting worse. You can feel the bed pressed against the side of your leg. You feel the cold, soft boniness of her hand in yours. You have been grieving her loss for weeks. The doctors have said her death is imminent.*
>
> *There are things you want to say to her. When she dies, she will be within you in memory. You want her to enjoy her life inside you. You want to enjoy her life inside you. You don't want it to knot your stomach, to pull you into old pains and patterns. You don't want her to be an alien living inside you, always stopping you from living your own life. What do you want to say to your mother?*
>
> *Start with your earliest childhood. You are less than five*

years old. Recall an incident in your childhood in which your mother did something that hurt herself terribly, or in which someone else hurt her terribly. When this happened, you wanted to protect her, to make her feel better.

See this incident from your earliest childhood as in a dream. Linger in it as you hold your mother's hand. Describe it to her, help her remember it. Was it a time when your father did something to her? Who hurt her? How did she hurt herself? Did you hurt her? Remind her. Tell her how you felt when you saw her hurt.

(Pause)

Keep your heart's eye in early childhood. See now the same incident or another in which your mother did something to you that directly hurt you and hurt you terribly. You were terrified, but she left you alone anyway. You needed her, but she wasn't there. You messed up at something, and she shamed you for it. She beat you. She was cold to you.

Where did this incident happen? See the furniture of the house or the trees in the woods. See the inside of the car or the building or supermarket. Keep looking at that incident and memory. How did you respond? Did you cry? Were there others around who watched it happening? How did they respond to what your mother did, and to how you felt?

(Pause)

Now move a few years forward. You are five, six, seven years old. You're in school by now. Recall an incident in which your mother did something that hurt herself terribly, or in which someone else hurt her terribly. When this happened, you wanted to protect her, to make her feel better.

See this incident from your earliest childhood as in a dream. Linger in it as you hold your mother's hand. Describe it to her, help her remember it. Was it a time *when your father did something to her? How did she hurt herself? Did you hurt her? Remind her. Tell her how you felt when you saw her hurt.*

(Pause)

Keep your heart's eye in those boyhood years. See now the same incident or another in which your mother did something to you that directly hurt you and hurt you terribly. You were terrified, but she left you alone anyway. You needed her, but she wasn't there. You messed up at something, and she shamed you for it. She beat you. She was cold to you.

Where did this incident happen? How did you respond? Did you cry? Were there others around who watched it happening? How did they respond to what your mother did, and to how you felt?

(Pause)

Now move forward to that strange time around ten, eleven, twelve, thirteen, the time of late childhood and early adolescence, the time when your body and voice were changing or, if not yours, then the bodies and voices of your brothers and friends and school enemies.

Recall an incident in which your mother did something that hurt herself terribly, or in which someone else hurt her terribly. When this happened, you wanted to protect her, to make her feel better. But now you may also have wanted to get away from her. And maybe you were the perpetrator this time.

See this incident from your early adolescence as in a dream. Linger in it as you hold your mother's hand. Describe it to her, help her remember it. Was it a time when your father did something to her? How did she hurt herself? Did you hurt her? Remind her. Tell her how you felt when you saw her hurt.

(Pause)

Keep your heart's eye in those adolescent years. See now

THE INVISIBLE PRESENCE

the same incident or another in which your mother did
something to you that directly hurt you and hurt you
terribly.

Where did this incident happen? How did you respond?
Did you cry? Were there others around who watched it
happening? How did they respond to what your mother
did, and to how you felt?

See this incident as in a dream. Linger in it as you hold
your mother's hand.

(Pause)

Continue later into your adolescence. You have pubic
hair now. You are growing too fast and in confusion. You
want girls all the time, and you're scared of the wanting.
You want to be a man. You are fifteen, sixteen, seventeen.

Recall an incident in which your mother did something
that hurt herself terribly, or in which someone else hurt
her terribly. When this happened, you wanted to protect
her, to make her feel better. But now you may also have
wanted to get away from her. And maybe you were the
perpetrator this time.

See this incident from your early adolescence as in a
dream. Linger in it as you hold your mother's hand.
Describe it to her, help her remember it. Was it a time
when your father did something to her? How did she hurt
herself? Did you hurt her? Remind her. Tell her how you
felt when you saw her hurt.

(Pause)

Keep your heart's eye in those adolescent years. See now
the same incident or another in which your mother did
something to you that directly hurt you and hurt you
terribly.

Where did this incident happen? How did you respond?
Did you cry? Did you keep yourself from crying and feel
utter rage? Were there others around who watched it
happening? How did they respond to what your mother
did, and to how you felt?

See this incident as in a dream. Linger in it as you hold your mother's hand. Linger in the feeling of needing to get away from your mother, to find yourself. Linger in your fear of moving away from her, your guilt.

(Pause)

Now enter your late teens, your early twenties. You may have moved out of the house by now. You have been thrust into a man's world. You may have had sex for the first time by now, or many times. You are beginning to see the future, still in confusion, but with sublime moments of clarity. Your dreams are big, and the world may not realize it yet, but you are the one it has been waiting for. Recall that time and that feeling.

Recall an incident in which your mother did something that hurt herself terribly, or in which someone else hurt her terribly. When this happened, you wanted to protect her, to make her feel better. But you may also have wanted to get away from her. And maybe you were the perpetrator this time. Maybe you've been perpetrating hurt on her a lot lately, even if just by not paying much attention to her.

See this incident from your late adolescence as in a dream. Linger in it as you hold your mother's hand. Describe it to her, help her remember it. Tell her how you felt when you saw her hurt. Tell her how it felt to hurt her.

(Pause)

Keep your heart's eye in those late adolescent years. See now the same incident or another in which your mother did something to you that directly hurt you and hurt you terribly.

Where did this incident happen? How did you respond? Did you cry? Did you keep yourself from crying and feel utter rage? Did you handle it like your father would? Were there others around who watched it happening? How did they respond to what your mother did, and to how you felt?

*See this incident as in a dream. Linger in it as you hold
your mother's hand. Linger in the feeling of needing to
get away from your mother, to find yourself. Linger in
your fear of moving away from her, your guilt. Linger in
your rage at your mother for holding on to you, or for
letting you go.*

(Pause)

*Now see yourself in your present age. You are sitting
with your mother in the hospital room. Recently you have
been involved in a difficult time with her. It happened last
week or last month or last year. It happened directly with
her, or you are not in contact with her but it keeps
happening in your memory. You keep remembering bad
times with her. You feel her working inside you, hurting
you, pulling at you, not letting you go, not letting you
have power.*

*In what way does your mother still control you? What
does she still do that makes you unable to trust yourself?
Remember incidents, memories, conversations. Let them
flow through you.*

(Pause)

*As you sit at her bedside, holding her dying hand, in
what ways do you distrust yourself? Recall one recent
incident to your mother aloud. Perhaps it was a fight with
your partner or spouse when you should have raised your
sword or your shield but you did not, and she turned you
to stone. Perhaps you made a decision concerning your
work or livelihood that you regret now, a decision you
would not have made if you trusted yourself.*

*You know that a man's lack of self-trust manifests itself
in his fear of taking risks, and his inability to hold his own
boundaries, commit himself, and let love flow. As you
recall your recent incident, you will notice that in it there
were risks you should have taken and did not take, boundaries, commitments, and love that did not grow. Grieve*

---

that incident. Grieve your lack of self-trust. Grieve it now as you hold your mother's dying hand.

(Pause)

When you have finished telling your mother how you feel, look into her closed eyes and say goodbye to her. Come back to this room when you wish to do so.

Write in your journal whatever feels important about the experience you've just had. Don't try to write everything, just what struck you the most. If the experience of early childhood, for instance, was most powerful, linger there in words, write whatever you can. Perhaps that will be the place you'll go back to with most power as you continue your epic story later. Whatever you write at this point, write about your relationship with your mother—memories, fears, guilts, deep confusions.

BECOMING YOUR MOTHER

Before doing this ritual, recall the incidents of the previous ritual in which your mother was hurt and hurt you: incidents from early childhood, middle childhood, early adolescence, late adolescence, early adulthood. You may have more than these incidents locked in your memory and your journal. If so, you can extend this ritual to include all of it.

For this ritual, you need to stand up and have a few feet of uninterrupted space around you.

Undo tight clothing. Close your eyes. Stiffen all your muscles, then relax them. Take three deep breaths. Continue through your rituals of meditation and relaxation.

When you are relaxed and ready, recall the first incident, the incident from your earliest memories of boyhood. See your mother clearly. See her face and posture as she is being hurt. Freeze the picture in your mind.

Now change your point of view. See your spirit step out of your boyhood body and step into your mother's body. Feel your spirit resist this step. Feel your spirit hold back. Wait a second, move in slow motion. Slowly let your spirit enter your mother through her navel, through that point of your early connection with her. Feel your spirit enter through the opening of her navel and spread through her.

Make a sound like your mother made when you were a boy, some sound you remember. She used to sigh or laugh through her nose. Use any sound she made. Take on her posture. Go into her body and go behind her eyes. Feel yourself in her breasts, in her organs. Spread out through her.

See her fingernails—they are your fingernails now. What do they look like? What kind of shoes are you wearing? Even if you can't remember, let your imagination show you. Your imagination holds all the imagery. What kind of clothes are you wearing? What does it feel like to have breasts, your mother's breasts? How old are you? Is there anything on your breath—booze, tobacco, garlic? How tall are you? Are your arms large, small, in between? Do something as you become your mother, something that your mother always used to do, some idiosyncratic gesture.

How does it feel to scratch your pubic hair? How does it feel to touch your mother's wildness? It is your mother's pubic hair! You have crossed the uncrossable boundary. You have gone inside your mother. All boundaries with her will make more sense from now on, they will be less confused by your constant tension not to cross boundaries with her. You have done it now. You have become your mother. You will not do it ever again outside the confines of this exercise.

Now speak. Say something in your mother's voice. Hear yourself talk in the feminine. Say something your mother always used to say. Look around. Take in the room, the car, the outdoors, wherever you are standing. Perhaps say something about that place.

(Pause)

Now return to the picture you froze moments ago. You are no longer the boy in that picture—you are no longer yourself—you are now your mother, the woman in that picture. You no longer need to imagine your mother's feelings and try to mold yourself to them. You can feel her feelings now. You no longer need to live in confusion.

(Pause)

What are you feeling as you are hurt by your husband, or someone else, or your son? What do you want to do? Do you want to cry? Let the tears out. Let the feelings out. Feel the fist or the verbal attack hit you. Respond to it with your feelings.

Look at the boy who is watching you, that little boy. Look into his face. Look how frightened he is. Look at how much he loves you and wants to protect you. What reasonable thing can he do for you? Through your tears and feelings, tell him that. He has spent a lifetime wanting to know if he has done right by you. Say to that boy what you need to say. And when you are done, say to him: "You have done your best, son. You are not responsible for me."

(Pause)

Feel the world around you shift now to the incident during these years of your son's early boyhood when you hurt him terribly. It is an incident he remembers vividly to this day. See the furniture, the car, the trees, the backyard. Feel yourself move to the surroundings of the incident. Feel yourself take up awesome female space there. See your son and see how tiny he feels as you hit him, or turn away from him, or push at him to do what you force him to do. See how frightened he is, how ashamed, how hurt.

You are that boy's mother, and you are hurting him.

THE INVISIBLE PRESENCE

You wish you weren't hurting that boy. Why can't that boy understand what it's like to be in your body, to feel the pains and frustrations and needs you feel? Why can't he just do the right thing and stop being himself, so rebellious, so passive, so wanting attention, so angry, so irresponsible, so mean to others, so much like his damn father? Why can't he just be my little boy and be good?

Stop what you are doing to hurt that boy. Stop it as if you have frozen your body. Freeze the whole picture.

Open your mouth. Tell the boy what you are feeling. Tell him your frustration and disappointment. Finish by saying to him: "Forgive me, my son. I am human."

(Pause)

Move forward now to the incidents of pain and fear that occurred in that boy's early adolescence. See the picture again of you being hurt. Play out the action of that picture. You are being hurt by your husband, or someone else, or the young man.

What are you feeling as you are hurt by your husband, or someone else, or your son? What do you want to do? Do you want to cry? Let the tears out. Let the feelings out. Feel the fist or the verbal attack hit you. Respond to it with your feelings.

Look at the young man, your son, who is watching you, or who is hurting you. Look into his face. Look how frightened he is, how angry. Look at how much he loves you and wants to protect you. Look at his confusion. What reasonable thing can he do for you? Through your tears and feelings, tell him that. He has spent a lifetime wanting to know if he has done right by you. Say to that boy what you need to say. And when you are done, say to him: "You have done your best, son. You are not responsible for me."

(Pause)

Feel the world around you shift now to the incident

during these years of your son's adolescence when you hurt him terribly. It is an incident he remembers vividly to this day. See the furniture, the car, the trees, the backyard. Feel yourself move to the surroundings of the incident. Feel yourself take up female space there. See your son and see how tiny he feels as you slap him, or turn away from him, or push at him to do what you force him to do. See how ashamed he is, how embarrassed, how confused.

You are that boy's mother, and you are hurting him. You wish you weren't hurting that boy. Why can't that boy understand what it's like to be in your body, to feel the pains and frustrations and needs you feel? Why can't he just do the right thing and stop being himself, so rebellious, so irresponsible, so disrespectful? Why can't he still be my little boy?

Stop what you are doing to hurt that boy. Stop it as if you have frozen your body. Freeze the whole picture.

Open your mouth. Tell the boy what you are feeling. Tell him your frustration and disappointment and fear that he is leaving you. Finish by saying to him: "Forgive me, my son. I am human."

(Pause)

Move forward now to the incidents of pain that occurred in your son's early adulthood. Look at your son now—he's a man. He's watching you get hurt, or he is hurting you. Play out the action of that picture.

What are you feeling as you are hurt by your husband, or someone else, or your son? What do you want to do? Do you want to cry?

Let the tears out. Let the feelings out. Feel the fist or the verbal attack hit you. Respond to it with your feelings.

Look at the man, your son, who is watching you, or who is hurting you. Look into his face. Look how angry he is. Look at how much he loves you and wants to protect you. Look at his confusion. What reasonable thing can he do for you? Through your tears and feelings, tell him that. He has spent a lifetime wanting to know if he has done right by you. Say to him what you need to say. And when you are done, say to him: "You have done your best, son. You are not responsible for me."

(Pause)

Feel the world around you shift now to the incident during these years of your son's early adulthood when you hurt him terribly. It is an incident he remembers vividly to this day. See the furniture, the car, the trees, the back-yard. See your son's house or dorm or apartment. Feel yourself move to the surroundings of the incident. Feel yourself take up a mother's female space there. See your son and see how he feels as you abuse him, or turn away from him, or belittle his spouse or friend, or push at him to do what you force him to do, or hold onto him too hard. See how tense he is, how ashamed, how embarassed, how con-fused. See his strange powerlessness to really confront you.

You are that man's mother, and you are hurting him. You wish you weren't hurting him. Why can't he under-stand what it's like to be in your body, to feel the pains and frustrations and needs you feel? Why can't he still be your little boy?

Stop what you are doing to hurt that man. Stop it as if you have frozen your body. Freeze the whole picture.

Open your mouth. Tell the man what you are feeling. Tell him your frustration and disappointment and fear that he is leaving you. Finish by saying to him: "Forgive me, my son. I am human."

(Pause)

Move forward now to the last time you saw your son. See the place. Stand or sit in it, or lie in it, if it is the time you died. This is the last chance you have had to be with your son and communicate with him. What was raising him like for you? Talk to your son awhile about what you really thought of him, deep down, beyond all the mistakes and all the hurt.

(Pause)

Now move to a time that probably has not existed between your son and yourself. It is the most recent time in his life when he needed to do something without the approval of others, the most recent time when he needed to trust his manhood to carry him through. See him in this time of decision and sit with him. What would be the most helpful thing you could tell him at this time of risk? Even if you disapprove of what his heart tells him to do, support him. This may be your only chance to do it. Even if you are a ghost now—even if you are dead during this time of your son's most recent risk—stand or sit by him without invading his process. Let him be and approve his being.

Ask your son if you may embrace him. If he does not want to embrace you now, accept that with grace. Do not make him feel guilty. Tell him how much you respect him for finding his own way in the world. Do and say what you must to show this son that you respect him as his own man. Begin with "You are no longer a boy, and here's how I know it . . ." continuing with incidents from his adolescent and adult life in which you've observed his manhood. Linger in these times. Point out to him parts of his own developed manhood he may never have seen himself. Give your son permission to be a man.

(Pause)

It is time to return now from your mother's body into your own. Take time to do this. You may find you miss her body a little. You may feel disoriented. Feel her body movements and idiosyncrasies give way to your own. Shake your arms and feel the manhood in them.

Your eyes still closed, run your fingers through your hair. Scratch your mustache, your beard, or your shaved face. Touch your chest and feel your muscles, your ribs.

THE INVISIBLE PRESENCE

*Perhaps reach in and feel your hair, if you have hair on
your chest. Touch the hair on your arms. Your hair carries
a lot of the wildness of your manhood. Scratch your balls,
reach down your legs toward your feet, feeling the stretch
in your hamstrings and lower back. This is your body, this
is a man's body.*

*When you feel ready, open your eyes, look around your
room, your house. There are ways in which your room and
house, or the woods you are in now, resemble your mother's
world. There are ways in which you and your vision
resemble hers. But this is your own world, and you are the
man of this world.*

Write in your journal whatever feels important about the
experience you've just had. Write how it felt to be in a
woman's body, your mother's body. Write how your
mother felt while she was being hurt and disappointed.
Write how your mother felt while she was abusing, neglecting, impinging on you. Don't try to write everything,
just what struck you the most. If the experience of your
early adolescence, for instance, was most powerful, linger
there in words and write whatever you can. If you need
to, do this guided meditation again for other incidents in
your boyhood, adolescence, or adulthood.

CONFRONTING YOUR MOTHER WITH
A MAN'S WORDS

When you are finished with these guided meditations, sit
down with your journal or at your computer and begin a
letter to your mother, a letter in which you tell her what
confronting her felt like, what you most feared as you did
it, how your feelings of rage and guilt rose and fell, and
how you feel now that the confrontation is over.

Write how it felt to be in her body. Write what part of
her you still feel in you, and what part of you is so

---

different from her. In doing this, go into your subtle intuitions. Go beyond the fact that you and she have different sexual organs.

Write how it felt to be female and be hurt. Write how it felt to be male, a son, and to do the hurting.

Write to your mother what she must do to let go of you so that, when you see her Medusa's face, you do not turn to stone, your soul does not whimper or wither.

Always remember that it's not important whether you send the letter or not. There is no critic, editor, or judging mother who will come around and review this letter. Your open heart and memory are all the letter needs.

Delton wrote:

> I remember an incident I had forgotten a long time ago. When I was nine you and Aunt Jane and another woman whose name I can't remember had me try on a pair of pants you were sewing for me. You and the other woman both checked my inseam, my crotch. Then since Annie [eleven-year-old sister] wasn't around but I was about the same size, you asked me to try on her skirt so you could measure it. I was so embarrassed at being paraded with the women, and also I was so embarrassed about the skirt. And at the same time I really wanted to do what you wanted me to do. I acted like it was OK. That's the important thing for me, see. I wanted to do what you wanted. I hid what I wanted.
>
> When I did the meditation where I was in your bodymind during that incident I saw that you had no idea how I felt. You didn't mean anything nasty. You were just asking for my help in doing this. You weren't purposely trying to embarrass me. You were ignorant of how I felt. I couldn't explain it to you. I don't even know where Dad was. Maybe he should

have helped you understand I was growing up. Or maybe I should have been able to tell you how ashamed I was. But even if he had told you I don't know how easily you would have listened. I don't think you respected Dad too much, especially as a parent.

Vince wrote:

I was an only child and you and Dad were always fighting, and Mom, what I felt during those adolescent years was that I failed at the mission you had given me, the mission to hold the family together. When you and Dad split up I felt like I failed. Dad hadn't taken very good care of you, I was the one who did that. I tried to keep doing it, I really did, but don't you see, I had to have something else, too, that couldn't be my only mission. Thank you in that meditation for telling me I didn't have to have that mission anymore. God, I'm so glad to not have it anymore. But I know I have to keep concentrating on not feeling I have it. It's the way I live my life, trying to always patch things up.

After you have written what you need to write, wait a day or two and then go on to the next task.

TASK 3: CONFRONTING THE SHADOW FEMININE IN YOUR INTIMATE RELATIONSHIPS

In accepting the gifts from the maidens, you accepted magic sandals that to this day, if you would but use them, allow you to hover over the Medusa and the Gorgons and discern your best way of confrontation; you accepted a bag capable of holding Medusa's head once you've cut it off; and you accepted a cap of invisibility by which to make your exit from the field of confrontation. Along with these gifts, you've also received a sword and shield from your male and female mentors. These are your power to confront the Feminine you are intimate with and your power to protect yourself against her Shadow rages, angers, and abuses.

Without the shield, we would look Medusa in the eye and die. Without the sword, we could not cut off her head. Without the magic sandals, we would not be able to move about freely in the field of confrontation—we would not be able to dance in it. Without the magic bag, we would not be able to control the Shadow Feminine—after we cut off its head, the head would just grow back and threaten us again. Without the cap of invisibility, we would not be able to exit the field of confrontation, for Medusa's sisters, the Gorgons, would chase us down.

Our confrontations with our partners need all our tools and skills. We especially need to find ways to understand what shadow elements of our relationship with our partner is "her stuff" and what is "our stuff." We need to develop a bond, and do the healthy confrontation essential for the growth of this bond, without giving up one of our five gifts—the sandals, bag, cap, sword, or shield. Much of our ability to do this depends on how healthy or unhealthy our partner is. Yet for this task, we can't do anything about that. What we can do is concentrate on how healthy *we* can be.

IN WHAT WAY DOES SHE FEEL DANGEROUS TO ME?

Focus on your present partner or your most recent long-term partner. If you've had no long-term commitments yet, focus on the relationship with a partner that has felt the most potentially long-term to you.

THE INVISIBLE PRESENCE

In your notebook, answer these questions as if you were writing directly to your partner.

1. What is dangerous about her?
2. What does she do to cling to me too much?
3. What does she do to verbally attack me?
4. What does she do that makes me feel I can't trust her?
5. What has she done to others that makes me suspicious of her?
6. When in danger, how do I respond?
7. Do I turn away from her anger and get her barbs in my back?
8. Do I charge at her and flail my sword to cut her to pieces?
9. Which of her attacks work best to take me apart?
10. Do I have the capacity to basically trust her? Does she have the capacity to do the same with me?

As you answer these questions, you need to focus on trust. Be honest about how much you trust her and how much she trusts you. Note very basic reasons why you do and don't trust her. Especially note connections between your relationship with your partner and your relationship with your mother. And if you should discover, as Verne did, that some of her shadow is really your own, honor that too.

> Basically, yes, I trust you, Colleen. We've been together four years. But you really push my buttons when you get onto how much time I spend away from you and Lionel [two-year-old son]. I ask you how much time would be enough family time and you say you don't know. You just feel like I should be present every second. And I think I know why this pushes my buttons so much. Until I confronted my mother,

I didn't realize it. But for my part I think I never felt I did enough for Mama, especially with Papa basically an asshole. I felt like I needed to give more to her. All the time. With you, it's the same. You mention maybe we ought to spend more time together on Saturday and I get pissed off at you. And you know in your heart how I've got this thing about Mama. You must. Because sometimes you use that weapon about how I'm not being a good father or doing enough for you. I'm just "another lazy blackass." You must know it hurts me. I can't believe you don't know.

But dammit, I do know part of it is about me too. I know that. You might just be talking kind of blandly about how we should be together as a family and I overreact. I know that too.

SHADOW POLITICS IN YOUR INTIMACY

In your notebook, answer these questions about gender politics and their impact on your intimacy and your ability to do healthy confrontation. Answer them as if you are writing to your partner.

1. What is my role as the man in our relationship?
2. What is my role as the father in our relationship?
3. What is my partner's role as the woman in our relationship?
4. What is my partner's role as the mother in our relationship?
5. If our roles are unclear, do we spend adequate time making mutual covenants of what our separate roles are going to be, and agreeing on those roles?
6. How much do we fight with each other just because there's a gender war going on in our culture, and we are a man and woman who have learned some of its barbs, daggers, and other weapons?

7. How much does she attack me for being a man? How much do I attack her for being a woman?
8. How much do we fight with each other because we have different communication styles?
9. What does she do to or say about other men that makes her seem dangerous to me?
10. What do I do to or say about other women that makes me seem dangerous to her?

Focus as you answer these questions on how each of you feels about being a member of your gender. What doesn't she trust about men? What don't you trust about women? What don't you trust about men, and how does your own self-distrust affect your relationship? What doesn't she trust about women, and how does her own self-distrust affect her relationship with you?

> So much of the time it's about just the fact that I'm a man. The other day I was being firm with Ted [twelve-year-old-son]. He really needs firmness now, I can see that. You seem to almost obsess about how men are abusive, violent. Some of this comes from your past, I can see that now, you had a terrible childhood, especially with your dad. And some of it just seems to be that old thing I've just heard too much of lately, how men have ruined the world. You devalue me constantly, Jill. My discipline style isn't right. I don't do sex right. You have a goddamn masters in art education, you should be able to see beyond all the stereotyping and bashing, but you do it anyway. It's getting to the point where I have to do something, I have to say something. I've been standing around taking this "men are pigs" stuff for too long from you.

Men and women bring primary and secondary fears to their relationships with each other. For men, the primary fear is of being devoured by the feminine, the secondary fear of being abandoned by her. In many men, of course, this is reversed. For women, the primary fear is of being abandoned by the masculine, the secondary fear of being devoured by it. Again, this is often reversed.

Why does this occur? We were probably brought up in homes where there was too much mother and too little father. This affected us differently. Girls grew up with so little father intimacy, they project their fear of abandonment onto the men they marry. As one woman put it, "I know I worry too much that he'll leave me, but I don't know how to stop." Boys grew up with the same hunger for the father, but more pressing for men is the fear of an adult lover becoming our mother. As one man put it, "The time when I really know I've lost who I am is when I feel like my wife is taking over my life."

This is not a pattern new or unique to American culture—it is age-old. For millennia, men/fathers have tended to be the ones who left to work elsewhere or go to war, their wives generally holding down the fort at home. Women/mothers have tended to be the ones who, without ritualized separation, held onto their kids too long, fearing the dangers the world had in store for their kids, especially sons who went to war. This age-old pattern is exacerbated in our industrial culture, in which the men are constantly away at work and now in divorce, and few grandfathers or mentors step in; and where, thus, mothers and sons don't separate, and daughters grow up to expect emotional withholding and abandonment from men.

In the average overmothering/underfathering home,

girls and boys are growing up at odds, women wanting more affection from men so they won't feel abandoned, men wanting less deep connection with women so they won't feel smothered. It is a tragic situation we bring to our adult love-mirrors, a situation that brings out the shadow in both genders.

This is the primary pattern couples live in these days, but your particular family of origin might not fit it. In yours, perhaps the mother was the abandoning one. As a result, your primary fear about women—the button her Medusa will most easily push—is your fear of her abandoning you, not your fear of being smothered. In the following questions, look carefully at your family of origin and what primary and secondary fears it has set you up for.

1. Can I say, unequivocally, that my mother loved me?
2. Can I say, unequivocally, that I have separated from my mother, feeling equally adult to her?
3. Here are five memories of my childhood with my mother. (Recall and detail five, leaving space after each.) In each of these, what was she doing to me— abandoning me, devouring me, leaving me unprotected, neglecting me? Explain and feel each of the five.
4. Can I recall incidents when I fought back against my mother? Are they incidents I can talk to her about now? (Recall these carefully and in detail. If they are not incidents you and she are comfortable with now, work through them with her or a therapist or friend.)
5. Do I recall a time when I got so much of a pattern from my mother that I just came to expect that

pattern (of devouring, domination, abandonment, nonprotection) from women?

6. Am I generally watchful of my partner's interactions with me, always looking for flaws in them? Is she doing this with me?

7. Do I feel closed off from my own power to handle my relationship, make it work, and have a good family life? Does my partner feel this?

8. Do I let my partner do most of the emotional work of the relationship? Does she let me do it?

9. Who usually "wins" our confrontations, she or I? How does each of us "win?" Who is devastated when one of us wins?

10. How does the way I do confrontation match the ways my parents did it (or avoided it) with each other? How does the way I do confrontation with my partner match the way I used to (and still) do it with my mother?

Concentrate as you answer these questions on the deep fears you and your partner bring to your relationship, fears you especially bring to its confrontations. Focus on how these fears were cultivated in your families of origin. Look especially at how your relationship with your mother set you up for primary fears of the Feminine.

Sonny writes:

#10. Confrontation. That's a big thing for me. Everything I read and hear about men is me. It's a huge blob. Yes, I'm scared of being dominated. But I'm scared of losing Ally too. I'm scared to get into confrontations with her. I know Dad was scared to do it with Mom, too. Dad wouldn't say it or act it but I know now what he felt like. I know why he would just tell her he wasn't gonna talk about it. Or he'd go out and get in the car. He'd take his dog, our dog, Andy, with him and be gone for hours.

When I get into a fight with Ally what happens is I kind of fold up inside, I forget things, I know I'm right but I can't prove it. She's got a huge list of items and I just feel lost. I don't want to be like Dad and get silent. But I don't know how to fight well either. Anywhere else in the world, like if we're traveling, it's always me who is ready to confront the world. But in my own damn house I'm not.

What is my primary fear? OK. I guess it's that fear of being devoured. When we have a fight I feel like it's fight or flight. I get stressed out immediately. No wonder I can't remember details and things. My heart pounds and I feel sure I've done something wrong. I feel like it's all my fault probably anyway, and that makes things worse. I know it's not all my fault but I don't know any other way to feel with Ally when it comes to a real fight.

Here's what it is. It's like she rarely loses her temper so when she really does and really wants to have a fight, then I figure she must really have something to be fighting about. I figure she must be right. And yeah, if I think about it, that is the way I felt with Mom a lot. A lot of guilt. Because she was so even-tempered, raising seven kids, but when she got mad we knew we had done something really wrong.

BRINGING YOUR SACRED WARRIOR TO FUTURE CONFLICTS

Throughout your relationship with the Feminine, you will face the Medusa. She is everywhere around you. Sometimes you ask for her rage, unconsciously, with your own behavior. Other times she just comes out, unexpectedly, with no substantial collusion on your part. How will you be ready for her from now on? What will you do from now on about your boundaries with her?

These are important questions. Many of us don't answer them because we can't see our own part in the Medusas we meet. Many of us don't answer them because we see our own part too well, and in our sense of guilt, we paralyze ourselves. In the first case, we put up such huge, fearful barriers against the Medusa that we wall out most other intimacies as well, quashing conflict as soon as it rises in a woman, or escaping it. In the second case, paralyzed, we let women brutalize us and figure it's our due; or we believe that men can't do intimate and loving conflict as well as women, so we might as well just take the blows. Sonny found some of both in himself. Neither case nurtures equal and growthful relationships.

Each man must develop a sacred warrior's plan for how and when to use sword, shield, sandals, cap, and bag. When the Medusa rises up, what are we going to do? Using the metaphors and objects of Perseus' journey, look at your own conflicts. Look at how you can better do conflict.

Isolate in your notebook your most recent incident of substantial conflict with your partner. Write it down in detail.

- What started it?
- What kind of mood were you both in before it happened?
- How did you hurt each other during the conflict?
- What "stuff" was working in it?
- Did it get distracted by anything—phone, kids, your own games?

- What ended the conflict? Who ended it and how?
- Did you practice the dance of swords in the conflict, or did one of you have to "win" it by putting the other down? The mythic dance of swords is a fencing dance in which both participants are skilled, practiced warriors who dance as a way of relating, playing, and resolving tension, rather than as a way of destroying the vanquished and revealing a final victor.
- What did you lose as a couple by one of you winning?
- How did you feel when the conflict ended?
- How do you think she felt?

If it is too hard to answer questions about this conflict, go to another conflict. Find one substantial enough to give you material for this exercise. Recall the exact words you used. Ask your partner to help with her recognition if you must, but try to do most of the recollection on your own.

Now apply the metaphors of the magic sandals, the magic bag, the cap of invisibility, the sword, and the shield to the conflict. If this feels artificial, try it anyway. Remember that these metaphors of the Warrior are universal to all cultures. They only feel artificial to us because we, unlike adolescents in tribal cultures, are not initiated into them from very early on. We are not given, by our fathers and mentors, a language that expresses their archetypal potency. Instead, we learn how to express anger and rage in external violence. We do not learn the adolescent male's necessary lesson about violence—that except when absolutely necessary in the outer world to protect or preserve, a male's and a female's sense of what violence is really should be seen as metaphorical of the complex inner world of consciousness and relationship.

1. How should I have used the magic sandals? In other words, how should I have danced and hovered around the Medusa for a while without getting overly defensive and too quickly offensive? What would I have learned? Would the fear and even rage of the middle of the conflict perhaps have been avoidable if I had hovered for a while, discerning what was really going on, and how I could best approach this moment's Medusa?

2. What was I doing with my sword during the conflict? How could I have better used it? Did I need to cut off this Medusa's head, or should I have left this Medusa in her cave to fight out her own rages? When do I need to cut off the Medusa's head?

3. What was I doing with my shield during the conflict? Did I, in the heat of the moment, forget to use it? Did I end up turning to stone or feeling killed by looking directly into the Medusa's face? Do I tend to do this in my conflicts? How can I better use my shield, better fend off her most terrible attacks, better hold onto my self-image even in the face of her power?

4. Did I use the magic bag? Did I put the Medusa's head in the bag and thus integrate her shadow into my power? Or did I do nothing with the head, leaving it there to find its way back to the Medusa moments later so it could come at me again, even more fiercely, in the future?

This is about making clear to a mate that her particular rage will no longer work against you, that you have bagged it and put it away, that you both must find a new issue to work with. Sometimes we can bag the Medusa's head in an authoritarian way, without giving her a say. Sometimes we just say, "Shut up, I won't talk about that anymore." That doesn't bag the head, although in the short term it seems to. Bagging the head is really about working through the conflict so that you in your healthy power get some agreement from your partner that the head is bagged. Without that agreement, there's no magic. The head will reappear another day, and you'll replay the same rages and conflicts ad infinitum.

5. Could I have used my cap of invisibility better? Did I, instead of putting it on when I had cut off the Medusa's head, try to stick around to kill her sisters too? Do I have the courage to put the cap on, the courage to finish my anger and move on? Or do I tend to linger, often with terrible silences and nonforgiveness, when my partner's Medusa shows up?

After you have answered these questions for one or more conflict situations, write down specific things you would like to change in the way you conduct future conflicts. Make a covenant with yourself to do these things differently. In future conflicts, return to this material to see how well you're doing. Keep conscious of your way of doing conflict, keep using this material as spiritual ground for its growth. Slowly but surely, you will find yourself empowered in your conflict, and more helpful to your partner's self-empowerment.

TAKING YOUR CONFRONTATION DIRECTLY TO YOUR PARTNER

Once you feel satisfied with what you have done in these tasks, set up a time with your partner, if you have one now, to talk to her about this material, and to show her what you've done. Show her only what you feel comfortable showing her. Ask her to read at least this chapter of this book so she has a sense of what you're doing. It would be best if she could read the whole book.

With your partner, explore very carefully how you both do conflict. Talk with her about what you feel her Medusa is. Remember in doing this that "her Medusa" is very much your perception of her shadow side. "Her Medusa" is not necessarily who she is or even *her* perception of her shadow side. If she is not involved in any kind of personal growth or sacred work that involves dealing with her side of what's going on in your relationship, try to help her see how her Medusa affects you, and perhaps volunteer to go into couples therapy with her.

Be especially conscious with your partner about the ways you felt abandoned, neglected, abused, nonprotected, or devoured by your mother. Your partner, once you get into this material in depth with her, will probably have a lot of wisdom about how those wounds from your mother are affecting your present relationship with her. Your lover can become a healthy mirror in this regard.

Be aware throughout this process of speaking directly with your partner that there is risk. You are being very vulnerable to her. You are giving her, if she wants to use them, weapons against you. She may be able to say, from now on, "You see, it's all your fault, you're just doing your mother-thing on me." As you become vulnerable with her (and as she becomes vulnerable with you), it is essential you work together, as co-creators rather than competitors. Know that even if she uses this material against you in future conflicts, you still have your shield, sword, and other magical tools of your dance.

When men have explored this material with their partners, partners have generally been receptive. But men have kept some of the magic for their own journals. Each of us needs to resist the temptation to get that mommy-love from our partner by showing her every nook and cranny of our inner lives and then, having given everything away to her, hoping she will take care of it all.

Save some of your psychic body for only you to know. Share with your partner whatever you safely and nurturingly can.

If you are not with a partner right now, or even if you are and want to do some preliminary inner work before sharing it with her, write a gentle confrontation with her (or your ideal lover) in a letter.

When you have finished the tasks of this chapter, take a break. You will probably be exhausted. After a few days or weeks, move on to the next chapter. In it, you will move from your confrontation with the Shadow Feminine to your meeting with the Beloved and Sacred Feminine.

Chapter 10: Meeting Andromeda: Reclaiming the Beloved Feminine

> The ultimate adventure, when all the barriers and ogres have been overcome, is commonly represented as a mystical marriage of the triumphant hero-soul with the Queen Goddess of the World.
>
> —JOSEPH CAMPBELL

AS MUCH AS THIS is a journey-book about mothers and sons, it is equally about sons and lovers. And as much as it is about these, it is about the son's claiming and reclaiming of his own female side, that femaleness and that femininity which, as psychologist Herb Goldberg has put it, "is a part of every man's core." No single heroic act claims and reclaims that empowering femininity; rather, the whole Goddess-Hero journey reclaims it. Yet in heroic myths throughout world cultures, a single episode invariably represents the integration of the son's femininity—his rescue of the Beloved Feminine from the Monster Masculine. The archetypal idea here is that a man, as a final act of his initiation, must recognize the shadow side of his masculinity that imprisons the feminine. He must confront that shadow masculine and rescue the feminine from it.

As we continue our Goddess-Hero journey, let us recognize the importance of his rescue of the Beloved Feminine to his continued growth as a man. Many of us barely or never rescued our Beloved Feminine from our Shadow, Monster Masculine. Because we have not begun or completed this rescue, we possess, consume, abuse, even destroy the women in our lives. We become easily enraged by our partner, losing our temper with her over little things. Our own Beloved Feminine unrescued, our balance of Warrior and Lover tips far more to the Warrior than the Lover, and when we use that Warrior, it is often in Shadow. Our Monster Masculine still has hold of our own femininity; thus, it will take hold of our partner's as well. With one woman being beaten by a partner every fifteen seconds in the United States, this is a crucial issue, a crucial rescue, for both men and women.

Most men, of course, do not abuse women, yet the Beloved Feminine remains unrescued in many of us. One of the reasons so many of us men turn away from our partners (causing our partners to complain that we don't say we love them enough, that we don't know how to relate, that we have no feelings) is that we are trying to protect our partners, constantly, from the Monster that keeps rising in us.

In this culture there are two very well-constructed barriers to our healthy integration of our own femininity. One, our cultural socialization, crushes our femininity from very early on, teaching us that "to be a man means *not being weak like a woman.*" The second involves our unresolved feelings toward our mothers. It is no accident, of course, that in the mother-son initiation myths—in the Goddess-Hero mythology—the rescue of the Beloved Feminine occurs *after* the man's confrontation with hag, mother, and Medusa. Mythology teaches wisely that until we confront our mothers, fully separate from them, and feel a strong sense of adequacy as men, we cannot fully rescue our own femininity.

The tasks of this chapter will lead you to confront your Shadow Masculine and rescue your Beloved Feminine.

TASK 1: CONFRONTING YOUR SHADOW MASCULINE

In what ways, in your love-relationships, do you act like a violent sea serpent, a jeering dwarf, a possessive giant, a manipulative magician? As you explore these questions, you will probably notice patterns of shadow masculinity in your interactions with other men, children, women other than mates, animals, even ideas. If material concerning these others arise, let it come, but soon return your focus to your interactions with intimate partners. These interactions will give you the clearest mirror into what shadow masculinity you must confront before you can rescue the femininity within you.

Return to your journal material on your Lover and your Warrior. As you did these histories, you re-encountered a number of girls and women whom you once knew. You also explored in depth your present or most recent love relationship. Read your entries about these women. Let your rereading of this material stimulate you to recall moments and experiences with these women in which your shadow came out. If in recalling a moment you feel confusion about what really happened, whether you were driven to your anger by her actions, or whether in fact your anger wasn't shadow at all but rather your sacred Warrior doing his job well, move away from these confusions. Find moments in which you know in your heart that you did wrong, that you hurt her unnecessarily.

In new pages of your journal, recall those clear and distinct shadow wounds, imprisonments, and dangers to the girls or women. Put the woman's name at the top of the page and write the shadow incident in detail.

Paul wrote:

> Jackie. Something about her. I don't know what it was. But she just made me mad. I hit her three, maybe four times. We were both sixteen. The last time, I beat her bad. I was different back then. I was already drinking heavy. My dad was a drunk and he beat my mom. But when he saw I beat Jackie he beat me real good.

Swayne wrote:

> There was a girl in college, Teresa. She was even darker black than I am. Real African black. I made jokes about her to her face. "You oughta be a slave girl," that kind of thing. I always put her down. I'm ashamed of myself now. She was really nice. Eighteen. Smart. But she was really black and pretty ugly. All Cro-Magnon bones. I was on the football team at S—. I could get any girl I wanted. Any black girl. But I stayed with this Teresa for a long time and she stayed with me. "You're lucky you're going with me," I'd say. "Who else would have you?" I hated myself. I hated her. I hated everybody back then.

After you have written the moments of shadow masculinity you can recall, reread your entries and look for patterns. What behavior did you tend to do over and over? Most obvious patterns will be patterns of physical and verbal abuse. Other patterns will be harder to discern. Did you punish girls and women by withholding what they wanted? Did you get easily jealous and possessive? There are many ways to cut off a woman's hair.

Swayne wrote,

> I never realized it till I really looked close like this. In one way or another, I told the girls they were lucky they were with me. Maybe I'd come right out and say it. Or maybe I'd just be so into my own way of doing things I'd take them for granted. Like they'd just stick around no matter what I did because *they were so lucky to be with me!* It's so obvious now. I could have saved myself a lot of shit if I'd seen it before. With Gladys, Tommi, now Joni [second wife, separated], I just took them for granted. They'll never leave me, I figured.

When you have finished writing what you can about your patterns, confront sources of these patterns. Look closely at the early masculine influences on your life. Look at your models. How did your father treat your mother? Does it match the patterns you've just written about? What other masculine models influenced you? Spend time here. Detail older brothers, uncles, teachers, mentors, male friends, coaches, any others who gave you messages that taught you the patterns of shadow masculinity you've detailed. Linger here. Linger especially in your memories of how they treated women.

> When I look back I can't think of one good model of masculinity. Not in the way I'm beginning to learn masculinity could be. Pop was a cold man. He treated Ma with coldness. He took me out to bars a lot. He got me laid at "Aunt Sally's." I was scared to death. He knew it but didn't say anything about it. I didn't dare mention I was scared. It's not like Pop beat Ma. It's not like he'd beat me, no more than the ordinary. He was just cold. He was arrogant, is what it was. He was an assembly line worker at GM, but he dressed up and he had a conceit like no one else.

I didn't want to be cold like him. I know I didn't. I
hated him so much of the time. I vowed I would be
different. I wasn't different. That hurts to realize that.
I was just being cold like he was.

For many of us, shadow masculinity toward women is
learned at the hands of our fathers. Confronting our
shadow masculinity requires that we confront our fathers.
If you have not made this long, difficult, and rewarding
journey, you may want to do so. *The Prince and the King:
Healing the Father-Son Wound,* my previous book, offers
you this journey of confrontation and forgiveness.

When you have explored the most profound male influences on your shadow masculinity, take some space in
your journal to decide what you must do to change these
shadow patterns. Are you involved in patterns of abuse,
distance, or addiction that force you to keep your intimate
partner imprisoned in some way? Can you get at the
source of these patterns? Do you need therapy at this time?
Do you need to confront a former mentor, who taught
you shadow patterns? Do you need to have it out with an
older brother? Do you need to break a friendship that is
taking you down a shadow path and pulling you away
from intimacy with the Beloved Feminine?

Start today on a path out of the shadow you have
discovered. Take one shadow at a time, one source at a
time. Work with it. Bring to your therapist, sponsor,
men's group, or good male friend your discoveries about
your shadow masculine. Unless you are already working
with a female therapist or guide you trust, I suggest you
seek out a male to work with. Let this task dealing with
the Shadow Masculine serve as a beginning point for your
confrontation with that shadow.

Whatever material of the shadow this task has brought

up for you, sit with it for a while. Don't move immediately to the following guided meditation, in which you will claim your Beloved Feminine. Some men I've worked with have not moved on to the next task for months. They have gone deep into their shadows, taking the Prince-King journey, and have confronted their fathers. They waited until they were on the way out of shadow again before they entered the sacred experience of the meditation. They have gone back into previous material in this book concerning their mothers, completing that. They have filled whole notebooks with shadow material from the masculine they need to discover.

TASK 2: CLAIMING YOUR BELOVED FEMININE

When you are ready to move forward, come relaxed and ready to this guided meditation. Loosen tight clothing. Take three deep breaths. Enter your personal ritual of relaxation.

Now prepare to move into your archetypal wilderness. There is deep affection and openness within you, waiting for you to trust it. Relax and breathe so that your mind's chatter is closed off as much as it can be. Concentrate on the sound and feeling of your own breath as it goes in and out, in and out. Feel your breath begin somewhere down near your navel and travel upward, out your throat, then back in again, downward toward your center.

Begin to imagine yourself becoming smaller. Take a deep breath and imagine yourself at half your present size. Let your breath out. Take a deep breath and imagine yourself at one quarter your present size. Take a deep breath and imagine yourself so small that you can stand on your own stomach. See yourself there, standing on your stomach, so light your feet leave no imprint.

You are standing at your navel. We all began connected by our navel to life itself. There is still a spiritual cord that is like a tiny tunnel going inward from our navel into our deepest and most sacred self. Find your navel, find that magical entrance to your inner life. Climb onto the lip of that entrance. Hang your tiny leg over it. Hang your other leg over. It's frightening to let go. It's frightening to let yourself fall down that tunnel. Push your tiny body a little further, a little further. Let yourself go. Feel the warmth. It's your own body you are moving into.

Come to a soft landing at the bottom of the tunnel. You are in a forest. You are dwarfed by huge trees and vines. Cries of animals are all around you. This is your inner wilderness. You have been here before. Feel at home as you walk in this wilderness.

Walk a few steps toward shadows and light that emanate from behind a mass of trees and vines. Push through the vines. Something important sits behind the mass of vines. Sweat rises on you. Pushing through the vines takes a lot of effort, a lot of breath. Feel vines and foliage scratching your skin.

Push through at last to see a huge lake. As you come to the lake, sense a huge presence there, a presence you cannot yet see, a presence that feels dangerous. What is the most fearful male presence you can imagine? Is it a monster, a vampire, a beast? That presence is under the dark lake. That presence is not one man alone; it is more than your father or any other single man who has hurt you. That presence is these men and other people and other hurts and fears and shadows, so massive in their combined dark energy you would rather not know what they are, what they look like—you would rather not confront them. But here you are, nervous at this lake. Don't turn away. Don't give the presence that satisfaction.

Call out to it, "Where are you? Show yourself!"

Know as you call out that you are a whole being, that you have more power than has the dark presence in the lake. Know that the dark presence is a part of you, a part you must embrace, a part who has lessons for you, a part whose energy you must integrate into your life. It is the dark shadow that walks beside you, that steals your energy unless you embrace it. Know that no matter what happens now, as the dark presence shows itself, you are safe in your inner wilderness. You are in control.

If the presence does not show itself, call to it again, and again, until it does.

Watch the dark presence slowly rise from the lake. Let it rise in its loud terror or its silent rage. Let it rise before you. If it must, let it even surround you. What is it? What shape is it in? What animal? What man or god? What mass? What size? Let it rise from the lake.

What does it say to you or yell at you? How does it feel to be awakened, to be summoned? Let it spew at you or croon at you, whatever its anger or its manipulation. Remember that this dark side of yourself is a part of you.

(Pause)

When you are tired of its spewings, its manipulations, even its silence, take a step forward toward the dark presence. Make this a strong, powerful step. Raise your voice above the din around you. Say to the presence, "I need you. I need your lessons. Will you answer my questions?" If at first the dark presence laughs at you, or comes at you as if to hurt you, or simply remains silent, do not give ground. It cannot hurt you. You are the whole. You have the patience to outlast the shadows. Repeat the sentences. Do what you must to quiet the shadow presence and make him your ally. As you are doing whatever you must do, concentrate on looking him in the eye. Penetrate him, penetrate down to his source of life, a source whose portal is the eye. If your shadow presence seems to have no eyes, keep looking for them. Find some way into his soul.

(Pause)

When you have control of the shadow presence, celebrate the moment. Notice what you did to quiet him, to open him to you. What you did with him here, in your deep imagination, may also be what you need to do with this shadow monster in your everyday life. Notice if you needed to make a deal with the shadow presence. Did he want something in return for his cooperation?

(Pause)

Speaking directly now to the dark presence, looking him in the eye, ask him to reveal hidden secrets to you. Tell him you want to be shown the ways in which, with the feminine, you cut off hair, you sacrifice your own heart, you consume again and again. Say to the dark presence that is part of you, "Show me my darkest actions. I am ready to see the dark side."

Let him do whatever he does to take you back through your life. Does he take you by the hand and fly you back into relationships, locations from the past? Does he put up a movie screen for you and show you scenes? Your dark presence will have a method. Let him use his method to show you your dark side. Ask him why you did what you did, why you still do it. What do you need to be healed?

(Pause)

Linger in the scenes of pain, fear, and darkness. Stay as long as you need to with the dark presence that has risen from the lake. Ask the questions you need to ask.

(Pause)

When you have finished with whatever revelations or confirmations you have gained, thank the dark presence. Tell him that now you have another job for him. Say to him, "You have imprisoned the feminine part of myself I cannot live without. I will do anything now to rescue her."

*How does the dark presence react? Does he feign igno-
rance? Does he roar? Does he go silent again? No matter
what he does, stay focused now on the task at hand. As he
does what he does, feel tools and strengths growing in your
body and on your clothes. If you need a sword to subdue
this monster, feel it at your waist. If you need a shield, or
a sudden knowledge of martial arts, or any other tool or
skill, feel that it is a part of you. Prepare to do what you
must do to rescue from this dark masculine side of yourself
the Beloved Feminine he is hiding.*

Speak to the monster. "Where is she? Show her to me!"

*Be patient. Be forceful. Follow the monster if he runs,
follow him deep under the lake. Follow him to an island
prison. Do what you must do to make the monster show
you the Beloved Feminine. Attack if you must attack.
Defend if you must defend. Grow as huge as he is, or as
small. Find your Andromeda trapped in the bowels of his
home. Find her.*

(Pause)

*When she is found, rescue her. If you have not already
subdued the monster, do it now. When you have done it,
free this trapped femininity from her chains, her cell, her
despair.*

(Pause)

*What does she look like, this representation of your
inner feminine? Who does she look like? What clothing is
she wearing? What color is her hair? What color are her
eyes? Look at her closely. In the presence of the subdued
monster, let her thank you, let her speak to you of her long
capture. Walk with her. Fly with her. Learn her history.
Share yours.*

Become her friend.

(Pause)

*It takes more than a little while to get to know the
Beloved Feminine who has been trapped within you. Ask*

her questions. Ask her, "How do you manifest in my life?"
Ask her, "How do I imprison you in my life?" Ask her
questions in which you seek to see her in your life, to
integrate her.

(Pause)

Pledge your love to this Beloved Feminine. If you can't
do it yet, share more of yourself, learn more of her. Do not
move forward until you can honestly pledge your love. If
the first impression you had of this female presence needs to
be transformed somewhat to become the presence you can
pledge love to, let it change. Help her change. Remember
that if you can pledge your love to the Beloved Feminine
within you, you will then know clearly and see clearly
projected onto the woman in your life what you need and
want from that woman. If you falsely pledge your love to a
female presence within you who is not freed from prison, or
who is not the Beloved Feminine, you will falsely pledge
your love to partners in your outer life.

(Pause)

After you have pledged your love to the Feminine who is
most authentic to your inner life, ask how you can better
love your intimate partner. Of the difficulties you have in
intimate relationships, ask her for wisdom. Be specific
about the difficulty; point it out to her on a screen or
through a window, or by flying with her to the scene.
What should I have done better there? you might ask.
Why do I always do that? How can knowing and caring
for you help me stop that shadow activity? How can loving
you help me find the right partner for me?

(Pause)

Wherever you are now, whatever scene you are in,
whatever place you have flown to, return with your new
partner to the edge of the lake. Know that the dark
presence you subdued will never go away completely. He
will return. That is the way of life. Do not try to bury him

or destroy him. Leave him where he is. Celebrate that you have the power to subdue him. Celebrate that you have the power to rescue and befriend and love the femininity within you.

Standing at the lake's edge, turn with your beloved to the undergrowth you earlier pushed through. Walk through it with her. Come to the path you began on. See it break in a Υ to two paths. Go down whichever path your beloved directs you to. She knows what is waiting down the path. Don't ask her. Just be patient. Walk with her.

Come to the archway of trees you have passed under before. Pass under it now and enter the meadow you have been in before, the meadow in which you met your mentors, the meadow you have returned to many times. See in the center of the meadow two female presences. You know them both. One is your present intimate partner, or your most recent significant partner. The other is your mother.

See them standing there side by side. Walk up to them. Your mother has come, even from the dead, to meet your Beloved Feminine. She has been called by your beloved. She has been looking forward to this day. Let her greet you. Let her greet the beloved beside you.

Your partner has come, even if you are separated from her, to meet your Beloved Feminine. She has been called by your beloved. She too has been looking forward to this day. Let her greet you. Let her greet the beloved beside you.

(Pause)

Hear your mother say to your beloved, "I have passed into you. I no longer need to be you, the beloved whom he must hurt and rescue. Now my son and I can be equals."

Hear your partner say to your beloved, "I no longer need to be you, the beloved whom he must hurt and rescue. He has rescued his own femininity. Now my partner and I can be equals."

Linger in these words. Hear them. They are important words. Hear how your Beloved Feminine responds. Celebrate the response. Celebrate this moment.

(Pause)

It is time for you to leave your mother and your partner in the meadow. It is time for you to find your way back to ordinary reality. Say anything now you feel you need to say to any of the three women in the meadow.

(Pause)

When you are ready, say goodbye. Hear their goodbyes. This may be a painful moment. Linger in the pain. When you next see your mother and partner in ordinary reality, you will love them no less than you ever have. But you will have left behind in this meadow an old, shadowy way of loving them.

(Pause)

Move with your beloved to the archway of the two trees. Walk under the archway. As you walk under it, you are moving with your beloved toward a hole in a huge tree that is like a cave just your size. Say goodbye to the female presence you have rescued, the female presence that is as much a part of you as is the dark presence you confronted. Say goodbye to her in whatever way you wish, knowing that you will never be far from her. Work out with her a way you can come back to your inner wilderness and find her here. Say goodbye and let her say goodbye to you.

(Pause)

Enter the huge hole in the tree. You are entering darkness again. Walk up the slippery incline, back up that tiny cord toward your navel.

It's difficult to return to ordinary reality. It's a hard climb. It is difficult to leave your guts and return to the distractions. It's difficult to return to your ordinary size. Yet it must be done.

As you climb, see light above you. Come to the entrance

*of your navel. Step out into the light. Take one deep breath
and find yourself growing in size. Take another deep
breath, and you have become half your ordinary size. Take
a third deep breath, and you are now your ordinary size.
    Slowly open your eyes.*

When you're ready, turn to your journal and record the
important moments of this experience. What was your
shadow presence like? How did it feel to confront him? Do
you need to go back in and confront him again? What
tools did you need to confront him? How can you translate
these tools to your everyday life?

What was your Andromeda like? How do you feel
knowing her better now? Can you enunciate what your
own Beloved Feminine is to you in your everyday life?
How does it translate? Is it your ability to perceive things
in a feminine way? Is it your ability to feel certain things,
to do certain things? What is it?

What was it like to meet your mother in the meadow,
with your Beloved and your partner?

When you have written what you need to write, go on
to the next section.

Task 3: A Letter to Your Mother

As you complete this chapter, write a letter to your
mother about your experience here. As with the other
letters, it is not a letter you will necessarily send to her.
What has it been like for you to confront your shadow
masculine? What roads has this taken you on since you
began this chapter? What do you want to say to your
mother about her contribution to your shadow masculine—how did she contribute to it in you? Do you feel she

did not protect you enough from the shadow masculine during your growing up? How do you feel about how the shadow masculine in your father, other men, and even yourself hurt her?

After you have completed this letter, consider writing a similar letter to your present partner, if you are presently in a love relationship. In that letter, explore the shadow masculinity you bring to your partner. Even if you don't show this letter to your partner, you may notice as you compare your letter to your mother and your letter to your partner some profound connections between your feelings about your mother and your feelings about your partner.

Tim found himself writing about "permission" to both mother and partner.

> It's about permission. That's what it is. Feeling like I have the permission to feel delight. It's about you giving me that permission, Mom. You're dead and I still want your permission for things! Kind of pathetic, I guess. But that's the way it is. I was supposed to take care of you and protect you. You never felt delight so why should I?
>
> Clare, I have a task. To live with more delight. To give myself permission to feel it. To notice the times when you are giving me permission. To notice when the kids are giving me permission. To push away the fog and see how Mom is in heaven giving me permission. To be a man is to be a guilt-ridden jerk. That's how it has felt. It doesn't need to feel that way. There is another way.

When you have written what you need to write, go on to the next chapter, your final episode of this journey. Your mother waits in that episode to be reunited with you.

Chapter 11: Reunion with the Goddess-Mother

> "But if you don't come back," his mother sobbed, "what will I do?"
>
> "I will come back," Stone Boy said. "I will come back with my uncles."
>
> And he did, many years later, after many adventures, and he came back to teach his tribe the ceremony of the Lodge.
>
> —From *The Stone Boy*

A MAN, TERRY, ONCE spoke of a dream he had. He walked up to his mother's house. His father was alive at the time of the dream, but in the dream he had the sense that his father was dead. As he came up the walk, he noticed that his mother's flowers were all dying, as if she had abandoned her garden.

He walked into the house and found no one, although he knew his mother must be there. At first, as he called out for her, no one answered, as if his mother didn't want him to find her. He called again and again. He began to feel worried, even panicked.

Finally, as he called out from the top of the basement stairs, she answered. He ran down into the basement, but he couldn't find her. He called out again. From behind a wall, she called back. He followed the sound and found it wasn't a wall—a padlock and a long metal bar held a door closed. He broke the lock, lifted the bar, and opened the door.

Inside the utter darkness, he found his mother. Shocked by her ragged appearance, he ran to her, embraced her, carried her out of the dungeonlike space. "What happened?" he cried. "What are you doing here?" She wouldn't say how long she'd been in there. She wouldn't say who had put her there.

She said, "I knew you would come back when you were ready. I'm glad you did. Now I can live, and I can die." The two of them walked upstairs, and his mother took him immediately out to the garden, where they started working together on resuscitating the flowers.

"Now I can live, and I can die." What strange words, Terry thought, as he wrote his dream into his journal. But he knew immediately what it all meant. He had turned a corner in his inner work around his mother. He felt a freedom coming with this dream. The mother inside his personal mythology was finally giving him permission to find his own way, and this time in a spirit not of confrontation but of communion.

In Goddess-Hero mythology, the hero reunites with his mother, sometimes by rescuing her from a prison or dark cave, as in Terry's dream; sometimes by rescuing her from an evil husband, as in the Perseus story; sometimes by bringing her a trophy or wisdom ritual from his journey; sometimes by taking her back to her husband, the hero's true father.

Part of the hero's mission in his work with the Goddess is to give to his mother a great gift that only he as a *man* can give her. It will be a gift so important—such as, for instance, her freedom, or rescuing her from near death— that it can come close to repaying the debt of the gift she gave him when she carried, birthed, and raised him—his very life. In giving her this gift of her life, in repaying his debt, he also becomes an adult equal, no longer her little boy who needs her protection. His relationship with her changes forever.

We, too, in the heroic journeys and vision quests we live in everyday life, feel our lives change when we are reunited with our mothers. In the quest we are making in this book, we have drawn boundaries with our mothers, we have even killed off the parts of her that need to be killed off. Now the time of forgiveness, gift-giving, and reunion has come. This is a time and place to feel connected, to feel equal to her, to feel respectful, to feel generous, and to feel that it is OK if she lives or she dies. She has a garden. She is tending it. When she is done, she will die. We will grieve over that, but it must be. If we are to have a functional, mutually supportive relationship with her (or, if she is dead, with her memory), and if we are finally to see her as separate from the other women in our lives, we must not only steal her eye, kill the Medusa in her, separate from her, and create clear boundaries with her. We must also, finally, reunite with her. In doing this we embrace her, help her walk to her garden, begin the work of a new kind of relationship with her there, then return to our own lives. Whatever our unresolved issues with her have been, it is time now to show her how much we care, even as we draw clear boundaries about what we will and will not do for her to prove our compassion and love.

In the quest we are making, premature forgiveness is not worthwhile. It acts like an antihistamine that masks symptoms without curing the sickness. If you do not feel you are ready for this step with your mother, do not proceed with this chapter. Seek, in earlier episodes of the journey, pieces that are not yet sufficiently resolved for this final reunion.

Task 1: Giving Your Mother the Gift of Your Adulthood

In the archetypal journey mothers and sons make, the son's reunion with his mother and the concomitant gift he gives her is most often connected with her rescue, her freedom, and thus her life—not only because the son is repaying her for his life, but because she cannot have freedom as a Woman until her son gives her freedom from being his Mother. Until she is free, she cannot wholly and completely become the Crone, discovering magic and mystery in herself she would not discover if still locked into the role of Mommy, a role that is no longer necessary after the son has become an adult male.

Children give their parents their freedom back by finding lives of their own—by breaking the invisible cord between parent and child. Sons and mothers have so much difficulty separating from each other in our culture that many women with grown sons do not realize how much magic and mystery they are missing by remaining umbilically tied to their sons. Many sons (and their fathers, mentors, and elders), uninitiated into the heroic quest, do not realize they are partly responsible for the mother's continued imprisonment, her continued exile from that magic and mystery—an exile which, over the years, she will probably find subtle ways to punish the son for.

When we give our mother the gift of our adulthood, we give her a huge piece of her life back. The homecoming at which we give her that gift can be painful, very emotional, and deeply rewarding for both mother and son. If you as a son find that your mother resists the gift, give it none-theless. If you find she won't accept it—that she still wants to hang onto you—give it nonetheless. You are not abandoning her. You are finding your own way in life. Initially these may feel like the same thing, but they are not.

This task requires you to write your mother a letter. Before writing this letter, you may want to converse with your mother on the phone, or face to face, in preparation. Unlike the other letters, I strongly suggest you send this letter to your mother, if she is alive. If she is not, consider taking this letter to her gravesite and doing a ritual, perhaps burning it there after you have conversed with your mother's spirit about it. This is a good letter to give to your mother, actually or in spirit, because it is a letter of reunion. Unlike previous letters, which you may not have felt comfortable giving, this one is a gift that should not threaten, intimidate, or hurt her—just the opposite, it should bring her joy.

If your mother is alive, converse with her about these things, and others you think of. If she is not, consider in your journal what her answers would be.

1. Mom, how did my growing up and away from you free you to do things you couldn't do before?
2. What are some of the things? Do you get joy from them?
3. What permissions do you need from me? What do you feel I withhold from you when we are together?
4. What do you remember as good times we had together during my boyhood?
5. What did you really enjoy about raising me?
6. In what ways are you unhappy?
7. Is there anything I can do to help? Which of these things do you have to take care of on your own?

8. Are you proud of me? What makes you proud?
9. Here are some of the ways I'm most proud of you, both in looking back at my boyhood, and looking at you now.
10. Mom, how can I better show you how much I love you?

Very importantly, converse with your mother about things you need to forgive her for. If you can't talk to her about these, look closely at them on your own. Before you begin your letter, reserve a page or pages in your notebook for your work dealing with forgiveness.

STEP 1

Write sentences with your mother's appellation (e.g., "Mom"), then, "I forgive you for . . ." Some of these sentences will become paragraphs.

What do you need to forgive your mother for? Write these things even if you don't feel you forgive her for each one. Write them even if there is still anger or unresolved issues for you surrounding many of them. Look back at what happened in the Medusa chapter. Look back at the childhood, adolescent, and adult incidents. What events in those periods do you need to forgive your mother for? What did she do to you and teach you that were hurtful?

> *"Mother, I forgive you for the times you beat me without any good reason. Nothing in life ever hurt me more, and I forgive you . . ."*
>
> *"Mom, I forgive you for being so cold to me and showing so little affection . . ."*
>
> *"Mama, I forgive you for the way you treated Dad during those years. You put him down and put men down, and I learned that men were bad and I was bad. I forgive you . . ."*

As you write this, your power comes in separating yourself from your mother. Your power comes from saying, "I am a man in my own right. I have the power to forgive my mother." There is an old saying: "Women forgive but never forget; men forget but never forgive." If you are the kind of man who pushes hurts out of his mind but does not let his heart forgive them, take some time here to forgive your mother.

STEP 2

When you are finished with step one, go back over each piece of forgiveness again. Identify which ones you really feel, in your deep heart's core, that you can forgive her. Run your fingers along these sentences, as you would if they were words carved onto the monuments in the meadow of your inner wilderness. Celebrate how far you've come over the years, the months, the days—how much healthier you are now than you may have been years ago, how much more easily you can forgive these things.

Then identify the things your mother did that you don't yet feel you can forgive. Feel your own anger, even sadness, as you run your fingers over these, and remember the incidents described by the words you've written. Honor these. Honor the fact that you're trying to forgive your mother for these, but you have more work to do. You'll come back to them. You'll be watchful in your own life not to repeat them.

Once you have enough material to determine what gift your mother needs from you, begin your letter. Remember that, no matter what dysfunctions you lived with in her house, and no matter what you still cannot forgive your mother for, this letter is a moment of focusing on the positives of her parenting, on her positives as a mother, and on your vision of who she is as a woman separate from that role.

Begin your letter "Dear Mom," or with any other appropriate endearment. Tell your mother about the journey you have been on through the Perseus story and this book. Tell her briefly (if you haven't told her in your work in earlier chapters) some of the painful things you've gone through concerning her. Make these brief and nonattacking. Just show her you've been working, separating from her, finding yourself.

Make sure to list positives in her parenting and give incidents and examples. Make sure also to tell her what you love about her as a woman separate from parenting. Give incidents and examples. Tell her what positive qualities from her personality and values you have gained and now use in your life.

Make sure to give her permission to let go of you in whatever language works between you both. Explain to her what separation is about, and how in your family it wasn't accomplished too well. Help her understand what it might have felt like for her, unconsciously, not to let go of you, and how it felt for you. Again, do this with no attack. Explain to her other issues your family hasn't dealt with well.

David wrote:

Dear Mom,

This is hard for me, to write to you. It's hard in the same way all my life with you has been hard. It's this feeling of knowing you loved me and adored me and also knowing we had a lot of problems together, you, me, dad, our whole family. It's so hard for me to speak honestly with you because honesty might hurt and I don't want to hurt because you did so much for me and I know you loved me, and then at the same time I know not being honest is hurting us all even more, now that Jim and Sarah and I are adults. It's like in not being honest we're replaying what we did as kids, but we're adults now and we need a new way of doing things.

Does this make sense, Mom? I'm writing you to try to create a new way of doing things that is good for all of us. That's good for you and me both. I want to have a reunion with you that also looks forward.

I have to tell you before I get into anything painful, I have to tell you how much I appreciated everything you did for me. You worked hard to support the three of us. There were so many things I didn't notice about you then, things I can see now. You were an amazing woman, really, and I don't think I've ever told you.

Alex began his letter this way. It was a letter that led to a whole new relationship with his mother.

Dearest Mother,

I am writing you to tell you that I can finally forgive you for leaving Father, and that I realize now how important it is for me to let go of you, and let you get on with your life.

Until recently I hadn't even understood that I had a problem with either thing. You kicked Father out and that was that. You had your reasons. Some of them were pretty good. I hadn't realized I was holding onto you like I was. But I was. I wasn't letting myself grow up. I was trying to stay thirteen years old. I was trying to stay that young boy/man whose father had just been kicked out and whose mother was all he had now. And I was trying to stay angry like that boy, even though I never admitted how angry I was at you. And I was so angry, so angry, but also I was trying to keep everything together, trying to be the good boy, the good little man, trying to make things OK for you.

In a way I am at the end of a quest I'm on, and in a way I feel like I'm just beginning another one. I feel like just now, at the end of my quest, I'm realizing how hard it is to be your son, and to be a man too. I want you to know that I'm going to start making changes in my life. I hope you'll help with those changes. We've been in this pattern for so long where I've stayed the boy and you've stayed the mom, it's going to take work on both our parts to change the pattern.

I got incredible strength from you. That I know in my heart. A lot of the strength I have now to make changes in my life comes from modeling after you. You were one strong cookie. You didn't take shit, not even from Father. I want to talk more about that later. But first, here's some of what I need to do now. . . .

When you feel ready, finish off the letter in any way you see fit. Consider sending it or a version of it to your mother. Actually, sending the letter could be a further step toward reunion. This will never be a perfect resolution— unresolved issues will still remain, and more may rise up when she receives it—but it is an act of reunion.

If you feel you cannot send the letter as written, see if there's any part of it you can send.

If you feel you can send none of it, if you feel sending it will just damage your relationship with your mother all the more, then hold onto the letter. You've made a powerful act of reunion within yourself just by writing it. Now all you can do is try to live that act when you see your mother, or, if you never see her, when next you remember her and think about her.

Whatever decision you make about this letter, make it from the vantage point of the Hero, your mother's equal.

If you feel you can share the letter with a spouse, friend, or men's group, you will feel strengthened by sharing it. You'll feel the Hero in yourself having the inner power to share the letter and say boldly who you are at this time in your life.

Epilogue
Dancing with the Moon

We have come a long way together. We have been on a vision quest in an inner wilderness. We have disturbed our fear of the feminine, and we have strengthened our embrace of the feminine. We have made covenants to get more of what we need out of love and give more of what we have. We have confronted our mothers and flourished. We have done things that took great courage to do, and in doing these things, we have discovered what mature male heroism is, and how we can live it.

When we began this journey, we stood on the earth and made statements about who we were at that moment. Celebrate those early statements. Celebrate, too, how far you have come, and how much stamina and courage you had for this journey.

In ancient Goddess-based and God-based cultures alike, the moon, the phases of the moon, and the moon's mysteries were most often associated with the feminine elements of life. These elements were balanced by the sun energy, which was associated with the masculine. At the end of the story of the Moon Children, you'll recall the islanders' moon dance, a dance that celebrated who they were and what they had survived in their pursuit of feminine mysteries. In Goddess cultures, after an initiation ceremony, a moon dance was often done to celebrate the new identities of the initiates. In these ancient ceremonies, dancers wore masks and role-played various archetypal elements and gender personae. In Egyptian, Native American, and so many other indigenous cultures, the male participation in the moon dance was marked by dances between masked Lovers and Warriors.

We are like these dancers. The long journey of initiation we have been on has mirrored our identities. The archetypal elements of the Warrior and the Lover have been mirrored especially. Because this Goddess-Hero journey began with our mothers, it is only fitting these two archetypal elements should pervade its process. Especially with her, there is tension between the Warrior and the Lover. There is confusion about when to adore and when to set boundaries. The moon dance celebrates initiation and the lifting of that confusion.

As you leave this book, dance your own moon dance. Finish your journey in a way that feels sacred to you. Sol finished his journey by sending his mother a revised reunion letter. When he sent it, he said he felt "weird, worried, I knew she wouldn't understand it, but I *had* to send it. And when I didn't hear back from her for a week, then two weeks, I felt my usual panic I feel with her, like she would reject me, abandon me. I was ashamed because I'd gone through a whole growth process and still the terror was in me.

"But I worked on the terror with my therapist and one day it just went out of me. And about a day after that, about 10:00 at night, my mother called. The moon was full and I took the phone outside and we talked a long time. She didn't understand the letter, she said, but I knew deep down she did. Our relationship changed yet again after that talk. Something finally clicked in her. And in me."

Following an ancient initiation tradition, John danced his moon dance in a prayer to Mother Earth. In this ancient tradition, a young man who separates from his mother does not lose the son-mother energy. He transfers it to the care of Mother Earth. John wrote this prayer:

THE LORD'S OTHER PRAYER

Our Mother Who art the Earth,
Love be thy name.
When heaven rains on you with its light,
You receive, and celebrate the union
with prolific birth.
Let us kiss you, and caress you tenderly.
Let us take some shreds of all the love
with which you nursed us
And return them to you as a well-worn cloak
And reverently drape you with care.

In both these cases, men danced with the moon in words. Other men have done other things: creating music to mark the end of their journey, actually dancing in the moonlight with an intimate partner. Find your own way.

As you dance, like the moon dancers who came before you, embrace the feminine moon without capitulation to the feminine moon. Accept the power of the mature masculine as a valued part of your life. Embrace women without fantasizing that their femininity will save you and your kingdom from pain. The moon dancer sings a song to the moon in the same male range and timbre as other men who are singing the same song and dancing the same dance. He loves his mate, who is his equal, with the adoration of the Lover, the power of the Warrior, and the clean, humble respect for an intimate partner that comes from inner balance. If he is not partnered, he brings his Lover energy to the Earth, waiting for the right circumstances for intimacy with a partner. He does not give up the rich solitude of nature for the constant desperation to be loved by Woman. The moon dancer, whatever his life circumstances, lives the life of a man, letting go of the umbilical cords of his adolescence.

Find a moon dance of your own. The first time you try "making it happen," it may not work. You may not be truly ready. Try again until it does work. As you well know, all your life problems will not be solved. You will still, throughout the rest of your life, suffer moments of guilt, fear of men, fear of women, self-image doubts that go back to your dance in your mother's mirror. But the moment of moon dancing will ritualize your new identity. That is what, in tribal traditions, the sun dance, the moon dance, or the finish of any initiation ceremony is about: showing the man what his new identity is, giving him his new name, so that now he can face future suffering with vigor and secure self-confidence.

Thank you for letting me help you with your journey. May you live in a balance of Warrior and Lover. May you and I meet some day. Heroes, brothers, and friends.

Selected Readings

Abrahams, Roger D. *African Folktales*. New York: Pantheon Books, 1983.

Afanasev, Aleksandr. *Russian Fairy Tales*. New York: Pantheon Books, 1945.

Berman, Morris. *The Reenchantment of the World*. Ithaca: Cornell University Press, 1981.

Bettelheim, Bruno. *The Uses of Enchantment*. New York: Vintage Books, 1977.

Bly, Robert. *Iron John*. Reading, Mass.: Addison-Wesley, 1990.

Bolen, Jean Shinoda. *Gods in Everyman*. New York: Harper and Row, 1990.

Bradshaw, John. *Homecoming*. New York: Bantam Books, 1990.

Brazelton, T. Berry, and Bertrand G. Cramer. *The Earliest Relationship*. Reading, Mass.: Addison-Wesley, 1990.

Campbell, Joseph, *The Hero with a Thousand Faces*. 2nd ed. Princeton, N.J.: Princeton University Press, 1968.

———. *Historical Atlas of World Mythology*. New York: Harper and Row, 1983.

———. *Myths We Live By*. New York: Bantam Books, 1988.

———, commentator. *The Complete Grimm's Fairy Tales*. New York: Pantheon Books, 1972.

Coles, Robert. *The Call of Stories*. New York: Houghton Mifflin, 1989.

Corneau, Guy. *Absent Fathers, Lost Sons*. Boston: Shambhala, 1991.

Druck, Ken, with James C. Simmons. *The Secrets Men Keep*. New York: Ballantine, 1985.

Eliade, Mircea. *Rites and Symbols of Initiation*. New York: Harper and Row, 1975.

Erdoes, Richard, and Alfonso Ortiz. *American Indian Myths and Legends*. New York: Pantheon Books, 1984.

Feinstein, David, and Stanley Krippner. *Personal Mythology*. Los Angeles: Jeremy P. Tarcher, 1988.

Frazer, James. *The Golden Bough.* New York: Macmillan, 1907.

Goldberg, Herb. *The New Male.* New York: Signet Books, 1979.

Greenberg, Jay R., and Stephen A. Mitchell. *Object Relations in Psycho-analytic Theory.* Cambridge, Mass.: Harvard University Press, 1983.

Grizzle, Anne F., with William Proctor. *Mothers Who Love Too Much.* New York: Ivy Books, 1988.

Gurian, Michael. *The Prince and the King: Healing the Father-Son Wound.* Los Angeles: Tarcher/Putnam, 1992.

Herdt, Gilbert H., ed. *Rituals of Manhood: Male Initiation in Papua New Guinea.* Berkeley: University of California Press, 1982.

Hillman, James. *Revisioning Psychology.* New York: Harper and Row, 1975.

Hopcke, Robert H. *Jung, Jungians, and Homosexuality.* Boston: Shambhala, 1991.

Houston, Jean. *The Possible Human.* Los Angeles: Jeremy P. Tarcher, 1982.

———. *The Search for the Beloved: Journeys in Sacred Psychology.* Los Angeles: Jeremy P. Tarcher, 1987.

Jung, C. G., ed. *Man and His Symbols.* New York: Doubleday, 1986.

———. *Psychology and Religion.* Princeton, N.J.: Princeton University Press, 1958.

Kaplan, Louise J. *Oneness and Separateness: From Infant to Individual.* New York: Touchstone Books, 1978.

Keen, Sam. *Fire in the Belly.* New York: Bantam Books, 1991.

———. *The Passionate Life.* New York: Harper and Row, 1983.

Keen, Sam, and Anne Valley-Fox. *Your Mythic Journey.* Los Angeles: Jeremy P. Tarcher, 1978.

Kiley, Dan. *The Peter Pan Syndrome.* New York: Avon, 1983.

Kipnis, Aaron R. *Knights without Armor.* Los Angeles: Jeremy P. Tarcher, 1991.

Lawrence, D. H. *Sons and Lovers.* London: Penguin, 1978.

Leonard, Linda Schierse. *The Wounded Woman: Healing the Father-Daughter, Relationship.* Boston: Shambhala, 1983.

May, Rollo. *The Cry for Myth.* New York: W. W. Norton, 1989.

Miller, Alice. *For Your Own Good.* New York: Farrar, Straus, and Giroux, 1983.

Mitscherlich, Alexander. *Society without the Father.* London: Tavistock, 1969.

Moore, Robert. *King, Warrior, Magician, Lover: Rediscovering Masculine Potentials*. Wilmette, Ill.: Chiron Publications, 1988. Audiotape.

Moore, Robert, and Douglas Gillette. *King, Warrior, Magician, Lover* San Francisco: Harper, 1990.

Napier, Augustus, with Carl Whitaker. *The Family Crucible*. New York: Harper and Row, 1978.

Nicholson, Shirley, ed. *Shamanism: An Expanded View of Reality*. Wheaton, Ill.: Quest, 1987.

Nin, Anais. *Delta of Venus*. New York: Bantam, 1969.

Osherson, Samuel. *Finding Our Fathers*. New York: Fawcett Columbine, 1986.

Pearson, Carol S. *The Hero Within*. New York: Harper and Row, 1989.

———. *Awakening the Heroes Within*. San Francisco: Harper, 1991.

Pirani, Alix. *The Absent Father*. London: Arkana, 1988.

Pittman, Frank. "The Secret Passions of Men." In the *Journal of Marital and Family Therapy*.

Richardson, Ron. *Family Ties That Bind*. Vancouver, Wash.: Self-Counsel Press, 1984.

Rico, Gabriele. *Pain and Possibility*. Los Angeles: Jeremy P. Tarcher, 1991.

Rubin, Lillian B. *Intimate Strangers*. New York: Harper and Row, 1983.

Sams, Jamie, and David Carson. *Medicine Cards*. Santa Fe, N.M.: Bear and Company, 1988.

Scarf, Maggy. *Intimate Partners*. New York: Random House, 1987.

Shah, Idries. *World Tales*. New York: Harcourt Brace Jovanovich, 1979.

Shaner, Paul. "Dan Quayle, Murphy Brown, and Fatherlessness." *Seattle M.E.N.*, August 1992.

Slochower, Harry. *Mythopoesis*. Detroit: Wayne State University, 1970.

Solomon, Marion F. *Narcissism and Intimacy*. New York: W. W. Norton, 1989.

Stern, Daniel F. *The Interpersonal World of the Infant*. New York: Basic Books, 1985.

Storm, Hyemeyohsts. *Seven Arrows*. New York: Ballantine, 1972.

Turner, Victor. *Ritual Process*. Ithaca, N.Y.: Cornell University Press, 1977.

———. *The Forest of Symbols: Aspects of Ndembu Ritual*. Ithaca, N.Y.: Cornell University Press, 1967.

Uysal, A. E., ed. *Selections from Living Turkish Folktales*. Ankara, Turkey: Ataturk Kultur, Dil Ve Tarih Yuksek Kurumu, 1989.

von Franz, Marie-Louise. *Interpretation of Fairy Tales*. Dallas, Texas: Spring Publications, 1970.

———. *Puer Aeternus*. Boston: Sigo Press, 1981.

Walker, Barbara. *The Crone*. San Francisco: Harper, 1985.

Wexler, David B. *The Adolescent Self*. New York: Norton, 1991.

Winnicott, D. W. *Human Nature*. New York: Schocken, 1988.

Woodman, Marion. *The Ravaged Bridegroom*. Toronto: Inner City Books, 1990.

Yolen, Jane, ed. *Favorite Folktales from around the World*. New York: Pantheon Books, 1986.

Credits

Robert Duncan's poem "My Mother Would Be a Falconress" is used by courtesy of New Directions Publishing Corporation.

The author gives special thanks to Lisel Mueller for her poem "Moon Fishing."

Study Questions for Women

For Mothers of Sons

You are the mother of a son who has read or is reading a book that is directed toward men. In order to help you gain deeper access to some of this book's joys and challenges for mothers, I hope you'll answer these questions with your mate, therapist, or other support person. If you are caring for an infant or toddler, some of these questions may not impact you right now—but you may want to return to them when your son is older.

1. What are your strengths as a mother? List them on a piece of paper, keep the list, and update it periodically.

2. What are the greatest gifts you've given your son? List them and keep updating them. On your list might be parts of his genetic inheritance from you, including personality traits that you're proud of. On your list might also appear social and economic opportunities you've given him, spiritual visions, and emotional tools.

3. Is your son aware of the gifts you've given him? If he is not, how can you transmit awareness to him? Who can aid you in helping him understand who you are, and what you are trying to give him?

4. What are the inadequacies that you feel as a mother—not the normal guilt any mother feels when her son does something wrong, but deeper, nagging guilt you identify as weakness in you as a mother of this son? To help you make a list, you can refer to chapters 1 and 2 and ask questions based on the content there, questions such as, "Am I enmeshed with my son?" "Am I impinging on my son's development?"

5. Do you have a support system in place as a mother, one that helps you with the hands-on development of your son, but also helps you constantly explore yourself as a partner of men, and a mother of boys? If not, list people you can go to, and institutions that can help you.

6. Do you know enough about how boys operate differently than girls? Do you understand the male soul as interdependent with, but also independent of the female soul? Review this book, looking specifically for ways you can sense the differences between boys and girls, even in their interactions with their mothers.

7. How does your relationship with your husband/partner positively and, perhaps, negatively affect your son's growth? Make a list of both the beneficial and detrimental aspects of this relationship. To help you make this list, review chapters 1 and 2, referring to the subheadings to ask yourself how your partner is doing in each category, and then look at the tensions that manifest in you and in your son from these categories.

8. How can you better facilitate your son's relationship with his father? Look again at the section on mother-son-father triangles in chapter 2, and list ways in which you might be able to help your son and his father gain deeper trust in one another. If no father is available—and even if he is—you can ask these questions regarding male mentors of your son as well. As you explore this material, consciously look at how to make sure there are two or more good men in your son's life by the time he becomes an adolescent.

9. Refer to chapter 3 and review the three categories of men that emerge in the Moon Children story, and then ask: "Am I raising a boy who cuts off his hair, or holds his heart in his hand, or drinks the whole ocean?" Your son is, of course, more complex than these categories, and if he's

too young to fit any of them, then put off these questions until later. If, however, you sense some truth in one of these categories, explore it with your support system, and look at how you are unknowingly participating in guiding your son toward one of these difficult ways of being a man, lover, and father.

10. As you think about Part Two of this book, the healing journey for men, make a list of ways you can support your son in taking these steps while he is still a boy. You can make this list based on the chapter titles themselves, since each is a stage of the male journey.

FOR WOMEN IN RELATIONSHIPS WITH MEN

You are the woman in a relationship with a man who has read or is reading a book that is directed toward men. In order to help you gain deeper access to some of this book's joys and challenges for women, I hope you'll answer these questions with your mate or a therapist or other support person. If you are not in a relationship right now, you can apply these questions to a previous love relationship. You can also return to them when you are in a new relationship.

1. What do you do well as a lover of a man? What are your strengths as a woman in a relationship with a man? On a piece of paper, list your strengths, keep the list, and continue to update it. Have you let your lover/husband know what you perceive as your strengths? Have you talked to him about them? If not, can you show him the list and have a conversation? Can he construct a similar list about himself, and can you discuss it together?

2. What are your partner's strengths? What are the gifts he gives you as a woman? Make a list and keep it updated.

Even if you are in conflict with this man, he has many gifts, and he is probably trying to give them constantly. Understanding these gifts can help heal your relationship.

3. To what extent do you feel your husband or lover is "dancing in his mother's mirror," according to the dream image that began this book? Review the introduction, and look closely at your husband's interactions with his mother and with you. What are the tensions you feel your husband experienced in his relationship with his mother when he was a boy? List them. Concentrate on one or two basic tensions, rather than trying to list many small tensions, which might have myriad causes within you and within him.

4. Were either you or your partner under-fathered during your upbringing? What are the inadequacies that you experienced in your relationship with your father? What are the inadequacies you feel your husband experienced in his relationship with his father? How has under-fathering negatively impacted either of you in your relationship? It is nearly impossible to deal with mother-issues if we are not also cognizant of father-issues, both as women and men.

5. Refer to chapters 1 and 2 and ask questions based on the headings in that chapter, such as, "Is/was my partner enmeshed with his mother?" "Did his mother impinge on his development?" "Was he abused, neglected, or abandoned by his mother?" If you feel a yes answer is appropriate to any of these, work with your husband or a therapist to talk about the impact of that yes on your love relationship.

6. Is your husband involved in adolescent-adult behavior? Go to pages 37–42, and review the material there, including the twenty questions. Answer these regarding your lover/husband from your point of view, following the model set up on those pages. Once you have answers you are satisfied with, get whatever help you need to discuss these with your partner.

7. Is your marriage or love relationship caught in a "mother-son" bind? Go to pages 43–45, and review that material, including the twenty questions. Answer these from your point of view, following the model set up on those pages, and the model set in number 6 above.

8. Go to chapter 3 and review the three categories of men that emerge in the Moon Children story, and then ask, "Is my partner a man who cuts off women's hair, or holds his heart in his hand, or drinks the whole ocean?" Your mate is, of course, more complex than these categories. If, however, you sense some truth in one or more of these categories, explore it with your mate and/or your therapist. If you are not in a relationship right now, look back at previous relationships to see which kind of man you tend to be attracted to. In this context, look at your mother and father and see if you can see links to this kind of attraction.

9. Did your mother-in-law give your mate denigrating messages about men? If she is alive, does she still do so? In either case, did she or does she personally denigrate your mate? How can you help rebuild his sense of manhood? List messages you can give that your husband needs, and compromises you can make that will allow him to feel needed, loved, and important again.

10. As you think about Part Two of this book, the healing journey for men, make a list of ways you can support your mate in taking these steps. You can make this list based on the chapter titles themselves, since each is a stage of the male journey. You know your mate—follow your kind and deep intuition about what he needs from you in order to help him heal his mother-son relationship. Encourage him in his journey, expect it to take a year or more, and be there for him as you can be.